WILD AND PRECIOUS LIFE

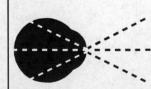

WILD AND PRECIOUS LIFE

DEBORAH ZIEGLER

THORNDIKE PRESS
A part of Gale, Cengage Learning

Farmington Hills, Mich • San Francisco • New York • Waterville, Maine
Meriden, Conn • Mason, Ohio • Chicago

GALE
CENGAGE Learning®

LIBRARY OF CONGRESS CATALOGING-IN-PUBLICATION DATA

Names: Ziegler, Deborah, 1956- author.
Title: Wild and precious life / Deborah Ziegler.
Description: Large print edition. | Waterville, Maine : Thorndike Press, a part of Gale, Cengage Learning, 2016. | Thorndike press large print biographies and Memoirs
Identifiers: LCCN 2016043172 | ISBN 9781410495129 (hardback) | ISBN 1410495124 (hardback)
Subjects: LCSH: Maynard, Brittany. | Brain—Cancer—Patients—United States—Biography. | Assisted suicide—United States—Biography. | Right to die—United States. | Ziegler, Deborah, 1956- | Mothers and daughters—Biography. | BISAC: BIOGRAPHY & AUTOBIOGRAPHY / Personal Memoirs. | BIOGRAPHY & AUTOBIOGRAPHY / Women.
Classification: LCC RC280.B7 M39 2016a | DDC 616.99/4810092 [B] —dc23
LC record available at https://lccn.loc.gov/2016043172

Published in 2016 by arrangement with Emily Bestler Books, an imprint of Atria Books, an imprint of Simon & Schuster, Inc.

Printed in Mexico
1 2 3 4 5 6 7 20 19 18 17 16

To Brittany, my sweet pea.
Fly freely in and out of my heart. Always.

Who made the world?
Who made the swan,
and the black bear?
Who made the grasshopper?
This grasshopper, I mean —
the one who has flung herself
out of the grass,
the one who is eating sugar
out of my hand,
who is moving her jaws back and forth
instead of up and down —
who is gazing around with her
enormous and complicated eyes.
Now she lifts her pale forearms and
thoroughly washes her face.
Now she snaps her wings open,
and floats away.
I don't know exactly what a prayer is.
I do know how to pay attention,
how to fall down

into the grass, how to
kneel down in the grass,
how to be idle and blessed,
how to stroll through the fields,
which is what I have been doing all day.
Tell me, what else should I have done?
Doesn't everything die at last,
and too soon?
Tell me, what is it you plan to do
with your one wild and precious life?
— Mary Oliver, "The Summer Day"

Do not judge the bereaved mother.
She comes in many
forms. She is breathing but she is dying.
She may look young
but inside she has become ancient.
She smiles, but her heart
sobs. She is here, but part of her is
elsewhere for eternity.
— Author Unknown

CONTENTS

PREFACE

Be soft. Do not let the world make you hard. Do not let pain make you hate. Do not let the bitterness steal your sweetness. Take pride that even though the rest of the world may disagree, you still believe it to be a beautiful place.
  — Iain Thomas, *I Wrote This for You*

This is a story about ordinary people who accomplished extraordinary things. A story of a family that weathered more than one horrific storm. The last storm was the darkest, leaving in its wake scarred human beings and broken hearts. No one can look into my eyes and miss this. The melancholy is there, even when I smile. I see suffering etched in my husband's face, as well. We are changed forever by what happened.

Often people ask me, "What did you learn from your journey?" In the early stages of grief I remember thinking, *Not only am I supposed to survive, put one foot in front of the other, but I'm supposed to have learned something, too?* It was an unspoken rebuke, a visceral reaction to the question. Over time, through the process of grieving, I have begun to understand that the effort put forth in answering this question is valuable, and perhaps even transformative. At least it has been for me.

Shortly after my daughter's death, I got a tattoo on the instep of my right foot, reminding me not to let pain make me hard or bitter. It says, "Be soft." Brittany's birth date is inked below the words.

This book is my "soft." In it, I'm exposing my underbelly. I'm revealing my daughter's beautiful spirit, her fury and fearlessness, her resolute determination, our frantic struggle as we staggered toward something that flew in the face of the natural order of things. No mother should bury her child. No child should have to drag her mother, kicking and screaming, out of denial and into ugly reality. My brave Brittany faced the truth sooner than I did. It took me a while, but ultimately I was forced to look death square in the eye. "Death is coming for me, Momma. Don't you get that?"

More than life itself, for twenty-nine years I loved my daughter. Yet I've learned that she doesn't have to be physically present in order for me to love her. I can love her even after she soared away from me. My heart is open for her to fly in and out of at will.

My daughter did the best she could. I'm rock solid in that truth. She tried so hard to do what was right. This idea sounds simple, but it is not. Look around at those who disappoint you, hurt you. Are they doing the best they can? Are you? Does it make us feel safer to think our best is better than theirs?

Now look at those who are terminally ill. Are they doing their best? How dare we judge them. How dare we tell them how they ought to die. How dare we impose our beliefs on them. How dare we try to manipulate them into fighting when they have no more fight left.

Everyone who walked Brittany toward death was fallible. We were angry, sad, brave, and frightened. We were human. But each of us in the little yellow house in Portland was doing his or her best. That is one of my big lessons, and it gives me great comfort. My daughter knew that she was loved. Even in the worst of it, she knew that, just as I knew she loved me. Love sustained us, then and now.

Our lives are wild and precious, and I've

promised to try to live mine with those words in my heart; in my laughter; in my plans for living boldly. That's what Brittany said she wanted for me.

■ ■ ■ ■

ONE:
CATASTROPHE

■ ■ ■ ■

I was a mother who worked ridiculously
hard to keep catastrophe at bay.
— Ann Hood, "What I Never Told Anyone
About Her Death," life@salon.com,
May 16, 2011

1
FOREBODING

December 31, 2013–January 1, 2014

The worst moments in life are heralded by small observations.

— Andy Weir, *The Martian*

The first step in leaving the world I formerly inhabited was more like a jarring shove. Not a tiny toe-out-the-door kind of move. Instead, I was cruelly pushed into a new life.

Late New Year's Eve of 2013, when Brittany should have been dining and dancing, my son-in-law called me from an ambulance. Dan said that Brittany had a very bad headache. They had gone to a hospital, where a CT scan revealed a shadow on her brain. Since the hospital didn't have an MRI, they were now heading to a larger one that had the proper equipment.

"Should I try to get on a flight tonight? I'm not sure there *are* any middle-of-the-night flights to Oakland."

Dan responded that she'd have to do admittance tests and take the MRI, so tomorrow morning would be fine. He put my daughter on the phone.

"Momma, my head hurts so bad," Britt said, her voice thick and slurred from the effects of pain medication. "They took a CT scan and found a shadow on my brain. It might be a brain tumor."

My heart dropped as my mind refused to accept this possibility. "Don't jump there, darling. Don't draw any premature conclusions. Baby, I'm coming. I'll see you tomorrow."

Gary booked my airline ticket as I haphazardly threw clothes into a suitcase. "Follow your own advice," Gary said. "Don't jump to any conclusions. I'll make arrangements for someone to check on your father and stay with the dogs. Then I'll come up later." He held me by the shoulders. "Try to get some sleep tonight. You'll need to arrive rested."

As I flew to Oakland from San Diego the next morning, I wondered what might have created a shadow on Brittany's brain. My daughter with a brain tumor? It just wasn't possible.

Brittany had always been a healthy, active

child. Over five feet nine, she positively exuded strength and vigor. As I looked out the plane's window at the cloudless sky, images clicked through my mind like a silent slide show:

Three years old. Feet up on the dash of her toy ride-on car, screaming in delight. "Faster, Momma, faster!"

Preschool. Curly hair hiding her face, dangling upside down on the monkey bars. "Look at me! Momma, look at me!"

First grade. Bent over homework, Britt printing her letters over and over until she developed a pressure bump from bearing down on her fat beginner pencil.

Elementary school. Green eyes gleaming, Britt as Princess Jasmine sang her solo parts as clear as a bell. Back and forth with the boy playing Aladdin, she fearlessly belted out lyrics about taking a free-spirited flight through a glittering sky. Trilling perfectly on key, she stretched out her arms to the beaming audience. How prophetic this song about seeing amazing sights would be, although Britt would never need an Aladdin to escort her anywhere.

Preteens. Tumbling, cheering, and ice skating her way through middle school, effortlessly excelling at sports.

High school. Alternately crashing and

soaring, Britt spiraled into wild rebellion as she fought for autonomy. With almost waist-length honey-brown hair and a smile that knocked the breath out of boys, she skipped school with gleeful abandon, yet somehow always excelled scholastically.

Young adulthood. A trip to Costa Rica to work on a women-owned farm filled Britt with a deep yearning to volunteer, to experience wild places, and to engage in adrenaline-producing activities. It was the first sign of the trekking, bungee-jumping, stranger-befriending young woman that she became.

As I flew toward my sick daughter, I envisioned her startling white smile, muscular legs, and powerful arms as she winged upward and plummeted, freewheeling, through life. I imagined her long tanned legs glistening in the white foam of a waterfall as she rappelled down slippery rock. I pictured my girl in a life vest and helmet, white water almost obscuring the raft, Britt the only occupant who somehow managed to grin impishly at the camera while everyone else grimaced and paddled furiously. I imagined the sound of her laugh — the very best sound I've ever heard — as she jogged across a hanging bridge, deliberately setting it in motion to unsettle others in the group.

I could not picture Britt lying still and quiet in a bed. My daughter was definitely more of a magic carpet girl.

Brittany's mother-in-law, Carmen, picked me up at the airport. We hugged, her compact frame rigid as she squeezed me hard. She drove me to the hospital where my only child slept on crisp white sheets in the Neuroscience ICU.

Carmen told me that they would get a clear MRI today, since the previous hospital only captured a fuzzy image with their CT scan. Her voice was precise, with the charming hint of a Cuban accent that I found endearing. Carmen and her husband, Barry, had bonded with me and Gary at our kids' engagement lunch. Carmen added that Barry was taking care of Britt and Dan's dogs, Charley and Bella. I thought of kind, strong Barry and how the dogs immediately calmed down in his presence. The whole family called him the "dog whisperer."

Carmen and I loved our children fiercely. Dan was Carmen's pride and joy, just as Brittany was mine.

I didn't know then that an MRI is the investigative tool of choice for neurological cancers. Carmen and I were silent for a few minutes as she negotiated traffic. "What

21

does a shadow on the brain mean?" I asked.

Carmen replied that she didn't know, but that Dan would explain when we got there. In the quiet of the van, I prayed silently all the way to the hospital. Brittany had been complaining of headaches for almost a year. Were they migraines? Stress headaches? Sinus headaches? She and I had posed many hypotheses as to what might be triggering the increasingly debilitating pain. Sometimes at night the throbbing of her head was so all-encompassing that all Brittany could think to do was go sit in the shower with warm water pouring down on her neck and head. I had looked online, but there were hundreds of potential reasons.

Brittany tried avoiding wine. She made sure she exercised regularly. She avoided nitrates, and bought farm-fresh, organic foods. Was it our imagination that the headaches seemed to get better when she visited me and Gary in Southern California?

Brittany had bought a Great Dane puppy to join Bella, her needy rescued beagle, soon after marrying Dan in late September of 2012. She said she was lonely living in Northern California, and longed for a puppy to keep her company. Had the teething Charley caused stress?

Soon after her wedding, Brittany saw a

neurologist. She chose him because he had training in both Eastern and Western medicine, and he advertised a holistic approach. Although Brittany described the headaches as coming on when she went to bed, severe enough to make her vomit, the doctor told Brittany that she was having "women's headaches" and that they might get better when she had a baby. Brittany was a bit insulted by this, thinking that he was suggesting that the headaches were potentially a combination of newlywed stress and hormonal imbalance. I didn't dare say it, but I thought he might be right.

Later, Britt and I discussed the fact that this neurologist hadn't ordered an MRI and caught her growing tumor. He missed a couple of glaring pieces of information. The headaches grew worse when Britt was lying down. It was at night that the pain caused her to forcefully throw up and to seek the refuge of a warm shower. But we also were told by other neurologists (do they always defend one another?) that a hundred million Americans report bad headaches each year, with 35 million of those experiencing migraine-level headaches. If doctors ordered an MRI for all of these patients, the medical system would go bankrupt. So our anger and desire to write a blistering letter died away with time. There was so much else to deal with — we had to let go and keep moving forward.

The doctor also encouraged her to avoid too much caffeine, red wine, processed meat, MSG-laden foods, and artificial sweeteners, as all of these things can trigger headaches. Brittany became very averse to the use of artificial sweeteners and adamantly opposed my use of sugar-free flavored coffee creamers.

He prescribed subcutaneous injections of pain medication, a selective serotonin receptor antagonist used to narrow blood vessels around the brain. It is a medication used for migraine headaches. Britt would find a place at the top of her thigh, wipe the area with an alcohol pad, and use an auto-injector pen. But the injections hadn't helped. "Are you going to tell him the medication isn't helping?" I asked.

"I don't know. Maybe I need to give them a chance." Britt changed the subject before I could jump in with more advice. "Mom, why don't you fly up here? I'm trying to find someone to go shark diving with me."

"Oh my god. No, I don't want to go shark diving."

"We'd take a boat out to San Francisco's Farallon Islands, where it's common to see a great white the size of a car! You could just watch them from the boat. I'll go down in the great white cage."

"I *would* meet you for a few days' retreat and massages. How about that?"

"You're such a mom. You've gotta break out of this wine and massage thing," she said, teasing me. "You know what that big galoot, Charley, did now? He ate both of my retainers. That's $750 dollars of orthodontic products down the hatch."

I hung up thinking the headaches couldn't be too big a problem if she wanted to go shark diving.

Now, on January 1, 2014, as I sat next to Carmen in her immaculate van, I wondered what a shadow on the brain might be. Could fluid cause a shadow? Could it be a blood clot? I refused to even think of the word "tumor."

That was highly unlikely; not even a concern, I told myself. No one would refer to a tumor as a "shadow." Could it be an infection of some kind? Although I tried to convince myself that we would get to the bottom of the headaches and then take Brittany home, deep inside me a warning sounded. Not a blaring mechanical siren; more like the muffled, mournful tones of a foghorn. This sorrowful pulse of warning stayed with me. I hear it even now, when night falls and I find myself thinking too much.

Carmen pulled into the parking lot of a sprawling, modern glass building, and we hurried to check in at the main desk. On the second floor, we sat in a small waiting room. Since only two visitors were allowed at a time, Dan would escort me back to the ICU while Carmen waited there.

Dan appeared in the doorway. I rushed over and gave him a hug. He reported that there was a large shadow on her brain, that they had scheduled more tests, and that she was awake. His calm demeanor made me feel less agitated.

Dan announced our names into a squawk box, and we were buzzed in. I scanned the glass windows in the rooms we passed, looking for my daughter. The hulking equipment in the rooms overwhelmed me; my eyes were already flooding with tears. Patients were connected to ominous machines that blinked and beeped.

Dan turned to enter a room, and I saw her. A nurse held Brittany's shoulders up, but her head was lax, elegant long neck arched back, dark hair stark against a crisp white pillowcase. The doctor repeated her

26

name in a loud and urgent tone. "Brittany, wake up! Brittany!" Her eyes were closed, and she didn't respond. In the background, one of the machines beeped endlessly, flashing a red number that meant nothing to me. The doctor pried Britt's eyelid open and shone a tiny flashlight in her pupils. She didn't react.

I hurried to her bedside and touched her hand, but didn't pick it up as two IV lines were taped to the back. "Brittany, darling. Momma's here. Wake up." I spoke loudly, leaning toward her ear. "Wake up, darling! Momma's here." Tears streamed down my face. "Sweet Pea, I'm here." I willed her to recognize my voice and come to.

Still nothing.

Dear God, she's dead, I thought as my knees wobbled. *I didn't get to say goodbye.*

What were they saying — something about me? Someone was pulling at my arm. Dan and I were being ordered out. A nurse jostled past us.

In the waiting room, I fell to my knees. "Take me," I begged. "Take me. Not her, not her!"

My entire face was soaked with tears. A thin sheen of perspiration dampened my hairline. I couldn't breathe. I felt like something vital had been ripped out of me.

Carmen came near and rubbed my back. I looked through blurry eyes into her troubled face. I felt I was operating on a primordial level, like a mother wolf separated from its pup. The most primitive part of me needed to stand vigil over my child. "I need to call Gary," I gasped.

Carmen got her cell phone and searched for his number.

Dan slumped on a chair. With a perplexed expression, he said that he'd heard them order Narcan, a drug used with drug addicts who have overdosed.

"Who ordered what?" I stopped whimpering and tried to focus. "The doctor overdosed her?" I asked and began to cry again as Dan strode out of the room on a quest to find out why Britt had been given Narcan.

Carmen held the cell phone against my ear and I heard it ringing. I grasped the phone. Gary's voice broke my last bit of reserve.

"Come now," I sobbed into the phone. "Britt's bad. Very bad. I need you."

"Honey, slow down. I can't understand." Gary's voice faded as I handed the phone back to Carmen.

I gave in to a guttural noise building from deep within. An animal-like howl erupted as I rocked back and forth on the floor.

My wails had quieted to sobs by the time Dan returned to the waiting room, a smile on his face. Brittany was conscious. The Narcan had worked.

She's alive.

I followed him down the hallway, where someone opened the double doors to let us in again.

The curtain to Britt's room was drawn, and the room was dimly lit. Machines blinked numbers, but nothing beeped a warning. The nurse said we must follow the brain injury protocol written on the whiteboard. "Dim light. No television. Speak softly." Brittany sat propped up at an angle.

"This angle must be maintained at all times," the nurse warned us. "Don't lower the head of the bed."

I approached Brittany and softly said, "It's Momma, Britt. Momma's here." I touched her hair.

Britt opened her eyes. Her pupils, tiny pinpoints, focused on me. One eye opened wider than the other. The heavy eyelid fluttered.

"I'm sorry, Momma," she whispered. "I'm not going to be able to take care of you when you're old, the way you take care of Grandpa." Tears welled up and rolled down her face. "I'm not going to live that long."

29

Where had this thought come from? Watching me care for my elderly father for the last three years? I touched her flushed cheek. "Hush, sweetness. Just rest. Everything will be all right. I'm here now. Momma's here." These words rushed out in a loving whisper, but the mournful warning continued to sound rhythmically inside me. I tucked her tangled hair behind her ear.

"I feel so bad. I want these out." She tried to reach for the IV lines, but it was as though she couldn't see where her hand was.

"Let's leave them in for now." I stroked her hair as Dan untangled each of the four lines running into Britt. He gently laid them out straight on her bed.

Dan talked to Brittany about keeping the lines in. "What happened?" I whispered to the nurse.

She couldn't seem to meet my eyes. "Oh my, yes. Well, we're not sure. She might have had a seizure."

My hackles rose. "But she was unconscious, not jerking." I didn't buy this explanation. "She's never had a seizure."

The nurse patted my back. "Well, nevertheless, it was a terrible way to see your daughter when you first arrived. Don't you worry, all of her stats are fine now." She busied herself punching buttons on the machines, and then bustled out of the room.

Dan left to update Carmen.

I was trying to determine if the nurse was someone who could be trusted around my child. My daughter was of me, and a great deal like me, but younger, smarter, prettier. She was the hope of my heart. She embodied the grandchildren I eventually hoped to have. She was the promising career, the result of the excellent university education I'd scrimped and saved for. She didn't owe me these things; she was already all of this, and more. She was my only child — my everything.

Sitting next to her bed, I felt old, even ancient. I felt my youth slipping away, my future sliding away, the rest of my life tumbling into oblivion. Inside my gut, I knew that Brittany, my baby, was going to die. Looking back, I realize that my animal instinct discerned this. However, the thin veneer of my purportedly superior human knowledge denied it. Everything I'd learned in the fifty-seven years of my life — from my parents, schools, and life experiences — told me to keep that mask of human superiority on and deny the warning whimper inside.

Science. Medicine. They would save Brittany. Or perhaps God, through a doctor using science and medicine, would save Brittany. *Yes, a combination of faith and science and medicine would be unbeatable.* Or so I told myself.

As I watched my daughter sleep, I felt no different, no less awed, than the day the obstetrician held her slippery naked body above me.

"It's a girl," the nurse announced, holding what looked like a tiny Martian near my head.

In that instant, I felt a love like nothing else in the world. I would have ruthlessly crushed anyone trying to hurt my baby. My daughter hadn't been outside my womb five minutes, yet I knew I would die for her if need be. It was as though a switch has been thrown, and from that moment forward I would think constantly about her welfare. I was already fixated on keeping her warm and safe, guarding her against danger.

Later, the nurse rolled a bassinet into the room. Inside was the most beautiful, tiny creature I'd ever laid eyes on. Her head was perfectly shaped, not flattened or pointed by having to pass through the birth canal, since I'd had an emergency C-section. She had dark hair and gorgeous skin, as though she'd been born with a tan. I loved my child with a fierce protectiveness that altered me forever.

Brittany Lauren was the name I chose for my baby in November 1984. I thought it was original; my mother was British, and its Celtic meaning was "from Britain." In truth, I'd fallen in love with a name that would become one of the most popular girl's names in the eighties.

A breech baby, Brittany arrived via cesarean because although I was already in labor the hospital classified first-baby breech births as "high risk." My obstetrician told me I'd have to go to a different hospital if I wanted to try to deliver naturally. Brittany kicked hard and broke my water almost a full month early, avoiding, by one day, a painful procedure whereby the doctors would have tried to turn her manually. She was born with mild dysplasia, a hip click. She looked tan because she had newborn jaundice. She was absolutely perfect.

Now standing beside my adult daughter's bed, again I felt my body and soul go through extremely powerful reactions, as I had postnatally. Brittany lay there, helpless and in pain. Disease threatened her brain. She was in danger, and just as when she was a newborn, I realized I would die for her.

However, a willingness to die for one's child was, in this instance, of absolutely no use. There was no such thing as a brain transplant. I sat next to my beautiful girl repeating a useless circular prayer of "Take me, not her. Take me . . ." This begging, this entreaty, didn't make any sense; it didn't make any difference, and didn't calm me in any way. But I couldn't stop.

2
BAD NEWS

January 1–3, 2014

In the real dark night of the soul, it is always three o' clock in the morning, day after day.
— F. Scott Fitzgerald, *The Crack-Up*

Two young men came rattling into the ICU room with a gurney. Brittany blinked awake for a moment, one eye droopy, and then disappeared into sleep again. Dan had left the room earlier to do research and make some important phone calls. "What are you doing?" I asked as they slid her limp body onto the gurney.

"The neurologist ordered a functional MRI. It scans the brain while she's asked to perform various tasks." He was already rolling the gurney out of the room.

"It's just an MRI," I said to Brittany, walking toward the ICU doors. "Nothing to worry about, sweetie!" I called to the gurney as it disappeared.

"Momma, stay with me," Brittany called out sleepily.

She was back too soon. I knew that an MRI should take longer. I looked over at Dan, who'd joined me. Something wasn't right.

"She couldn't do the MRI," the guy pushing the gurney said to us. "She was claustrophobic. We'll need to mildly sedate her and try again."

"She's never been anxious or claustrophobic. She's had MRIs before." I didn't want Brittany being drugged anymore; not after finding her unresponsive.

Dan reiterated this, and stood up as they moved Britt back onto her bed.

"She was trying to climb out of the machine. She was talking about paradigms." The guy shrugged and left, passing a doctor entering the room.

"She was most uncooperative, and very vocal about not wanting to do the test." The doctor raised his eyebrows. "We may need to sedate her."

I locked eyes with him. "I think she's *too* out of it. I don't think she needs more drugs to make her even *more* out of it."

"I suppose we could wait awhile, let the

Dilaudid wear off a little, and try again," he conceded. "She'll be better able to follow the directions to complete the tasks. I'll try to reschedule for later today."

The afternoon ticked by. Dan went in and out of the room, making phone calls and sitting by Britt's bed. When Britt surfaced, I told her that she'd been a little out of it before, and that they'd thought she was claustrophobic. I explained that they hadn't been able to complete the test.

"Can you do the MRI without any anti-anxiety meds, baby?" I asked. Dan pulled the curtain aside and slipped into the room.

"Of course I can. I'm not claustrophobic. *You* are, Momma. That's your issue." Brittany sounded incredulous that anyone would think she was claustrophobic. "I want my laptop, Dan. Where is it?" Brittany spoke authoritatively, her heavy eyelid fluttering.

Dan explained that computers were not allowed in her room while Brittany fiddled with her bed, trying to lower the head.

"The nurse said your bed has to stay up at this angle. It's not supposed to be lowered," I told her.

Dan reached out to stop Brittany from pushing the control.

"I don't give a shit what she says. I'm not comfortable like this." Brittany continued trying to operate the bed. "And my head still hurts."

Thankfully she was interrupted by the young men with the gurney, back again.

"Ready for a ride?" They smiled and chatted with her as they carefully transferred her to the gurney.

"Dan, I want my laptop!" Brittany called, as once again the double doors swished closed.

This time she was gone a good while, so I knew she must be successfully completing the MRI. I flinched at the thought of her poor hurting head, subjected to loud tapping and thumping inside the narrow cylinder of the machine.

"How long do you think we can keep her computer away from her?" I asked Dan, who replied that we should for as long as possible.

I stayed busy by googling what they were doing to her. During a functional MRI, physicians identified regions linked to critical functions such as speaking, moving, sensing, or planning. The goal was to detect correlations between brain activation and the task the subject performed during the scan. This sounded like a logical test. Then I looked up what happened in a Dilaudid overdose. The situation I walked into at the hospital, when Brittany was unresponsive, had lost consciousness, was described as a Dilaudid reaction requiring immediate emergency help. I found out that Dilaudid is eight times more powerful on a milligram basis than morphine. Brittany's weak pulse, low blood pressure, and pinpoint pupils were all consistent with such an overdose. Finally, I found that the antidote was Narcan, the very medicine the doctor had ordered. Narcan was described as a pure opioid antagonist used to counter the effects of opioid overdose. While I do not know what exactly happened with Brittany, this information did not give me comfort in the care Brittany was receiving. I would need to talk to Gary about this when he arrived.

I mulled over Brittany's mention of paradigms when they first tried the MRI. Even though she was loaded up on Dilaudid, her reference seemed perfectly coherent to me. Brittany excelled in science. As a science teacher, I had hoped that she would go into the field. At one time she'd expressed interest in studying to be an immunologist.

In the past we'd spoken of paradigm shifts, or great shifts in thinking; and also of paradigm paralysis, the refusal to see beyond current models of thinking. I wouldn't know until later that my daughter would be leading a good bit of the country's population toward a huge paradigm shift. My mother's instinct told me that even on heavy medication, even before results of the MRIs were shared, Brittany was shifting her focus. She was always three steps ahead.

Carmen thoughtfully picked Gary up at the airport and brought him directly to the hospital. He met me in the waiting room.

I must have looked a sight with swollen eyes, smeared makeup, and a panicked expression. I rushed into his arms. He held me and smoothed my hair. "What have the doctors said?"

"Nothing yet. But it's bad." I wept into his shoulder.

Later I offered to stay with Brittany in the ICU that night, but I was firmly told that there was a "no overnight visitation" policy. I argued that I didn't think it was a good idea to leave her alone, but the wall was up.

Gary and I returned to Brittany and Dan's house with him to catch some sleep, and found a giant pot of fragrant lentil soup simmering on the stove. As I ladled the hearty soup into a bowl, I thought of how kind it had been of Carmen to do this in the midst of running back and forth to the hospital. She was such a good cook. The soup was comfort food, and felt like a giant hug from her.

The three of us sat eating dinner with our glasses of red wine. We were tired, hungry, and quiet. I wanted to cry again. The house was full of Brittany's Christmas things. Her love of the holidays surrounded me. In fact, their whole house was infused with the very essence of Britt. Her wedding photos and pictures from her trip to Africa livened the family room walls.

Dan insisted on doing the dishes himself, so Gary and I went to bed. Before I turned out the lights, I stood gazing at photos that Brittany had taken at the elephant sanctuary in Thailand where she'd worked for a while. A close-up of a giant elephant eye was my favorite. The elephant's kind, expressive eye gazed at me as if she knew and understood my fear and sorrow. Brittany had told me mother elephants often became deeply despondent after the death of their calves. She said that a mother would stand over the remains of her baby, touch the body with her sensitive trunk, turn it over, and caress it. There was no greater love in an elephant herd than maternal love.

Help me, Mama Elephant, I thought as I turned out the light.

In the wee hours of the morning, Dan

received a phone call from the night nurse. Brittany had pulled all her IVs out and was trying to walk out of the ICU. Could he come help? I slept on, unaware of the call.

Gary and I awakened the next morning to find Dan gone. We drove Brittany's car to the hospital. A succession of doctors came and went. Over and over, she was asked to sit up and do a series of tasks. The doctor seemed pleased that Brittany was acing these tests. She was asked to stare at his nose, and her peripheral vision was checked. The doctor used a pen-sized light, watched her pupils react, and asked her to follow the light from side to side. He gently tapped just below her kneecaps with a rubber hammer, and they bounced in response just as anyone's would. She was asked to smile, grimace, and frown. She was asked the name of the president, what day of the week it was, what year it was. I was amazed; *I* could have easily answered 2013, since it was only January 2. But Brittany answered all questions correctly.

Even when they listed three objects and then asked her to list those objects after more tests, Brittany was on it. She felt the pinpricks, and was able to identify a number traced on her back. She was able to move her finger from the tip of her nose to the physician's finger. She could identify the stethoscope when asked to feel it with her eyes closed. With each test, my heart swelled with hope and reassurance. She could smoothly rub one heel up and down the opposite shin. My daughter could perform every task with ease. Surely, nothing was seriously wrong. It had to be an eye problem, I thought; just that one drooping eye.

Late in the afternoon of the third day at the community hospital, a doctor we'd seen before entered Brittany's dimly lit room. He repeated the tests: the light, the hammer, the pushing up and pushing down. Dan, Gary, and I watched as he checked Brittany's chart, scribbled something on it, and prepared to leave. He was dressed casually, in what looked like a jogging suit, almost as though he planned to take a run after this quick look-see.

He was almost out the door when I heard Brittany's voice. "Hey, are you my doctor? Don't leave. I want to talk to you."

The man hesitated, and then stepped back into the room. "Yes, I'm the neurological surgeon on this case," he said.

"Have you seen my scans? Can you tell me what's going on?" Britt's voice seemed to emanate from the shadows of the room. "I've been here for more than forty-eight hours, and no one's talked to me."

The doctor shifted his weight. He opened the file in his hand and flipped through some pages, buying time. Those few seconds did not bode well.

"You have a large infiltrating nonenhancing lesion present in the left prefrontal lobe, and it extends posteriorly into the left temporal lobe. It is also crossing into the left hemisphere and pushing on the right ventricle." The neurosurgeon spoke in a soft but clear voice. He looked up from the file for a moment, and then back down. He moved toward the door.

Stupidly I felt relief. A nonenhancing lesion didn't sound too bad. He hadn't said *tumor.* He hadn't used the C-word. I'd had a lesion in my mouth after oral surgery; wasn't that sort of like an ulcer?

"So I have a brain tumor. A *big* brain tumor?" Brittany's voice was firm, and much louder than the doctor's. "Can you elaborate a bit? *Infiltrating?*" Brit's eyebrows arched up. "Can you tell me what a 'large infiltrating lesion' is? What does that mean?"

I looked at my daughter, who was trying to lock eyes with the doctor. Her green eyes were laserlike. I'd heard the word "infiltrating," too. I hadn't liked the sound of it, either, but I hoped Britt was jumping the gun.

The surgeon was clearly uncomfortable. "Based on the MRI, I would say that you have a glioma, a primary brain tumor. This means that the tumor started in your brain. It didn't metastasize from some other place in your body." The doctor shifted his weight and glanced around the room, avoiding eye contact. "Based on the scans and your age, I suspect that it is a glial tumor, possibly astrocytic."

I felt the slap of information, like a sucker punch to the gut. Reeling with the impact of the words "brain tumor," I frantically dug around in my purse for pen and paper to write down "glial" and "astrocytic," The doctor was talking fast and using medical terminology I didn't understand.

"We suspect this tumor has been developing for some time, because of its size and because in the functional MRI we detected that some brain function in the prefrontal lobe and the temporal lobe has relocated. These changes in creating new connections between neurons happen very slowly. The tumor is quite large, and has increased intracranial pressure. We're giving you steroids intravenously to reduce brain edema."

The neurologist took a quick breath and

45

continued. "The reason the tumor is described as infiltrating is that as seen on the MRI, it has undefined edges and has invaded quite a bit of the surrounding brain tissue. A biopsy will be needed to be absolutely sure of the diagnosis. We need to collect tissue and do the histology to know what we're dealing with."

"So, this thing is going to kill me, right?" Brittany said. In the dim light, her face was a pale dispassionate moon. I'd detangled and braided her hair the day before, and long plaits hung on either side of her face.

The doctor held up his hands. "Not immediately. You have some time."

"But it will kill me eventually?" Brittany's voice rang out forcefully.

"Over time, yes. This tumor presents as a low-grade glial tumor. Historically these tumors evolve into malignant gliomas. I would like to use a stereotactic needle and take a biopsy, collect some cells to have analyzed. That would be the logical next step."

"How long do you think the tumor has been growing?" Again, Brittany's clear voice asked hard questions I couldn't even contemplate.

"I'd estimate somewhere in the range of seven to ten years," he answered.

Again, another slap of information. *Ten years?* I felt a wave of nausea.

"Do you transfer patients to Oregon?" Brittany asked.

A ripple of recognition crossed the doctor's face. It undulated across my brain more slowly. Oregon? Somewhere in an old file in the dark cobwebs of my mind, I had a fuzzy recollection of a controversial law in that state. It had something to do with doctors helping people die. "Why would you ask about Oregon?" Here, the doctor made a strategic error in choosing to play dumb.

"If you don't know why I'd want to transfer to Oregon, this discussion is over." Brittany's voice was filled with disgust.

I shivered. Gary wrapped his arm around my shoulder before quietly asking, "Is the tumor operable?"

"Because the tumor grew out of the brain, it has tentacles, or roots. So no, in my opinion it is not operable." The surgeon looked around at our stricken faces.

"Are other doctors operating on these types of tumors using new technology, like gamma knife or laser?" Gary asked. My Harvard-educated husband was the first of us, other than Brittany, to form an intelligent question. The engineering company we owned had been involved in the design

47

of similar technology.

"There's a surgeon over at UCSF who's really out there doing some crazy . . ." The surgeon's hands circled in the air. "I should say, cutting-edge things." He shrugged his shoulders. "I don't really agree with his approach, but you could see what he has to say."

This was how he referred to a colleague? The way he delivered this terminal diagnosis enraged me. Why didn't he sit down? Why didn't he go over the MRI images with us? Why was he slowly backing out of the room?

"If Brittany were your sister, Doctor, what would you do then? Would you handle everything *here* at the community hospital — or would you perhaps consult elsewhere?" I heard the bitterness in my voice.

"I suppose I'd see what the UCSF neurosurgeon had to say, and go from there."

Immediately Dan suggested that we work on getting Britt transferred to UCSF.

Yes, I thought, *let's get out of this hellhole. I hate this cold fish of a doctor.*

The neurosurgeon started to slip out the door again, his desire to have this meeting over palpable.

"I'd like you to send someone with information about transferring to Oregon," Brittany called after him.

Gary looked at my face, and took my cold hands in his. He suggested that we might step out for an hour to let Dan and Brittany have some private time.

I bent and kissed Britt's forehead. From behind a painful lump in my throat, I squeezed out a hoarse whisper. "We're going to get a second opinion. Don't give up, darling. I'll be back soon."

As unidentifiable sounds bubbled out of me, Gary pulled me into the hall and around the corner. The sounds I was making weren't controllable, or recognizable. I sputtered and moaned, trying hard not to let go of whatever was dammed up behind the lump in my throat. Gary tried to get me outside the ICU so Brittany wouldn't hear what was coming.

We stopped at the elevator, and I hit my husband hard in the shoulder. "No," I said. "No . . . no . . . no!" Each "no" was louder than the preceding one.

"Come on. Let's go outside and get some air." Gary pulled me into the elevator. I slid down the wall and sat on the floor sobbing uncontrollably. In the reflection of the door, I saw my mouth stretched and contorted, mascara running down my face, snot running from my nose. For a split second, I laughed a pig-snort of a laugh, because the

49

image I saw was what Brittany called "ugly crying." She hated ugly crying. Brittany always cried in the shower, because she wanted to avoid others witnessing it. My daughter once pronounced Claire Danes one of the best ugly criers in Hollywood. As I rubbed my streaming nose on the sleeve of my sweater, I knew that Claire had nothing on me.

"Deb. Come on, honey." Gary tugged me up and propelled me out of the elevator. "Hold on. We're almost there." Gently he pushed me toward the entrance.

The cool night air hit me. I released a pent-up, god-awful wail. People coming in and out of the hospital walked faster to get away from the ear-piercing noise. I fell to my knees in the planter area before Gary could get me to the car. I got out my phone and flipped furiously through my contacts. My sister Sarah, in Atlanta, knew that I'd flown here. She'd been waiting to hear what was going on with Brittany.

"Deb. Oh my god." Sarah responded to the hideous noises that I was making. So far, I hadn't been able to utter anything intelligible.

"My baby," I finally wept into the phone.

"What is it?" Sarah paused, then tried again in a wobbly voice. "What's wrong with

Brittany?"

"She has a huge fucking brain tumor!" I managed to scream before I threw my head back and wailed in anguish again. Only this time, I heard someone howling with me.

"Oh God, no!" Sarah cried out. She was screaming "No, no, no!" over and over again. Her husband had come to take the phone away from her. But, even over his calm voice, I could hear my sister howling, just like I was. Gary took the phone from my hand, and I looked up at the moonless sky. It felt right to be screaming together with Sarah.

When I returned to the ICU Brittany was asleep, and a male nurse was on duty at the computer outside. I'd picked at some dinner and attempted to pull myself together.

There was something new written on the whiteboard: "Push Dilaudid slow — 3 to 4 minutes to admin. Patient sensitive."

I left Britt's room to ask the nurse what that meant.

"Your daughter's upper body flushes and she gets nauseous when this medicine is given to her too fast. She needs it delivered to her system slowly." He paused and shook his head. "How long did it take the nurse to push the Dilaudid into the IV line earlier today?" he asked.

"Just a few seconds." I thought back to when Britt got nauseated. "Less than a minute."

"That's wrong. The IV administration should take about four minutes. The push should be very slow. Pushing Dilaudid too fast can be dangerous."

"Is it in her record that she was unconscious yesterday after this drug was pushed too fast?" I asked.

The nurse established eye contact and held it long enough to confirm that he'd heard the question. His head moved almost imperceptibly up and down. "From now on, ask what they're giving her. With Dilaudid, point to the note on the board and remind them to administer slowly." He looked into my bloodshot eyes. "I'm so sorry. I know this has been a hard day."

At his kind words, tears spilled down my cheeks again. "I think Britt needs someone with her tonight. She's frightened and anxious. Last night she pulled all of her IVs out. She tried to leave the hospital." I took a breath. "I brought mindfulness recordings on my iPad. They might help in the middle of the night. It's a meditation technique."

"The neurologists always say no. The brain injury protocol strictly restricts visitation and stimulation." He continued to type into the computer. When he looked up and saw my puffy eyes, his face softened. "To be honest, the literature clearly shows that Intensive Care patients do better with family nearby. All their stats are better. Let me look up who the neurologist is on her case."

"He's an ass," I answered.

"Believe it or not, he's the warm and fuzzy one." The nurse smiled at me, and I tried to smile back.

"I want to be with my daughter. She heard some very frightening news today, and the diagnosis was delivered in a callous and unfeeling way." My chin quivered. "I can help keep her quiet and calm. Believe me, it will make your job easier."

"All right, I'll call the doctor that's on call. But he's going to say no." He picked up the phone. The nurse put up a fight, referencing the research information, recounting last night's attempted breakout. Finally I heard what sounded like capitulation.

The nurse hung up and gave me a high five. "Let's try to find a cot for you."

What they found looked more like a chair you might be electrocuted in. It was a transfer recliner, high-backed, with metal arms and wheels that locked. I was grateful when they showed me that it could lay flat.

The good thing was that it was almost the same height as Brittany's bed. Sheets, a blanket, and a pillow were provided, and I stretched out next to my sleeping daughter.

Brittany hated the puffy devices strapped to her legs that rhythmically filled up with air and applied pressure to her veins, then abruptly released pressure, only to click on again minutes later. She saw this contraption as a torturous sleep interrupter. Its function was to squeeze her legs in a "milking" action, forcing blood and lymph out. Then when the leg sleeves deflated, the veins would replenish with increased blood flow. This was done to avoid deep-vein thrombosis or pulmonary embolism.

After her attempt at leaving the hospital, Brittany was also required to sleep on a sensor pad that alerted the nurse if she tried to get up. "Momma, come here," Brittany whispered to me. "I have a plan for this stupid antiwandering device." She pointed at the pressure-sensing pad on her bed. "I want to pee without a nurse in the room, like a normal human being."

"Oh, Britt. I don't want to get in trouble. Let's just call the nurse."

"No way. Shush!" Britt hissed at me. "Here's how we do it. As I slide off the pad, you slide on. It's just like in *Indiana Jones*."

Britt winked at me.

I burst out laughing, "Except I'm not a bag of sand, and you're not the Golden Idol." I smiled. "If this thing is calibrated it'll notice the difference in weight. When your chubby momma slides on, it's going to sound off."

"I think we could do it. You have to slide in flat on your back." Britt gave me a thumbs-up.

"You do remember that this ploy didn't work for Indiana, right? I'm guessing a nurse will come rolling in here just like that boulder in the movie."

"Where there's a will, there's a way." But she went ahead and pushed the button for the nurse.

After the potty break, we listened to the mindfulness relaxation tape again, and eventually Britt drifted off. I closed my eyes and thought about her willfulness; how she fought each new contraption the doctors brought in. I could only hope that this fighting spirit would help her in the long run.

3
WILLFUL CHILD

1986–1988, Ages Two and Three

"I never knew a girl to have such gump-
tion," she'd say. "But I'm not too sure it's a
good thing."
— Jeannette Walls, *Half Broke Horses*

Two-year-old Brittany wore a red-and-white
romper with white leather sandals. She had
a lightweight watering can with a long spout
in her hands. Through the screen door, I
heard the slap of her sandals on the back
porch. She was getting more water on her
new shoes and on our dog, Heather, who
was following her about, than she was on
the flowers.

"Mo'," she demanded as soon as I slid the
screen door open. "Mo', Mommy."

I added a little water to the can, not so
much that she couldn't pick it up. Off she
went to pour a steady stream on the pave-

ment near the flowers.

"How about we give doggy a treat?" I asked.

Britt unceremoniously dropped the can and ran to me, sandals slapping the cement doubletime. I gave her a piece of dog jerky.

Brittany kept the jerky just out of the dog's reach. Each time Heather tried to get a bite, Brittany yanked it away.

"Brittany, give the doggy her treat. That's not nice," I called.

"No." Brittany held the treat above her head as the dog panted at her heels. "Mine."

"Sweetheart, that isn't your food. It's dog food." As I said this, ever so slowly she began to move the jerky toward her lips.

"Brittany," I said, using my serious voice. "Do *not* eat the dog's treat."

Her eyes locked with mine. The treat hung from her fingers, just in front of her mouth.

"Give it to me." I started toward her, my hand out.

Brittany popped the jerky in her mouth and chewed, screwing up her face at the taste.

"Spit that out!" I ordered, holding my open palm in front of her mouth.

Brittany swallowed it. "Mine!" she called out triumphantly.

The dog and I could only look at each other in disbelief.

I had graduated college in Texas and married my Dallas high school sweetheart. When it became apparent after seven years of marriage that Brit's dad and I couldn't live together another day, I asked him to move out. Within weeks, we were involved in a contentious divorce.

I soon realized that I needed a job that paid more than teaching. A neighbor told me about an opening at a semiconductor sales office almost an hour away. Although this sounded like a foreign world, I did well in the interview and found out I could equal my current pay. My new bosses were supportive of my doing what was necessary to take care of my child. They could be lenient about appointments in a way the school district could not. So I packed my teaching things and became their new administrative assistant. After six months, I was promoted to distribution manager.

With my new work schedule, Brittany's bedtime ritual became both the delight and bane of my existence. Putting her to bed took over an hour each night. This meant that from age three to six, my child and I engaged in the routine for more than a thousand hours. Not to mention the time invested in watching the Disney movie that the ritual was based on. For some time, we watched *Mary Poppins* at least once a week. The routine became more detailed when her father moved out of our home that Christmas. Britt had an old trunk that I'd filled with vintage hats, bridal veils, and the tiniest high heels I could find. My best friend, Sherri, scoured garage sales and thrift stores for things to add to the trunk. Brittany's scarves, gloves, and fanciful dresses that dragged on the floor behind her were accessorized with long strings of pearls, and even a sparkling magic wand. The dress-up trunk was a never-ending source of joy.

Sherri bought Brittany a vintage black ladies' bag to represent Mary's carpetbag. Soon it contained a mirror, a tape measure, a pair of gloves, a skein of yarn, and knitting needles. But still Brittany wandered around the house with a bereft expression, looking for something she called a "cee-jewel." For the life of me, I couldn't figure out what we were missing. Eventually, I figured out that she was trying to say "cathedral." What she wanted was a glass globe with birds flying around St. Paul's. An ordinary snow globe sufficed.

My British mum, tickled that Brittany was obsessed with an English character, supplied a crisp white pinafore apron, a cameo pin, and British coins, including a tuppence. The nighttime ritual was born. First, I, as Mary Poppins, tubbed and scrubbed Brittany, and then, spit-spot, rolled her hair in sponge rollers. After she donned pajamas, it was time for the tape measure to be drawn from the bag. I had written a note in marker at Brittany's height: "Brittany Maynard, practically perfect in every way." This simple measuring never failed to delight her. At my five-feet-seven-inch mark, the tape was inscribed, "Mommy, rather inclined to giggle and *always* picking up."

After that, I carried Brittany to her bedroom window, where we gazed out at the night. Brittany wanted to know if storm signals were up, winds from the East. I always assured her that there had been no wind change, even if it was raining. No wind change meant Mary would stay. With all the changes that divorce precipitated in our home, I wanted Brittany to know I would never leave, no matter how hard the wind blew.

Back at her bed, I climbed in beside her and read three stories. I slipped out of bed, pulled her covers up, and stroked her hair, the way Mary Poppins smoothed little Jane's hair while singing the "Stay Awake" song, a tongue-in-cheek admonishment to not fall asleep.

When Brittany and I moved to a smaller rental home, I continued playing the role of the all-knowing Mary as I struggled to gain footing in my new life as a single mom. Eventually Brittany's father stopped visiting her. His absence resulted in her idealizing him for some years. He became the absent but perfect daddy that would have solved all problems, had he only been there.

I tried to model myself a little after the marvelous Poppins. I didn't have her uncompromising authority and confidence, but I did my best. Unlike Mary, I tried to explain the unfathomable: why Brittany's father never came to see her. Both mother and daughter gleaned lessons from revisiting Poppins's world so many times. Britt imagined herself in far-off and exotic places, and as a young adult, she made those journeys happen. In fact, she traveled alone like Mary, with a duffel bag instead of a carpetbag. I tried to imitate Poppins by being resourceful and taking Brittany on adventures: seeing plays, visiting museums, and going for walks.

Brittany carried Mary Poppins with her

throughout her life. She exuded authority and confidence. She knew that if she truly listened to those who lived very differently, they had wisdom to share. Brittany became a nanny in her twenties while at Berkeley. Like Poppins, she instigated questions and then left it to her youthful charges to search for answers. The children adored her. She was matter-of-fact, trustworthy, and in command of just about every situation.

Mary had a knack for knowing when to come and go. She traveled on the wind, and she left when she had served her purpose. Leaving was hard — even for Mary Poppins. For the briefest of moments, we saw her blink back tears at the end of the movie, as she listened to the parrot head on her umbrella talk about how he wasn't fooled; he knew how she felt about the children. Ever-efficient Mary just clamped the parrot's mouth closed, snapped open her umbrella, squared her shoulders, and rose into the sky.

In many ways, I think my daughter followed suit. She closed the mouths of those who tried to muddle with sentiment her decision to die; she squared her shoulders and decided for herself when she would catch the next wind out of this world.

4
NOT ON THE SAME PAGE

January 3, 2014, the Night After Diagnosis

Everyone must sing from the same hymn
book.

— Dean Lombardi

"Momma."

I awakened in the middle of the night. In
the dim light of the hospital room, I saw
that Brittany was sitting up, pulling on her
IVs. "Sweetie, what is it?" I sat up and
reached for her hands, worried that the bed
alarm would trigger.

Britt shook me loose. "I can't breathe."
She placed a hand on her chest. "I've got to
get out of here. I need to get to Oregon,"
she said, throwing back the covers.

I got off my makeshift bed and leaned over
her. "Brittany, we don't need to go anywhere
right now," I whispered as I held her hands.
"Please don't pull your IVs out, darling. You

63

hate them searching around for veins. You're so bruised already."

Brittany looked down at both arms. It seemed as if she was noticing the bruising for the first time. There were several knots on her hands, one protruding worse than the others, from previous insertion sites. At the bend of both elbows were large blue bruises where veins had blown or the IV cannula had migrated outside the vein.

"Brittany, you only make it worse when you pull out your IVs. You don't want the doctor to order wrist restraints, do you?" I gently touched the knot on her right hand. "You already have a bed alarm."

"Momma, I need to get out of here. This brain tumor is going to kill me in a horrible way. I don't want to die like this. Please help me." Panic filled her eyes. "They can't do a damned thing for me here."

"Let's try to take this one day at a time. I think we need to get more information. I don't trust this doctor." I stroked her hair, and pulled her covers back up. "It's cold in here at night. Let me get you situated."

"I *am* cold." Britt tried to pull the thin blankets higher. "I can't sleep. I keep thinking about dying a horrible death." She moved her arms around on top of her thin blankets. "My heart feels like it's beating too fast."

Mine stopped, then jolted back into a faltering rhythm. I wanted to crawl in her bed and hold her close to me, smooth her brow with my fingertips and draw circles on her back; simple things that used to soothe her as a child. But she wasn't a child, and I couldn't crawl into her bed. My mind raced, thinking of how I could calm her, redirect her thinking.

"Here's what we're going to do." I recalled the mindfulness recordings on my iPad. "First, I'm making sure all your IV lines are straight, okay?" I straightened the lines, careful to ensure they weren't tugging the injection site. "Then I'm putting one blanket lightly over the top of everything, so your arms and hands have some warmth." I pulled a blanket off of my makeshift bed and fluttered it over her still body. "Then I'm going to turn on my mindfulness recording."

"Oh, Momma. I don't do that meditation stuff." Britt started to lift her head.

I smoothed Brit's braids on either side of her face. "If you hate it, I'll shut it off. My mindfulness teacher has a really soothing voice. It's better than lying here worrying."

"I'll try. But you have to promise to turn it off if I don't like it." She sounded drowsy.

65

I sat cross-legged on my bed so that if Brittany opened her eyes, she'd see me doing the breathing exercises. I pushed "play," and closed my eyes.

A flute and violins sounded softly in the quiet of Britt's dark ICU room. Karen Sothers's beautiful voice read a quote from Thomas Merton about there being places of peace in the midst of noise and confusion. Merton said that in this place, love could bloom. I felt my heart loosen and let go. Hot tears rolled down my cheeks.

The voice on the tape continued. "Serenity is the quality of being calm, clear, quiet, composed. Equanimity is the spacious stillness that accepts things just as they are unfolding moment to moment."

How, I wondered, would we be able to ever achieve this state of mind? Karen's voice asked us to settle into a relaxed posture. I saw that Brittany had placed her hand on her belly.

Good.

I mouthed the whispered words "in" and "out," just as the tape directed me to do. For the first time in days, I let go. As I breathed, I prayed that Brittany would feel some calm.

I sat upright and listened to the voice talking about being in the present moment, as if my life depended on it. In a way, it did.

Once Britt was asleep, I shut the recording off and climbed under my covers. But she awoke three more times before breakfast. Each panic attack was as bad as the one before. Each time she wanted to unhook her IVs and leave the hospital. "Momma, please get me out of here. Nothing good will happen here. We need to leave."

During one of those times, the nurse and I brought the portable toilet to the side of the bed and I held her lines while she peed. "Momma, I'm dying. There is nothing to be done about it. Please help me get to Oregon."

I handed Britt some toilet paper and looked at the nurse. His back was toward us as he tried to give Brittany some privacy. *How many times is my daughter going to stab me in the heart with this sentence? Don't we still have some checking out to do before we accept this diagnosis?*

"We need to wait and get a second opinion." I helped her straighten her hospital gown and hold it up.

I knew the nurse was listening, but he stayed occupied with paperwork, his back to us.

"I need my computer. Why hasn't Dan brought my laptop?" Britt asked.

"The doctor doesn't want you looking at the television or computer. They want to bring the swelling down in your brain first. I know it bothers you, but there will be time later for doing research."

Once she starts researching her illness, she'll become a walking encyclopedia of information about it, I realized. *She will see some of the disturbing things I've already read. But how can I protect her from the pain of that? I've always told her knowledge is power.*

"I don't care what the damn doctor wants. There isn't a lot of time. Mom, I need you to get this." She held both of my hands as she prepared to sit on the bed. "Did you hear what the doctor said? I have a big-ass, fucking brain tumor!" She sat down and turned to swing her legs up. "It's going to kill me. You do get that, don't you?" She tugged at my arm, eyes full of terror. "I need to plan."

Gary and I are planning. We are not giving up. There is a doctor somewhere in the world that can buy us time. Gary has some ideas already. But this isn't what Britt wants to hear right now.

My child grasped at me like she was being sucked down in quicksand. The nurse helped me get her covers pulled up and her pillow placed properly. He turned on the pressure pad beneath her, and put the pneumatic compression devices on her legs.

This is not real. I know that we're going to get a second opinion that makes a liar out of this cold fish of a doctor. I was focused on getting better news, a path forward, a treatment plan that would buy us time. *My daughter isn't going to die. She can't. I won't let her die.*

"I'm right here at your side, baby. We'll get a second opinion. We'll research every avenue, I swear."

"A second opinion. That's a good idea," echoed the nurse. "For now, you need rest."

"Do you want to listen to the mindfulness recording again?" I asked.

"I'm not into this meditation shit." Agitated, Britt rearranged her pillows, tangling her IV lines again. "I'm utterly terrified. I can't believe it. How out of all the people in the world did I get a brain tumor?"

I was wondering the same thing. *Was it the traveling to foreign countries? The stress of trying to excel at everything she did? The stress of losing her father when she was so little? Could this have all started when she hit her head on the windshield as a teen? Was it genetic? Her paternal grandmother had died of a metastasized melanoma on her head.*

Over time I mentioned all of these things to doctors, but received no answer as to whether any of them could have caused the tumor.

"I know, but for now, all you have to do is just breathe." *This is all I have right now. This mindfulness tape is all that I have in my Mary Poppins carpetbag. It's all that lies between me being here for you and me running down the hall screaming. Please, please . . . listen to it with me.*

"It helped you go to sleep last time, sweetie," I said.

"We can listen with the volume down. I don't need to hear what she's saying; I just want to hear the rhythm of her voice." Britt allowed her head to rest and closed her eyes. The recording continued. "Each moment that you reconnect to the still point within your breath, you connect to the sacred sanctuary of peace and calm that lives inside of you."

I knew that I needed to find this sanctuary, but in that moment, there was no safe place in the universe, much less inside of me. I had no peace; no calm. I was a tangle of panic and fear. There were many times in my life when I'd been afraid, but I'd never experienced terror at this level. I'd never felt this powerless as a mother. Never this vulnerable as a human being. Never this alone as a spiritual being.

Brittany had been the center of my life for so long. Unacceptable emotions — despair and hopelessness — were beginning to prevail, but I was determined to hide them. I had to make sure Brittany didn't give up.

I needed Gary to find someone who could buy us time. I asked this of him because when I'd tried to read about Brittany's diagnosis, I couldn't take it. It made my stomach hurt when I read about star-shaped astrocyte cells dividing and multiplying. When I read that healthy astrocyte cells were long considered the "glue" or supportive tissue of the brain, and are now known to be integral to sophisticated brain processes, I involuntarily shuddered. My gut churned when I read that brain tumors formed from cancerous astrocytoma cells were called "diffuse astrocytomas" and were typically diagnosed in young adults between twenty to thirty-five years of age. *Oh my god, this sounds like the specific type of glial tumor she probably has.* The worst part for me was the description of tiny, microscopic, tentaclelike fingers invading healthy tissue in the "thinking" part of the brain.

Unfortunately, this research stripped me of my naïve belief that the tumor was just a thin layer of abnormal cells floating on or draped across the top of Brittany's brain. After reading just a fraction of the information, I knew, although I recoiled from the knowledge, that the tumor had infiltrated her brain and taken over some of the surrounding healthy tissue. The brain and the tumor had entwined as one. Worse, most of the MRI images in the literature showed small distinct areas lit up by the contrasting dye. Brittany's MRI showed a huge portion of her brain fuzzy and softly glowing. I'd read that a complete resection or surgical removal of a diffuse astrocytoma was impossible because of the insidious penetration of a tumor's tentacles into normal brain tissue.

The information I had absorbed tormented me, even when I closed my eyes and tried to rest for a few minutes. Inside my daughter's beautiful head — in her frontal lobe, the part of the brain responsible for the higher functions of thought, memory, and judgment — function had been moving around over the last ten years. I marveled at the plasticity of her brain, which had adapted as best it could to being invaded by small, star-shaped cells. For some reason, it was important to me to envision what the tumor looked like. Perhaps creating an image in my mind made me feel as if I had some sort of control; as though I would be better able to look for medical hope if I could somehow create a blueprint to work from. I'd read that the infiltration of the brain by astrocytes made the brain matter firmer and ivory-white. I'd also read that as the tumor advanced, the brain took on a softer consistency and even created its own blood supply by mutating into blood vessels.

Of course, I wanted to know what caused this hideous monster that had attacked my child, but all I found out was that for some unknown reason, there had been a change in the genetic structure of her brain cells. Only a minuscule percentage of people inherited this deviant genetic structure. Researchers thought that environmental factors might cause brain tumors, but there was no conclusive evidence. It appeared that people exposed to petrochemicals or pesticides (Brittany hadn't been) were at higher risk. Studies about high electromagnetic fields had been conducted, too, but no one really knew what caused brain tumors.

Earlier in the day, I had turned my iPad off and gone to the bathroom to throw up. I'd told Gary that I couldn't do any more research. "Maybe later," I said. "Right now part of me wants to know, but part of me can't know."

None of these reality checks stopped the plan that was forming in my mind. We would find a way to buy some time — probably surgery to remove some of the tumor — and during that borrowed time, a cure would be found. This popular cancer myth was the one we hung onto, and it gave us an emotional buffer. Unfortunately, translating the latest pivotal research into real-world advances is an agonizingly slow process in the United States. Gary and I hadn't yet grasped that cancer research is a grueling marathon (approximately three decades from lab discovery to FDA approval), not a quick sprint. Britt, on the other hand, had already comprehended that she didn't have that kind of time and stared death squarely in the eyes.

5

THE TWO OF US

1987–1988, Ages Three and Four

Children will not remember you for the material things you provided, but for the feeling that you cherished them.
— Richard L. Evans,
Richard Evans Quote Book

After the divorce, Brittany and I moved to a modest one-story home I'd bought in Orange County, California. I turned it into a girl house. The walls were painted the palest hint of pink. We had beautiful flowered wallpaper in our tiny dining room. It was about a fourth of the size of the home we'd lived in with her father, but it was peaceful, and it was ours.

My parents drove all the way from Dallas, Texas, to help us move into our tiny new home. My mum, Iris, whom Brittany called "Nanna," commented with typical candor,

"You need Barbie furniture for this house. Your furniture looks oversized, as though we're stuffing sardines in a can. It's all out of proportion."

"It'll have to do." I tried not to snap at my mum; after all, she'd driven all this way to help. But, honest to God, if there was a way to make me feel worse about a situation, it seemed she knew how to do it.

My father, who was raised in Oklahoma during the Dust Bowl, was quiet as usual. He mumbled something and took his tools outside to build Brittany a little playhouse with a real shingled roof.

I grew up in Dallas with this odd pair, an Okie and a Brit. My mother said *tomahto* and my father said *tomayto.* Mum spelled it "colour" and Daddy spelled it "color." They were as different as two people could be. Even as a child, I knew that Mummy couldn't have picked a place to land that was more barren for her spirit. At Sunday school, I learned about sowing seeds on fertile ground. I pictured my mum as a British seedling landing on the clay-and-alkaline soil of Texas. Mum was named Iris, a flower born in rich, loamy soil; but here she was in an environment where soil was thin with a solid layer of limestone beneath it.

Mum's crisp British accent couldn't have

been more different than my Daddy's drawl. My Oklahoma/Texas relatives were huggers, cheek pinchers, and "bless your little heart" kind of folks. Mum and her family were a reserved, penny-pinching, "stiff upper lip" kind of crowd.

Mum made sure we had the fear of God (and her) put into us, and that we were clean and well fed. She found the hugging in my dad's effusive family "a bit queer." Iris was no shrinking violet and enjoyed, indeed thrived on, a good confrontation. Mum and Dad fought loudly and even physically all of my life. I made a rule that if they wished to be around Brittany, they couldn't quarrel in front of her. My siblings, two sisters and a baby brother, and I grew up practically living on the buckle of the Bible Belt. I learned conservative religious values, while at the same time observing that the folks who talked the talk sometimes didn't walk the walk. At my house, what you saw was what you got. My parents weren't strangers to giving a good whipping, and Mum could shriek our names loud enough to be heard a block away.

All four of us excelled in school. We toed the line for the most part, living in terror of our mother's wrath. And there was always Daddy, a sleeping volcano that Mum could

turn on and off with a good tongue wagging. Often my mum said, "When you
children move out, I'm divorcing your father
and never looking back." Once all four
children were out of the house, Mum still
grumbled about divorce, and Daddy even
once stunned her by saying, "Let's do it."
However, faced with the prospect of living
alone, Mum decided to stay. It was a shock
to find out that when push came to shove
my mother was, as Texans say, "All lime and
no tequila."

As I faced life as a single mother, it was
good to remind myself that living with two
screaming, fighting parents hadn't been a
walk in the park. Though Brittany had only
one parent, at least she wouldn't live on pins
and needles, as I had.

Growing up, I'd ridden horses and spent
summers barefoot, chasing fireflies in the
long evenings. All of this made me who I
was, and in turn it shaped Brittany. My
daughter called me "Momma" because my
daddy called his mother "Momma." I had a
deep sense of family obligation and loyalty,
something instilled in me by my father's
parents, Okies who would stay put and
hunker down in the face of triple trouble:
drought, wind, and economic depression.
Britt and I put our drinking glasses mouth-

side-down because that's how my family did it in the Dust Bowl.

Sometimes I felt a bit prickly and unable to express an emotion (behavior I'd watched my mother struggle with). And was it a British obsession that caused Mum to constantly wish aloud that her stout-legged and full-bosomed girls had been born to be "reed-thin, willowy, or lean," like her? Brittany's Nanna, Iris, laughed at the oddest things, including the misfortune of others. And surely Brittany and I had acquired our freakish devotion to the hunt for and acquisition of a good bargain from Iris. My daughter and I had the best and the worst of the Okies and the Brits to draw from — an interesting combination.

One day, four-year-old Brittany stood watching me attempt to dig with a trowel around our broken sprinkler. We had settled into our new home. We'd brought our rescued dog, Heather, with us. Determined to make life seem much like it had been before the divorce, I wanted to turn the backyard into a green oasis, where we could play croquet and kickball. Brittany would run and play here with our dog. She wouldn't even miss her father.

"We need Daddy," she said, her little face solemn.

"No, Sweet Pea, what we need is a proper shovel." I stood and wiped my muddy hands on a rag. "We just need the correct tools and a little advice. Let's go to the hardware store."

Brittany sat in the seat of a gigantic cart at the store and listened as I explained what I thought the problem was.

"We really need a daddy," she said again. "Could you come and fix it for us?"

I smiled at the older gentleman who was assisting us. "Brittany doesn't know that mommies can fix things just as well as daddies." I gave him a prompting look, hoping he'd pick up the thread.

"Well, sizing your mom up, I'd say she has as good a chance of fixing it as I do." He smiled at Brittany. "And if she has any questions, she can come back for more advice."

We left the store with a big shovel, a pink tool kit, PVC pipe, and glue.

This time, Britt watched while coloring in her coloring book. When I'd followed all the directions and glued the pipes in place, I left the hole and scooped her up for a shower.

After allowing time for the glue to dry, I

turned the sprinkler on and watched for leaks. "Look, sweetie," I crowed. "I fixed it!" I filled the hole with dirt and pressed it back in place with the shovel.

"Mommy, you did it!" Brittany danced around me as I patted down a chunk of sod.

I didn't like the job that the gardeners were doing on my small yard. I was paying them money I could ill afford, and they were at my house for less than five minutes. Three men jumped out of a truck and it was mow, blow, and go.

One Saturday I decided I would do my own darn yard. So Britt and I went back to the hardware store and got a new electric mower, a weed whacker, and an electric hedge trimmer. Over the next few weeks, the fireman who lived across the street would sit in his garage and have a beer with his buddies on Saturday afternoons while watching my efforts. I was sure he was amused by my gardening routine, but I just waved at them and continued working.

The long orange mower cord was a pain in the butt. I had to learn how to whip it hard enough so it would jump the mower and land on the other side, each time I made a turn. There was also a learning curve in using the weed whacker as an edger without hitting the cement or brick. Every time I hit the stucco of the house, I bent over to inspect the damage I'd done.

I afforded further amusement for my audience across the street when I tried to edge the privet. Sizing up the task, I climbed on top of my cement block wall and began swinging at the hedges with the electric trimmer. This made me feel like a genuine badass, but this was also when I heard the most laughter coming from my neighbor's garage.

The fireman's wife came over to chat one day while I was watering, and mentioned that her husband had asked why she couldn't do *their* yard. "After all," he told her, "that woman has a full-time job and a kid. You're a stay-at-home mom."

I laughed. "Well, I bought all these tools in a fit of exasperation with the gardeners. To be honest, with each passing week, I'm finding it harder to remember what was so bad about them."

Actually I kind of liked mowing. Unlike housework, the yard stayed nice for a few days. I could drive home with Brittany in her car seat behind me and admire the fruits of my labor. I did my own yard for several years, until I was promoted to account sales representative and made enough commission selling semiconductors that I could afford a gardener again.

A light breeze carried a faint, pungent odor of moist earth. Standing in our backyard, Brittany lifted her face to the sky. "Mommy, I think it's raining," she whispered in wonder.

The dainty dusting of freckles across her snub nose twisted at my heart. She didn't think her coppery splotches were cute, but I adored the way they accentuated her green eyes. I'd told Brittany her freckles were where angels kissed her nose while she slept, but she didn't buy it.

Tilting my head back, I felt drops. A slow smile spread across my face. Southern California was in its fourth year of severe drought; the ground was parched, the grass browning in patches. Would this bring relief from the relentless heat?

The drops began to fall faster. I lifted my arms to embrace honest-to-God rain, and blinked as a drop caught me squarely in the eye. Brittany began to spin in a slow circle. She stopped and stuck out her tongue.

"Rain tastes good!" she called to me.

"It smells good, too," I said.

"Raindrops keep falling on my face," I improvised from the *Butch Cassidy* song, "and just like the mom whose feet are too big for her bed . . ." I grabbed Brittany's hands and began to swing around with her. We spun as I sang, off-key, the words of "Singin' in the Rain," inserting Britt's name in the lyrics to make her laugh. We slowed to a stop, grinning into each other's dripping face.

I strummed an imaginary guitar and sang Eddie Rabbitt's "I Love a Rainy Night." Britt took up the beat clapping. We did our best rendition of strumming air guitars while we butchered the song, getting soaked to the bone. Brittany's eyes sparkled and her ears peeked through ropes of damp brown hair. We ran to the porch, the air redolent with the tropical odor of white jasmine. Britt shivered in delight.

I drew her toward me. "Time to get out of these wet clothes," I said, pulling her shirt over her head.

"Momma, we're outside!" She held the dripping shirt in front of her narrow chest.

"So?" I pulled off my wet shirt and wrung it out. "We're going to strip down and go indoors." Glancing at our high cinder-block walls, I kicked off my tennis shoes. "This backyard is totally private."

I crouched to untie Britt's wet shoelaces. She kicked off her shoes, and I helped her step out of shorts and panties that were plastered together.

My little naked jaybird ran into the middle of the yard and spun in circles, face up to the sky. Before running out to scoop up her slippery happiness, I stood watching the rain kissing my little girl.

Brittany took a kindergarten readiness test at her preschool because her November 19 birthday was referred to as "on the cusp." She could go on to kindergarten the following fall and be one of the youngest in the class, or she could stay in pre-K for one more year and be one of the oldest. The man who did the testing classified Brittany as gifted and talented. He said the first grade curriculum would be easy for her. However, he suggested that I consider whether I wanted her to be the youngest in her class. She was considered premature at birth, which he said was somewhat important in evaluating readiness. I also knew that she was emotionally needy due to the divorce. Ultimately I decided to give Brittany the advantage of being one of the older students in her class.

As a preschooler, Brittany liked continuity. When her daily schedule changed, it threw her off-kilter a bit. I tried to provide structure by having Brittany cared for by women whose children were in Britt's classes. That way, she would go home with a friend until I picked her up after work. Britt was blessed to be cared for by two very kind women who could give her the love, attention, and security she needed to grow strong and independent.

Brittany's preschool and elementary school were aware of the absence of Britt's father and of her deep attachment to *Mary Poppins.* The teachers would pull Britt into their laps and read a book if she became anxious.

Books provided solace for Brittany at school and at home. At the top of the list were *Madeline* by Ludwig Bemelmans, any of the *Amelia Bedelia* books by Peggy Parish, and *Matilda* by Roald Dahl. With the help of her excellent preschool teachers, I was able to guide my daughter gently through the worst of the divorce by giving her plenty of cuddling, attention, and a way to escape into books.

6
PROMISES

January 5, 2014, Transferring to UCSF

Promises and Pye-Crusts . . . are made to be broken.
— Jonathan Swift, "Polite Conversation,"
The Prose Works of Jonathan Swift

The next couple of days at the community hospital were tense because now we just wanted out of there. We were waiting for our request for transfer to the Brain Tumor Research Center (BRTC) at UCSF to be processed. We were asking the BRTC to accept Brittany as a patient, and to find an open room for her. *U.S. News & World Health Report* rated UCSF fifth best in hospitals for adult neurology and neurosurgery. None of the four hospitals that rated higher were geographically close. For now, until we could get the pressure lowered inside Brittany's cranium, UCSF was the

87

absolute best place to go on the West Coast.

Dr. Mitchel Berger was director of the BRTC. A Harvard-trained, nationally recognized neurosurgeon specializing in brain tumors in adults and children, he also had extensive training in intra-operative mapping of the brain. UCSF's BRTC was rated highly for advanced technology with imaging done with a 3-Tesla MRI, which had superior imaging capabilities. Edward Chang, an associate professor in residence of neurological surgery, was the admitting doctor. Dr. Chang had done significant work in trying to gain understanding of the speech mechanism of the brain, which Brittany's tumor was invading.

Dan and I had been trading off nights ever since Britt was admitted to the community hospital.

"You can't do this by yourself, Dan. We need to become a team, sharing and dividing responsibilities," I'd said to him.

Looking exhausted, Dan had agreed.

"We're in for a long haul," I'd said, worried that he felt he needed to handle everything. "We have to keep our strength up. We need to double-team this."

On the last night at the community hospital, it was my turn to stay with Brittany. Since her doctor's abrupt and clumsy diagnosis and his disrespectful introduction to Dr. Berger, Brittany's mood had naturally sunk. She had been told she had a fatal tumor, and that the only person who might attempt surgery was "really out there." How had he expected that description to leave her with any enthusiasm or trust?

Brittany spiraled into a dark and hopeless place; an understandably angry place. Where else do you go when given zero percent chance of defeating a cancer that is strangling your brain? This gaping maw of terror was worst after dark. We'd wake up in the middle of the night and have circular conversations, me firmly holding on to hope, Britt repeating the things that she had learned about her disease from reading. We'd lost the battle with Brittany over reading on her laptop. She was furious that anyone would even think of trying to stop her from researching her condition.

In spite of what was a perfectly understandable reaction on her part — anger at the diagnosis and terror about the future — I couldn't understand why Brittany had gone directly into acceptance mode. What happened to the other stages of grief, denial and bargaining? I wanted to fight. I wanted hope. I wanted a miracle.

I was firmly in the land of denial, where I

stubbornly imagined that we'd find a solution. Gary was furiously researching, even calling doctors in other countries. We were working on a plan.

"I'm toast, Momma." Brittany continued, "I need you to get that. I have a giant tumor that is going to kill me in the most horrible fucking way if I don't do something about it."

"No one has said you're going to die in a horrible way." I tried to placate her. When she spoke this way, I felt like I was being stabbed in the gut.

"Don't you get it? Have you read anything about this? It's what they *haven't* said that we need to fear." She cracked her neck, holding her head with her hands and jerking it to one side. "Haven't you noticed no one wants to talk about it? Hell, this *doctor* can't even talk about it. He barely got the diagnosis out." Britt jerked her head in the other direction, eliciting a second loud crack.

I grimaced. "Please don't do that. It can't be good for your poor head." The sound of her neck cracking made me nauseous.

"God, Momma! Cracking my damn neck didn't cause a brain tumor. Who cares what it's doing to my vertebrae? It doesn't matter if my bones are crumbling to dust, because that's all I'm going to be in less than a year. Dust." She cracked her neck twice more.

Pain knifed my heart. I breathed in tiny fearful wisps of air. My head itched, and I felt fiery bumps along the nape of my neck. Golden fluid seeped from an open blister-like sore on my left cheek. I feared it was contagious impetigo. Who knows where I could have picked up staph bacteria — my dad's memory care facility? On the airplane, or here at the hospital? I definitely didn't want Britt getting it. All of this was easier to think about than what my daughter had just said.

"We aren't giving up, darling. Gary will leave no stone unturned. We're getting out of this incompetent hospital, and we're finding someone who knows what the hell they're talking about." I scratched the burning bumps until my fingertips came away stained with blood.

"My neck, Momma. It hurts so bad." Brittany sighed and leaned back on her pillows.

I washed my hands with warm water.

"Lie straight, baby. I'll give you a massage." I slid my hands under Britt's neck, and using firm pressure searched for knots, trying to relieve the endless pain. Pain that interrupted every conversation. Pain that

91

pinched her brow. Pain that glazed over her eyes. Pain that robbed her of empathy. Pain that deprived her of sleep. Pain that she had borne for almost a year.

"You have to help me establish residency in Oregon. We have to move fast. I don't have much time." Her voice was soft and small.

Finding a knot, I applied pressure. I massaged her almost in my sleep, as I'd done so many times. I used my thumbs to knead the knots while Brittany asked me to make her promises that I didn't know if I could keep.

"Promise you won't let me suffer, Momma. Please don't ask me to lose my sight, hearing, and speech. The pressure inside my head's so bad. It feels like it's going to explode."

My daughter's beautifully shaped head was loose and heavy in my hands as I gently manipulated it this way and that. "The prognosis isn't good," Brittany continued. "Primary brain cancer is rare, so research isn't funded. They don't know what the fuck they're talking about. If I had any other kind of cancer, it'd be better. I have the worst damn thing you can get."

I listened to my logical daughter as I massaged the muscles on either side of her spinal column. If only I could heal her by sending love through my hands.

"A primary tumor like this is an outlier. It's not curable. It's a death sentence." She rolled carefully to the side and bent her slender neck as I pressed the heel of my palm between her shoulder blades and made long deliberate strokes.

"You heard that asshole doctor. This monster tumor isn't going to stop. It's going to change grades, and stage four brain cancer is cruel. I'll be paralyzed. I'll lose my memory. I might not even know who you are anymore." There was a sad hiccup in her voice. "I'll lose everything that makes me who I am."

I listened, but every cell in my body screamed no. It took all my will-power not to shout it out loud. Everything I'd learned from my mother, father, grandparents, and early church training flooded my mind. Childhood lessons, imprinted in my brain and drummed into my very corpuscles, made me reject what I was hearing.

All I said was "Lay on your back, sweetie. I'm going to do your head and face." I helped her straighten the IV lines again, made sure they weren't tugging, and dabbed her cheeks dry with a corner of the sheet.

"Momma, please help me. Brain cancer isn't like other cancers. The glioma on my

MRI is going to become a glioblastoma. That's the most malignant, fast-growing tumor. My brain will turn to mush. My eyes will bulge out of their sockets."

The image of my child's eyes, the window to her soul, protruding from her sockets from so much intracranial pressure, was hellish. My stomach churned. Rubbing her temples, I remembered what I'd read about the brain becoming softer and darker.

God in heaven, help me . . . help us.

"I promise," I whispered. "I promise I will help you, darling."

A vivid image of hell flashed into my mind. Every sermon I'd listened to in Texas had a little bit of hell built into it. My minister had taught me that hell was as real as any other geographical location; that Jesus (who I grew up loving) believed in hell and routinely sent people there; and that people I had known were now in hell. There was an unquenchable fire in hell. People in hell were eternally thirsty, everlastingly tortured by flames, their mouths stretched wide in agony while horned winged creatures tormented them day and night.

As I gently smoothed my daughter's forehead, I prayed for a miracle. *Please God, heal the brain that is beneath my fingers. Only you can help us now.*

Brittany gazed up at me, locking eyes. "Promise me. I need to know that you will help me die, that you won't let this tumor slowly torture me."

I looked down at her precious, worried face and promised again. "I will not let this tumor torture you. I will do whatever I need to do." As I said those words, I realized that I would have to keep this promise, no matter what. I'd break the law, I'd take her to another country. I'd do whatever I had to do.

The terrible thing was, at that moment I didn't know how I could help her. I just knew that I wanted her to stop talking about dying. I wanted her to sleep. *I* wanted to sleep. I wanted to wake up and find out that this had all been a bad dream.

"Go to sleep, darling. I'm right here at your side." I stroked her face and returned to my folding chair. Still praying for a miracle, I pushed thoughts of hell away. But that night I dreamed that Brittany and I were there. We couldn't walk; we could only crawl through the flames as we tried to escape from horned creatures that pierced our skin with their three-pronged pitchforks as Brittany screamed out to me.

■ ■ ■ ■

I awakened when a nurse whispered in my ear, "I'm so sorry to have to ask you to do this at this hour, but we need to move you to another room."

"What time is it?" I sat up, disoriented. I looked over at my daughter. "Brittany, are you all right?"

Before Britt could answer, the nurse said, "Oh yes, she's fine. We'll get her a gurney. I just thought you might like to start gathering your things." She handed me some plastic bags with handles.

So this was the abrupt end of the sacred brain injury protocol that we'd been following for days. Brittany was rolled into the brightly lit hall. I stumbled behind her, carrying our belongings as we traveled through a portion of the hospital that seemed to be under construction, with empty rooms and furniture in the halls as if they were readying for a thrift sale.

Finally, Brittany was wheeled into an odd-shaped corner room where we heard a loud television next door. This wing seemed crowded, and all the doors were open. There were no drapes on the windows. It was as though the hospital had washed its hands of us. We were now in a noisy area of the hospital with minimal nursing staff — a far cry from the ICU. Rest was impossible.

For the next twelve hours, Brittany talked almost nonstop in ever-tightening circles. The main gist of the circle was: Life sucked; life had been particularly unfair to her, to us; she'd worked hard all her life to be a healthy and good person; there was no God, because no God would let this happen; the universe was just a gaping maw of darkness and death; she knew deep in her soul that she was dying; she knew that the death would be a torturous process of loss upon loss; she loved me, but she needed me to help her get to Oregon; she deserved a peaceful death; she had done nothing to deserve the death that her brain tumor had in store for her; no one was going to stop her from seeking asylum in Oregon; she was afraid that she would lose the ability to speak and she would be stuck in her body; she would lose the right to advocate for herself; would I please be her advocate if that happened; knowing the way she would die was hell. What did we do to be given this hell?

I tried to pray with her or talk to her about hope, to encourage her to listen to the meditation tapes, but this only infuriated her and precipitated another full circle. All I could do was promise that I would support her. I said that I understood, but in reality I didn't. I said that I would do whatever she needed me to do, but deep down, I didn't know if I could. I said whatever I thought might make her stop fretting.

Aunt Sarah was already researching the death with dignity law in Oregon, finding out what Brittany needed to do to qualify. She was the right person to call. Her husband had had a bad heart all his life, and he and Sarah had talked about this very subject. She said that yes, she could do the research without losing her mind. My brother-in-law, Charles, was a smart and thoughtful man, and he had gone there in his head. This thought comforted me the tiniest bit.

Hours ticked by. Dan and Gary joined us after breakfast. I was reading out loud to Britt a book that she had been given for Christmas. The title was *David and Goliath,* and I loved Malcolm Gladwell's lean writing and provocative ideas. It was perfect for Britt, an inspiring book about looking at obstacles and disadvantages in a completely different way. "I'm David," Brittany said when I paused. "The tumor is my Goliath."

■ ■ ■ ■

Twelve hours after we'd been transferred out of the ICU, a nurse finally came to remove Brittany's IV lines. I rode with Britt in the critical care transport unit to UCSF, a trip that was made more miserable by getting caught in rush-hour traffic. I'd specifically told the critical care ambulance nurse that my daughter had just been taken off of all intravenous meds and a saline drip and was urinating frequently, and yet there was no bedpan for Britt to use.

When we got stuck in traffic, the nurse and I told Britt it was all right to just wet herself, and we'd clean her up at the hospital.

Brittany answered, "Nothing is all right. I am fully aware that life will never be 'all right' again."

7
SWEET PEA

1990–1994, Ages Six to Ten

What would it be like to feel so attached,
so intrinsically bonded, so protective of
one's own best connection with time and
the ages, of generations past and future,
of another human life, of their time?
— J. R. Tompkins, *Price of the Child*

One day when I picked up six-year-old
Brittany after work, Cheryl, her warm and
loving sitter, handed Britt her backpack and
reminded her that she had homework.

"Oh no," Brittany complained, her face
collapsing from joy to complete dejection.

"Well, you want to grow up smart and get
a good job like your mommy, don't you?"
Cheryl said.

"I never want to be like my momma,"
Brittany answered. "I want to be like you
and stay home with my children."

Pangs of regret, guilt, and sadness braided together, twisting at my heart, but I quickly recovered. Looking at Cheryl's stunned face, I said, "I understand that emotion. I wish I could stay home with you every day, Sweet Pea."

The sales job had grown by leaps and bounds. I'd never received any training, but maybe selling science to middle schoolers prepared me for the job. Whatever the case, it turned out I was quite good at it. I carried a briefcase, wore a beeper, and had one of the first cell phones on the market. None of that looked glamorous to Brittany, though. She knew how dead tired I was when I got home at night.

Within six months, I was the number one salesperson for my company. All of this success came with stress, from competing companies and within my own office. At least I was socking away money for Brittany's college. My goal was to be able to give her the gift of graduating with no debt. I put the money into savings, and pretended it didn't exist.

In first grade, Brittany made a smeared mess of her homework with her dirty pink eraser. When I suggested that she start afresh with a clean sheet of paper, she howled in agony.

"No! I won't! This is good enough," she yelled from the kitchen table.

I quietly picked up the paper, wadded it up, and threw it in the trash can.

"How can you be so mean?" she wailed.

I picked her up and carried her to the hall, where I had hung a collection of sepia-toned family photographs dating back to my great-grandfather. The pictures spoke of poverty, of the Dust Bowl and days of endless work. The photos spoke of desperation, aging before your time, and dying too soon. I carried her down the hall. "This is your grandpa," I said, pointing at a little boy in a wagon in front of the lean-to tent. "This is your great-grandma," I said, indicating a white-haired woman holding up a dead wild turkey by its spurred feet. "These are your grandma's sisters, eight of them. They all died of tuberculosis before they reached the age of thirty." I pointed to a family photo with eleven children grouped around their parents. Heavy on my hip, Britt calmed down.

"You come from these people, Brittany." I watched her eyes widen as she examined the photos. "These are your roots. This is your family from way back."

Brittany reached out to touch the picture

of my father. "Grandpa?"

"He lived in that tent. His family never quit. They just kept going." I tucked her hair behind her ears. "In the dirt, and in the wind, with no money. They weren't quitters."

"They don't look happy," she said softly.

"No, Sweet Pea, they don't. But when Grandpa talks about these days, he calls them 'the good old days.'"

"Why?" she asked. "They don't look like good days."

"Because they did the best they could with what they had. And that felt good to Grandpa." I smiled as she wiped her tears with the back of her hand. "Doing the best you can feels good."

"It doesn't feel good! It feels sad that I have to start over."

"I know it feels sad now, baby." I kissed her cheek. "But wait until you see how great it feels when it's finished."

That July, we traveled to Dallas to see my parents and my sister Donna, who'd flown out several times during the divorce to help with caring for Britt. Closest in age to me, Donna had been a source of calm strength during the emotional divorce proceedings.

Nanna, Grandpa, and Auntie Donna all

climbed in the car with Britt and me, and we explored the Fort Worth Historic District. Britt also got a taste of my mum's strictness, which did not go over well. Later, I took Brittany to the creek that ran near my childhood home. I showed her the school I'd attended, and the stable where I'd boarded my horse. It was an important trip, as Brittany was old enough to see that I'd grown up quite a bit differently than she had.

Brittany's first grade teacher had told me that my daughter was gifted and would do well in a private school with smaller classes. So Brittany started second grade at St. George Academy, where there were only fifteen or so children in her class.

In the third grade, Brittany was chosen to sing a solo part of Jasmine, with a little boy in her class singing the part of Aladdin. My friend Sherri and her son Tyler came to see Brittany's amazing performance. I couldn't believe children so young could step forward with such confidence and sing their hearts out. By this time, Britt was becoming less likely to say we needed a daddy, and more likely to brainstorm with me about ways to solve problems. She was into girl power, and she definitely wasn't happy when I decided to marry for a second time.

By that point, my daughter and I were as powerfully bonded as the neutrons and protons of an atom's nucleus. Our temperaments were quite different, but we balanced each other out. We were interdependent, but we'd learned that we could live happily without a man in our home. Unfortunately, the man I'd been dating for three years and who ultimately became Brittany's stepfather did not bond with her. From day one, the odds were stacked against us surviving as a married couple. Ultimately after six years of working at it, we separated and divorced.

At ages eight and nine, Brittany and her best friend, Jennifer, zoomed up and down the street on inline skates, their legs becoming more muscular with every stroke. Brittany organized practical jokes on the phone, head thrown back, mouth wide in laughter. Britt and Jen went to equestrian camp, climbed trees, did cartwheels, performed chemistry experiments, and danced like no one was watching. They put on plays, modeled in pretend runway shows, and went on nature explorations on nearby walking trails. Fearless and courageous, they were an absolute joy to watch. These two little girls, on the tender edge of blooming into pre-teens, wrote a note to their future selves full of whimsical wisdom.

Always believe in yourself. Always be friends. Stick together no matter what. We believe in you girls that are ladies now succeed through everything in everything. You are now 21 and probably in a good collage. Stay out of drugs and alcahal. Don't ruin your life that you have ahead of you. Remember all of your good and bad times through your childhood and always remember god is with you and loves you. Remember that poem, footprints in the sand! Love yourself and be confident!

Love
Us

Meanwhile, Brittany grew steadily in height, social skills, and scholastic ability. She needed vertical support, just as the flowering sweet pea's vinelike stems needed something to climb. Her tendrils twined around me for structure and sustenance.

Sweet peas are hardy flowering plants, with enchanting delicate flowers in a wide spectrum of colors. They need rich, well-drained soil and sun. With proper support, the canes can grow to fourteen feet. According to the pediatrician, my little girl might reach a height of nearly six feet.

Sweet peas grow heartier when their heads are in the sun and their roots deep in cool, moist soil. Britt's face was sunny and happy, and I felt that she was putting down a strong root system fertilized with my love.

I adored the fact that when I picked Brittany up from school, she jumped into my embrace and twined her arms and legs about me. I couldn't wait for each workday to end, so I could hear her latest joys and sorrows. I loved being Brittany's trellis, her support.

The image of Brittany as a climbing cane of delicate flowers stayed with me throughout her childhood, into her teens, through her illness, and right up to her death. Robert Kirkland Kernighan's poem, "Sweet Peas," captures my feelings perfectly, although I still cannot read it aloud without breaking down. He writes about his loved one dying, and planting sweet peas around her grave. He imagines the sweet incense of their scent floating up to God.

There are sweet peas in my garden now.

8
CRANIOTOMY

January 6–10, 2014, the Week of Surgery

When push comes to shove we can afford
to lose an arm or a leg, but I am operating
on people's thoughts and feelings . . . and
if something goes wrong I can destroy that
person's character . . . forever.
— Henry Marsh, consultant neurosurgeon
at Atkinson Morley/St. George's Hospital
in London, author of *Do No Harm*

The decision had been made. Dr. Mitchel
Berger, professor and chairman, Department of Neurological Surgery at UC San
Francisco, was out of the country. His
protégé, Dr. Edward F. Chang, would
perform a craniotomy on January 10, 2014.
Brittany was fine with this substitution, as
Dr. Berger had indicated in a personal
phone call to her that she was part of his
patient family. He added that when he

returned, they would schedule another surgery and try to get more of the tumor. But for now, to reduce the pressure, Dr. Chang would do a conservative surgery and get as much of the tumor as he could without risking the loss of any of her eloquent skills.

Young and fit, Dr. Chang inspired confidence in Brittany and yet she repeatedly warned him, "I don't want you going into my brain and riding around like a rodeo cowboy."

Dr. Chang smiled at the unlikely image, and assured her that he was aware of the risks. Edward Chang specialized in and excelled at neurophysiological brain mapping to safely perform neurosurgical procedures in the eloquent area of the brain. He knew his way around the hospital, and he knew his way around the human brain. Dr. Chang looked Brittany directly in the eyes and patiently listened to her as she told him about her plans to move to Oregon and use the laws there to facilitate a peaceful death.

"I need to know just how fast this son-of-a-bitch tumor is growing, and I know that means surgery to collect tumor tissue." Brittany was talking fast. "I also need a DNR form."

Chang looked down at the floor, then back

at Brittany. He asked why she needed a DNR now.

Britt's statement had felt like a knife wound to me. I wondered what it had felt like to him.

"Because if something goes wrong and I flatline during surgery, I want you to let me go." Britt's voice was steady and firm.

Dr. Chang shifted his weight and said that, in his opinion, having a DNR during her craniotomy was not a good idea.

"I think it's a great idea. If for some reason fate gives me the chance to die earlier rather than later in this process of dying from a brain tumor, I don't want anyone intervening."

Dr. Chang studied Brittany for a few seconds. Then he asked what she would think if he could buy her five years of time.

My heart fluttered. This was the most hopeful thing anyone had said so far.

"Can you tell me with certainty that you can do that?" Britt stared at him, her eyebrows arched.

The doctor said he would know more after the surgery. The tissue would tell them a lot. But he felt that she should hold off on plans for a DNR. He held Britt's gaze for a moment, then asked that she not tie his hands during the surgery. He asked that she

110

trust him.

In the end, Brittany had the DNR take effect immediately after the surgery. Dr. Chang honored this request.

They let Brittany go home for a couple of days, to rest, relax, and be with her husband and her beloved furbabies, Charley and Bella. Gary flew home, but I stayed with Dan and Britt.

Their house was still decked out for Christmas. The first thing I did there was race around cleaning. My priority was her bedroom and bathroom. One of Brittany's Berkeley buds, a former roommate, wandered in while I scrubbed furiously at the grout in the shower. She asked how I was doing.

"Okay, I guess." I pushed hair out of my eyes with the back of a gloved hand. As I gazed at her youthful face, it dawned on me that I was anything but okay. I was freaking out of control. I had just been thinking that if I could only get the shower clean enough, Brittany's cancer would disappear. As I scrubbed at the tiles, I imagined scrubbing tumor cells away.

"I'm cleaning because it feels like I'm attacking the tumor," I admitted, my tears welling up. I stood and turned the water on to rinse the walls.

"I get that," she said. "And if that strategy worked, I think it's safe to say she'd be cured."

I laid down my squeegee, stepped out of the shower, and clung to her neck.

On January 9, just before midnight, Brittany sent Gary and me an email with a link to a YouTube video she'd made to send to a doctor in Oregon. I think she emailed the information because it was too hard for us to talk about. In the video, Brittany spoke of using Oregon's death with dignity law. Because we were engrossed in the outcome of her surgery and her post-surgery care, it would be a couple of days before either of us viewed the video. We needed to get past the first forty-eight hours before watching her talk about aid in dying. In the hospital, I had promised her that I would back her up. I'd vowed that I'd support her no matter what. I had wanted her to stop talking about dying. I would have promised anything. Though it terrified me, I was prepared to keep my promise at all costs.

As a single mom raising a child, I had become a bit neurotic about honoring my word. Gary, who was by nature a promise-keeping kind of person, knew that if he told

Brittany he would do something, I expected him to do it. We tried to keep every promise, big and small.

Now I would keep this promise to my daughter, even if it killed me. When Brittany spoke of dying in Oregon, I immediately wondered if there was a way to go with her — and I didn't mean go to Oregon with her. This thought came naturally. It didn't shock me, but I was aware that it would shock others, so I kept it to myself.

For the hospital trip, I bought Britt a new nightshirt, fluffy warm socks, and an eye mask for light sensitivity. I was more prepared after our experience at the community hospital. Dan, Gary, and I took Brittany to UCSF on January 10. Soon she was prepped and gowned for surgery, with a hospital bracelet on her wrist. I looked at her name on the plastic band, and wondered if she would be the same Brittany when she came out of surgery. I looked at her waist-length hair, wondering if I should braid it. I knew the doctors were hopeful that they wouldn't have to shave her whole head. But there was no time to ask about braiding.

However, I did make sure to ask for permission to stay in the ICU with Britt after her surgery. I listened as various people told me that this was impossible. I explained that Brittany had tried to rip IVs out of her arms and escape from the ICU at the first hospital. "No one stays in the ICU at UCSF," an assisting doctor told me. "There are no accommodations. None."

Brittany was listening as I waged this war. Finally the doctor acquiesced.

"I'll be there when you wake up." I leaned over and touched the wisps of hair curling at her hairline. "Come back to me," I whispered into the pink curve of her ear as they wheeled her out.

Dan and his family were in the cafeteria. I stayed there for a while, but then realized I needed to be in a quiet place. "Gary, I'm going to find the chapel," I said.

He packed his laptop and went with me to the "meditation room" off of the main lobby. We entered a small room with a few chairs, sacred and inspirational texts, and a prayer request book. I dropped to my knees in front of a chair and leaned my elbows on the seat.

I prayed that God would guide the minds and hands of the surgeons. I prayed that He would keep Brittany's strong heart beating steadily throughout the surgery. I prayed that Dr. Chang wouldn't accidentally remove brain tissue that allowed Britt to think, speak, hear, or see.

"This is my child's greatest fear," I shared with Him.

I prayed that the pressure in her skull had been reduced enough by the drugs she'd been taking so that the surgery could be done without brain matter trying to escape the confines of her skull. I prayed that God would heal my daughter. I prayed that, even though I'd been told they only expected to get part of the tumor, that somehow, miraculously, they'd be able to remove it all. I prayed that I would know how to care for her and calm her when she got out of surgery.

After a while, Gary quietly left the room. Carmen came in and prayed for a while. She touched my shoulder in empathy when she left. When Gary returned and urged me to break for lunch, I joined the others in the cafeteria, but I couldn't wait to get back to the meditation room. I wanted the quiet, the sound of my breath and heartbeat the only things I heard. I excused myself and retreated to the little room.

I no longer prayed the ridiculous prayer "Take me instead" over and over. I tried another angle, concentrating on praise. I praised God for the miraculous neuroplasticity of Brittany's brain, making adjustments over the years so that she functioned normally. I felt awe at her brain's ability to remap itself. God had not hardwired Brittany's brain, and therefore it showed flexibility in restructuring its functional organization. I thanked God for her brain's ability to allow the healthy tissue to take over functions that were lost to the tumor's invasiveness. Brittany, articulate Brittany, remained so because the right side of her brain had taken over most language functions.

"My daughter's brain is already a miracle. Thank you for this miracle," I whispered.

I had been kneeling for several hours when I decided to prostrate myself before God. Perhaps with me in this most humble of positions, He would listen to my prayers.

Two thoughts entered my mind. These phrases were so different from what I'd been thinking and praying, so different from the way I normally stated things, that they sounded like someone else's words.

The first was "The tumor is the work of the devil. It is not of God."

The second was "I will take back what is mine."

I was startled. Never had I equated the abnormal cells growing in Brittany's cranium with a supernatural force. I'd only thought of her tumor as renegade star-shaped cells taking over the brain. I'd thought of the tumor in scientific terms.

The first statement, about the work of the devil, sounded ominous. Menacing. Brittany's tumor, the huge tangle of cells that no one understood, seemed to me more like a strike of lightning. A rare aberration coming out of nowhere, creating a shock wave in our family. The second statement sounded even more ominous to me. It didn't seem to contain any promise of Brittany's recovery. And yet it contained elements of a promise.

Does our mind create these answers, these voices from nowhere? If it was just my mind, why didn't I invent more comforting statements for myself? Had I tuned into the right channel, somehow accidentally ridding the air of all the static that I normally heard in life by prostrating myself in this quiet place? Or was I getting answers from a Zoltar-like voice in some kind of cosmic fortune-telling vending machine?

This was not a burning bush. This was not an angel speaking to me. It was just a clear voice, speaking in a way that I didn't speak. My college education was predominantly in science. I had taught science. Of course I thought it was coming from my own mind. However, I also left room for

117

other explanations, and in my heart, I laid claim to what I'd heard.

Whatever happened with this terrible tumor, God (the Supreme Being/the divine energy of the universe/the mother/father of all mankind) would claim Brittany as His/Her own. I held tight to that. It was so simple, really. As much as I loved my child, something bigger than me, someone infinitely more powerful than me, loved her more.

I couldn't even comprehend a big love like this. Loving Brittany was the biggest thing I knew. As her mother, I would do anything for her. Deep in my heart, I knew that this divine energy and power loved my daughter, did not want her to suffer, and that all the stuff people had said about going to hell was hogwash.

In a sudden moment of clarity, I also realized that the scene in my dream, of Brittany and me in hell, was something I'd seen on a trip to Italy. It was painted on the dome of the cathedral in Florence, Italy. No wonder the dream had been so vivid and scary; it was created from the terrifying images of Satan and his workers in Vasari's fresco of the Last Judgment.

My mind and heart felt opened up. The cobwebs of childhood thinking still hung in corners, but light was shining bright on the subject of a powerful all-encompassing love, illuminating the truth. The divine would never hurt my child. No matter where she went with her terrible illness, she was loved.

Eight hours. I hadn't seen my daughter in that long. We'd had a message about four hours into the surgery that all was going well. I didn't feel that I could leave the tiny meditation room for more than a few minutes until Brittany was out of surgery. Could a neurosurgeon buy my daughter her life in eight hours? In spite of all the information to the contrary, I held on to this hope. I knew down to my bones that the best he could do was buy her some time. But the stubborn part of me, the part of me that was still in denial, kept pushing this thought to the front of my mind: What if he came out and said, "We got it all"?

The other part of me asked, *What if he comes out and says, "I'm sorry, but we lost her"?*

While I prayed, Brittany was given general anesthesia. There had been discussion of doing an "awake surgery," and those conversations had caused a great deal of anxiety. Ultimately, Dr. Chang, conferring with Dr. Berger, had decided on a two-surgery approach. In this first operation, Chang would remove as much cancerous tissue as he could without risking loss of skill sets. It would be less aggressive than the surgery that could be done in an awake state. Later, Dr. Berger would do a second, awake resection surgery to target more risky tumor tissue.

Britt was prepped using a hair-sparing technique, shaving only a quarter-inch-wide area along the incision. The neurosurgeon made an incision behind the hairline above her left eye and curving in front of her left ear, a bit like a question mark. As he cut through the membrane, he sealed off many blood vessels because the scalp has a rich blood supply. He then folded back the scalp tissue to expose the bone. Using a high-speed drill, he bored holes in a pattern on the cranium. The holes were connected using a fine wire saw until a piece of the bone could be removed.

A protective covering of membrane, called dura mater — Latin for "tough mother" — was cut with surgical scissors and folded back to expose the brain. The dura is tough and inflexible or leatherlike. When I read about the Latin meaning of "dura mater," I cried. I needed to be a tough mother. But most of the time I felt vulnerable and soft, like brain tissue.

Using various instruments, Dr. Chang removed tumor tissue that could be safely taken without damaging speech or the ability to read. Since the surgery was being conducted in the eloquent area of Brittany's brain, the margin of error was less than a millimeter.

When the surgery was over, the dura and the bone plate were put back in place. The bone was held in place with titanium screws. A drain was put under the skin of Brittany's forehead to remove excess blood and fluid from the surgery site. Finally, the muscles were sewn and the skin was stapled.

Gary was in a waiting room across the hall from the meditation room. The irony for Gary was that I, who suffered from claustrophobia, had stayed in the small and suffocating room all day, yet he'd been unable to take its close confines for more than a few minutes. At times we spoke in the hall, asking each other questions that neither of us had answers for.

Is this unusually long? How does a surgeon concentrate on the intricacies of someone's brain for so many hours? Is the surgeon standing? Poor Brittany. Her head has been clamped in one position for so long; what will this do to her already aching neck? How much of the tumor is he able to access? Does the length of the surgery mean that it's very difficult to get at? Do the chances of a problem increase in relation to the time spent in surgery?

While Brittany was watched closely in the recovery room and her vital signs were being monitored, Gary came to get me. "She's in recovery. The surgery went well."

In the hall, I hugged him.

"They got approximately 45 percent of the tumor and necrotic brain tissue." Gary spoke softly in my ear.

Was it then that I thought, *Only 45 percent*? I don't think so. That thought came later. At that moment, all I could think of was that Brittany had not died on the operating table.

My daughter was alive.

■ ■ ■ ■

Two:
Renunciation

■ ■ ■ ■

Begin challenging your own assumptions. Your assumptions are your windows on the world. Scrub them off every once in a while, or the light won't come in.
— Alan Alda, *Never Have Your Dog Stuffed and Other Things I've Learned*

9
DENIAL

January 10, 2014, Day of Craniotomy,
Continued

Denial helps us to pace our feelings of
grief. There is a grace in denial. It is
nature's way of letting in only as much as
we can handle.
— Elisabeth Kübler-Ross,
On Grief and Grieving

I was terrified to see my daughter in the
Neurosurgery Intensive Care Unit, having
envisioned all kinds of things. I expected
her to have a bruised, swollen face and possibly blackened eyes. I expected her to look
like she'd been in a fight and lost. I expected
her to look frail.

But Britt looked beautiful after her craniotomy, although her hair was matted behind a headband of stark white dressing.
Her eyes were clear. Her color was good.

She was conscious.

The wave of relief was visceral. For a fraction of a second, I felt my knees wobble. I looked around, but there was no chair in the ICU cubicle. Lots of IV tubes and machines were attached to Britt; not much different than she'd had when first admitted to the ICU ten days ago at the community hospital. I wanted to pinch myself, to make sure I wasn't dreaming that she looked so good. So well. So alive.

I was filled with a rush of excessive love. I wanted to hug Brittany, the doctors, the nurses — anyone associated with the hospital. I felt that I'd witnessed a miracle.

Dan kissed Brittany on the forehead repeatedly, whispering something in her ear. Her big green eyes fluttered open and then drooped closed again. Dan moved away and I went to where he'd been standing.

I, too, bent to kiss her forehead. "You came back to me," I whispered.

Britt croaked, "Water."

We were told she couldn't have any water for a while, but the nurse got me a tiny cup of ice chips and a plastic spoon. I also asked for a chair, as I was staying the night. This resulted in a long explanation about how "no one ever stays with a patient in the Neurosurgery Intensive Care Unit."

After more conversation, the suspicious nurse checked the chart and made several phone calls. Someone came with a bucket-shaped molded plastic chair. The back was low and curved, so you couldn't rest your head. In fairness, a bigger chair would have made it impossible to get to Brittany on that side of the bed. I realized that it would be a long night after a long day, but I wouldn't leave her alone.

Before Dan and Gary left the hospital, Gary was allowed to come in with me to the ICU. Gary brightened as soon as he saw Brittany. "You look amazing, sweetheart." He held her hand. "You came through this with flying colors — just like you do everything. How do you feel?"

"Like crap," Brittany said.

I pulled Gary aside and told him, "She's complaining of jaw pain. I don't understand."

"She looks great. She's a trooper." He kissed me on the cheek. "Our Britt is very strong."

I clung to his shoulder and whispered, "Someone has to come and get me early in the morning, like eight o'clock. I'm going to be falling-down exhausted by then."

Gary rubbed my back. "I'll be here. I'll take you back to Britt and Dan's, and you

127

can catch up on your sleep. Dan is taking tomorrow's night shift." He held me for a long moment, and then he was gone.

The male nurse came in every hour to do the same neurological exam that was given to Brittany prior to surgery. The questions. The light in her eyes. The test of pushing and pulling against his arms. As she had before the surgery, Brittany seemed to complete each test easily, though she became increasingly annoyed at being awakened.

"It seems like every time I escape the pain and fall asleep for a few minutes, you come in again and wake me up," she told the nurse.

"I'm sorry, these tests are very important in the first twenty-four hours after surgery," he answered. "How is your pain right now?"

"It's a nine, and getting worse. My jaw is killing me. What did they do to my jaw?"

I didn't understand this at all. The nurse seemed concerned about giving her too much pain medication, and asked her if she could wait another thirty minutes. He got an ice pack to place on her jaw. As I sat next to her trying to help keep the ice pack in place, tears rolled down her face.

"Momma, my jaw is really hurting." Her

lips quivered, and she drew a breath. "It's hurting way more than the banging of my headache. Why is he making me wait?"

"Don't cry, sweetie." I dried her cheek. "Crying is likely to make you feel worse. I'm going to go talk to him. I'll be right back."

I sought out the nurse and asked him if jaw pain was unusual. I told him that pain strong enough to make Brittany weep couldn't be good for her recovery.

"Well, it isn't unheard of," he said, "but it is somewhat unusual. Sometimes the surgeon has to move or even cut the muscles of the jaw. I'll be right in with some pain medication."

Around midnight, when she drifted off, I grabbed my overnight bag and went to a restroom to change into sweats, wash my face, and brush my teeth.

When I returned, the nurse was sitting at a computer outside Britt's room. He gave me a smile. "Wish I could offer you better accommodations. I can't imagine that you'll get any sleep, but I can bring you a blanket and pillow."

"That would be nice. Can I ask why you're holding back on the pain meds?"

"Well, we don't want painkillers to cover up important symptoms. But with the jaw pain, it's tough."

I went back in and sat watching Brittany's sweet face. She looked angelic to me. I knew that the pain meds would wear off, and that each time we would have to beg for more. We were in for a long night, but I was still awash in relief and gratitude. Hope rose in my chest and fluttered like a wounded bird. Maybe this surgery had bought enough time. Maybe Gary could find a new procedure somewhere in the world that would save Brittany's life. Hope flailed and thrashed, twisted and turned.

I wrapped myself in the blanket, moved down until the back of my head rested on the chair back, and closed my eyes in a prayer of thanks.

I fervently prayed for God to show us where the answer was. Where in the world was there a neurologist or neurosurgeon who knew more than the doctors at UCSF? It was my version of asking for a miracle. It was my version of faith. It was my version of denial. I confused hope with denial, but now I know they are sometimes one and the same.

I know that denial is seen in a negative light and hope is seen in a positive one, but I'm not sure if they should be. Denial is an unrealistic hope; a false hope. Some would call it unfounded optimism. I would say that defining "unfounded" is hard for those faced with terminal illness.

I think there is a lot of pressure in our country for cancer patients and their families to keep a "good attitude." There is an unspoken belief by many that if you don't keep a positive attitude, keep up the fighting façade, the cancer will spin out of control. This line of thinking implies that we can stop cancer from spreading with our minds. There is no scientific research to support the concept that a hopeful outlook stops cancer cells from multiplying.

It is difficult for the families of those faced with terminal illness not to be in denial. Both hope and denial distanced us from the pain. These normal self-defense mechanisms acted as a distraction; we spent precious time looking for something to support our belief that there was reason to hope. At this stage, Gary and I were still clearly in a place where we were asking, "What if?" We weren't yet ready to ask, "What *is*?"

My husband said, "Let's hope for the best, and prepare for the worst." Even though he said this, he was invested in trying to find some research to support the hope, while leaving the preparation for the worst to others. I was so invested in wishing for a miracle that I welcomed this as our strategy.

On this first night after her craniotomy, Brittany was in too much pain to engage in conversation. Since she was only able to surface enough to ask for water, pain medication, or ice, I was left to my own thoughts.

I had envisioned that after waking from her surgery she, too, would be filled with a sense of promise. Perhaps she was. Perhaps for a brief period of time when she came to, she was able to only feel a kind of blissful gratitude. Maybe she thought, *Oh my gosh, I made it.* Or maybe she thought, *Shit. Why didn't I go on the operating table?*

I think I know the answer. I think she was happy to be given some more time. I also think that articulating any kind of expectation for recovery was just too painful for Brittany. In view of what her MRI revealed and what doctors had said, confidence in the future was equivalent to self-torture. If it crept in, she chased it away. There is a difference between wanting to live and having a likelihood of surviving. Brittany hungered for life, but she had no *hope* of living.

On that night, the nurses, clean white sheets, blinking screens, and signaling alarms comforted me. The sights, sounds, and smells of the hospital made me feel that we were doing all we could do. My sitting next to her all night — feeding her ice chips, changing her ice packs, advocating for pain management — was my way of fighting for her. That night I allowed hope to bloom in the shelter of my heart, away from the barren land of logic and scientific fact.

10
MIDDLE YEARS
1996–1998, Ages Twelve to Fourteen

"No," the mother told her. "It's too danger-ous there." A small incident, but when multiplied a hundred, a thousand times in a little girl's life, she learns that she's not as capable as a boy of handling life on the edge. She learns to hang back.

— Sue Monk Kidd,
The Dance of the Dissident Daughter

When does your carefree daughter — always in motion, legs ablur — change? When does she stop doing cartwheels, running through the house chasing the dog, bringing in pond water and caterpillars for observation? When does she stop pulling quirky hats out of the dress-up trunk to wear? When does she stop having fun with her mother? When does a daughter stop acknowledging that her mother has even spoken to her?

134

In 1996, when Britt was in sixth grade, I quit my job in semiconductor sales and became a science teacher at the Episcopal middle school that Brittany attended. I took this enormous cut in pay because I thought I could be a more attentive mother if I had basically the same school hours as Brittany. I could allow her to participate in more activities. We could remain close if I quit the energy- and time-sucking sales job. I probably didn't factor in how hard it is for a child to attend the same school that her mother teaches at.

At the same time, she and I moved out of our house, leaving the stepfather who never became a stepdad behind. Marrying him had been the second worst decision of my life. I felt that he didn't deserve me, or my little sweet pea of a girl, in his life.

We moved back into the house that I'd purchased after the divorce from Britt's father. I'd converted the one-story into a rental when I remarried, holding on to it as a safety net. Now we were downscaling again, returning to our safe place surrounded by sword lilies, the jacaranda now huge. I told myself that it didn't matter that I'd failed at marriage twice. I told myself that Margaret Mead had married three times, and she didn't consider herself a failure. The night we moved, Brittany and I turned on the boom box and jumped with glee on the queen mattresses laid out on the floor. We felt free.

In the half-light of that first morning in our old home, I swore that I would never trust a man again. I would never marry again; from now on, it was just the two of us. I no longer trusted my judgment regarding men, and I would not subject my daughter to any more losers. I couldn't wait to get my maiden name back. I was never going to give it up again.

Brittany attended sixth grade at the private middle school near our home, where I taught seventh and eighth grade science. My daughter was interested in absolutely everything. She had an unquenchable thirst for knowledge, tearing through books and poetry, drinking in the underlying meaning and themes in great gulps. Brittany excelled in all of her classes, and her teachers adored her. She quickly made friends with a gaggle of girls who were forever doing the Macarena.

When a few of the older kids talked about the strict new science teacher, I think she felt conflicted. I made light of it. "Just tell them they're lucky they don't have to live with me," I laughed. Most of the time Britt seemed to neither rely on me nor be ashamed of me. She started developing her own distinct tastes. She wanted her bedroom painted green, which we did. My friend Lola and I took our preteen girls to Melrose Place one Saturday afternoon and walked up and down looking at the shops.

Brittany's bedroom had a cathedral ceiling with a recessed area that she wanted to decorate. Looking in one shop window, I called out, "Hey, Brittany, look at this beautiful narrow vase. It looks like blown glass. It's so pretty."

Lola's older daughter, Kylie, and Britt came to look. Kylie started laughing uncontrollably, holding her sides. She said, "Wow, Britt, your mom rocks! She wants to buy you a bong."

Brittany's surprised face revealed that she didn't know what a bong was, but she laughed along with her friend.

"What's a bong?" I asked.

This was my first inkling that I would soon be navigating uncharted mother-daughter waters; a place where even the language we spoke would be foreign.

Brittany was now at an age where she listened to boy bands and some intensely depressing songs by female singers. She watched several television shows I didn't particularly approve of, either, such as *Friends.* I felt I needed to pick my battles, so I settled for just discussing the lyrics and inappropriate scenes with her.

"Gawd, Mom." Britt rolled her eyes. "I know what you're doing. You're trying to ruin *Friends* for me with all this psychobabble."

Brittany seemed to hold her own about me being not only *a* teacher, but *her* teacher. When she entered seventh grade, she was in my earth science class, and in eighth grade I taught her physical science.

I ran a hands-on science program and, as such, a classroom with strict rules. I couldn't have middle schoolers getting hurt because they were larking about in the middle of a lab activity. I knew I was one of the strictest teachers, but there was also a lot of learning going on in my classes.

One morning I forgot to bring some supplies in, so I asked Brittany to take my keys and get them from my car. She and her friend were happy to go to the teachers' parking lot. After a while, Brittany returned looking chagrined. "Mom, your keys are locked inside the Saab."

"Oh dear. Did you get the supplies? I'll

just call Triple A at lunch, if I have the stuff to do this morning's lab."

"Um . . . well, we have the supplies, but there's something else you should know." Brittany's friend tucked her chin so I couldn't maintain eye contact.

I raised my eyebrows at Brittany. "What?"

"The radio's on." Brittany smiled the tiniest bit. "Really loud."

"Are you kidding me?" The bell rang, and I ran downstairs to see if by some wild stroke of luck the key I'd hidden years ago in a magnetic box was still affixed to the undercarriage of the car. Brittany and her friend made a break for their next class.

Was it my imagination, or could I actually see my little Saab's canvas roof pulsating? The music was pumping, the side mirrors were vibrating, and the car seemed to be straining with the effort of containing the sound. Of course there was no longer any hidden magnetic box. So I dialed Triple A and returned to my classroom. I had to smile, wondering how many reports of rap music emanating from the beat-up Saab in the teacher's lot would make it to the main office before the Triple A guy arrived.

Brittany and I had several after-school routines that we loved. In between running her to the ice-skating rink, or cheering practice, or to the store for supplies for a project, we did little things that brought us comfort and togetherness. We loved to look for something yummy for dinner. We called it "Trader Joe's therapy." We also liked to drive through Wendy's. The reason we went there was for the long, bendable French fries. We fought each other for the "Wendy Bendys."

We also enjoyed evening walks around the tiny man-made lake that sat in the shadow of Saddleback Mountain's twin peaks near our home in Trabuco Canyon, California. I walked the one-mile path twice while Brittany jogged ahead in the dusk. I always insisted that Britt circle back before I lost sight of her in the twilight.

In middle school, Brittany changed from a tall, lanky girl into a taller, voluptuous young woman. Her hair darkened and grew longer, streaming down her back. Brittany developed a classic Sophia Loren figure, but she hated her hips and breasts. It didn't help that a list sent around by the seventh grade boys listed her as the girl with the "biggest tits." I tried to explain to her that our brains are programmed to look for symmetry, and that having a large bust, small waist and curvaceous hips was a good thing. I told her that historically and scientifically, her shape was considered alluring. "You have an archetypal hourglass figure," I said.

In our teens, my sisters and I had narrow hips, small waists, and large breasts. My mother was six feet tall and lanky, with small hips and breasts. She made us aware that she felt utter dismay at our bourgeoning bosoms. She seemed to think if we exercised enough, or dieted enough, our cup size could somehow be controlled.

I was determined not to have this dynamic in my relationship with Brittany. In some ways, I was successful. In other ways, I failed miserably. I accepted that Brittany's figure was beautiful. I thought that if you were genetically predisposed to a big bust, it was better to also get the curvaceous hips. I complimented her figure and told her she was lucky. I failed not so much in what I said to Brittany about her body, but in what I said in front of her about my own body. If I could do one thing differently, this would be what I'd change.

I complained about my weight all the time. Britt saw me try the grapefruit and boiled egg diet, the tuna, carrot, and celery diet, and the Atkins diet. I did encourage taking regular walks and outdoor exercise, but my unhappiness with my weight shone through. My self-deprecating remarks couldn't help but spill over to my daughter. I regret this thoughtless behavior, and always will.

Brittany's young body began to draw unwanted male attention. It was frightening and disturbing to have grown, even old, men ogling my child.

One day, I was driving with Brittany in the passenger seat with our windows down. At the stoplight, a truck pulled alongside us on the passenger side. Brittany yelled "As if!" as the truck pulled away. The middle-aged driver had offended her by ogling her and winking at her.

I told Britt that when I was in my teens and twenties, I pretended that the rude men didn't exist. I wouldn't give them the satisfaction of letting them know I'd even seen them. I also said that I didn't feel like that was enough sometimes. "Men who stare inappropriately or harass females with catcalls or whistling are rude, sexist jack-asses," I told her. "Some of this attention" — *Damn it, did I really have to tell my child this?* — "is just the way life is. When you're in a safe situation, you can call a guy out on this behavior; but *not* if you're alone.

"Always trust your gut," I said. "If the situation feels a little scary, don't be bold and take risks just because you think, *He can't do that.*" I paused. This topic was fraught with my own painful memories, strengthened by my instinct to keep my daughter safe. "Studies show that women who are attacked usually have a moment where they think, *Maybe I should go back and get someone to walk with me,* or *Maybe I shouldn't go to the car in the parking garage because there's a guy standing over there.*"

The silence in the car was heavy. I knew I hadn't nailed it. I wasn't sure there *was* a way to nail this. How could I say that it wasn't right to walk around afraid and embarrassed, and at the same time say that if you felt that way, you should heed it?

I didn't want this blooming sweet pea of a girl to get the message that she must still her voice, become shy, or doubt herself. I didn't want to put fear in my bold, willful girl's heart, but in my own heart, I knew that women feel fear because they *are truly at risk.* More than one out of four women will be assaulted in their lifetime.

I'd taught Brittany the single mom's habit of religiously locking doors. I'd taught her never to answer the door to a stranger. I'd taught her to come home before dark. I had already been teaching her fear as well as boldness.

No mother wants to teach her child to be anxious. I wanted Brittany to continue to run, jump, and climb trees. I didn't want her to cower in shyness or cringe in fright. I tried to teach Brittany that most people were good. At least that's what I said, but did she feel my worry when I had to stop in strange parts of town? If I'm brutally honest, middle school was the beginning of a long stage of apprehensive parenting for me. From age eleven to thirteen, something important stirred between Brittany and society. Between Brittany and her body. Between mother and child.

And not just for us; this was happening for a lot of the girls I taught. I saw trepidation in other mothers' eyes, too.

It happened slowly, just as a summer day fades. First a gentle lengthening of shadows, then the gradual loss of light until you find you're jogging in darkness and nowhere near home. That was how fear crept into my parenting. Niggling in the back of my mind was a growing sense that Brittany could somehow be hurt, and I wouldn't be able to prevent or fix it. I also felt somewhat wounded and abandoned as Brittany began to try to define herself as an individual. My mum had always frightened me into doing what she wanted me to do. She also had my dad as a backup drill sergeant. Brittany defied me in little ways, and I felt anxiety nibbling at the corners of my confidence.

"You're the worst mother in the world!" she shouted at me on the way home from school one day.

I took a deep breath. "Thanks, Sweet Pea. I'd hate to be the *second* worst." I'd hoped to make her laugh, but this comment only made her angrier.

"You think you're such a good mother, but you aren't!" She turned her back to me and stared out the window. "And stop calling me Sweet Pea!"

It hurt. Britt's childhood had been marked by that nickname. Sweet peas produce long-stemmed sprays, adorned with ruffled, winged blossoms that emit a blissful scent. Mothering her when we were truly intertwined had been just as sweet. As a little girl, Brittany remained within touching distance. We held hands or walked together, her arm around my waist. She climbed into my lap and looped her arms around my neck. My best friend, Sherri, Tyler's mom, called Brittany "the Velcro child" when she watched me drop her off at summer camp one year. She said she could actually hear the tearing sound when the camp counselor took her from my arms.

Like tendrils of sweet peas, Brittany twined around me as her support. And just as tension generates along the stem of the plant because it cannot hold up its own weight, tension crept into our relationship. I felt I had to intervene in any situation that threatened to upset Brittany. I tried to be the combination of a mother and a dad; a supermom.

Reality set in in middle school, when it became obvious that I was mere flesh and blood, with weaknesses, foibles, and faults that made it impossible to protect my daughter from all pain. In fact, it became obvious that I *should not* protect my daughter from all pain. She had to feel the pain in order to understand consequences. I didn't like this process of becoming an ordinary fallible human being, and I certainly didn't like seeing Britt hurt.

The speed at which Britt now wanted to disentangle was frightening. I wanted to peel each tendril of curling, climbing vine gently, to tenderly unwind fragile shoots, and snip and pinch off wilted or damaged stalks. Teenaged Brittany moved at a different pace, willing to lose some vines and blossoms in her hurry to separate and become autonomous. Indeed, sometimes she seemed to want to use something more like a dual-action, precision-blade hedge trimmer. Even as I contemplated this, I realized that whacking at the plant with a hedge trimmer might leave permanent nicks and scars, but the plant would recover and bloom even more profusely.

11
RECOVERY

January 11–13, 2014,
First 78 Hours After Craniotomy

Laughter is the closest thing to the grace
of God.

> — Karl Barth, quoted in
> *The Harper Book of Quotations*

In the wee hours of the first morning after
the craniotomy, there was a shift change.
Our male nurse went home and a female
nurse arrived. I ached all over from my
night in the plastic chair, and Brittany's pain
had been mounting. The new nurse was approximately the same age as Britt. "Craniotomy patients don't suffer a great deal of
pain," she said, her face a mask of indifference.

"Call the doctor," I said. "Do whatever
you need to get authorization. If my daughter says she's in pain — she's in pain."

The nurse heaved a sigh and left the cubicle. She returned with a syringe.

"I need a slow push because I get nauseous," Brittany said as the nurse flicked the needle.

The nurse pushed the Dilaudid faster than I'd ever seen it pushed, and Brittany vomited. The nurse did not apologize. She just held out a plastic dish.

"Bitch," said Brittany, as she slid into sleep.

When Gary came, I told him about the nurse. "We'll deal with her when you've had some sleep," he said.

Later that day Brittany was moved into a room in the Neurosurgical Acute Care Wing. It had a chair that folded into a bed, and was luxurious compared to the ICU.

At Gary's insistence, I went to Britt's house to get some sleep. I collapsed on the guest room bed, and slept for eight hours. When I returned to the hospital, I was thrilled to find Britt out of the ICU and in a regular hospital room where we would both sleep better.

Brittany had already had a postoperative MRI. That bit of news from Dan surprised me. The jaw pain had continued and made her extra cranky. She had a drain from the surgery site that I hadn't noticed last night.

I could see some bloody fluid in the clear tube. I tried not to think about what the fluid was. Brittany was twenty-four hours out from a surgical smack-down with her tumor. She was grumpy, bloody, and feeling the pain of battle.

I tried to think of what I could do to distract Britt from the pain. Digging through her overnight bag, I found *David and Goliath.* I hoped that as I read the fitting analogy, Britt might feel that she could continue her fight with the monster, cancer.

The next night, while making up the sleeper chair with sheets, I heard Brittany gasp.

"Shit," she said. She held up one of her IV lines. Blood trickled across the back of her bruised hand.

I hit the call button, grabbed a paper towel, and pressed it lightly on her hand. "Ouch," Brittany said. "It hurts so bad. There's a knot there."

A nurse came in and tried several times to get an IV started. The steroids that Brittany was taking made it hard to find veins due to swelling. It was excruciating to watch as silent tears rolled down Britt's cheeks. I held up my hand. "Stop. We need a different nurse. No more tries."

The nurse seemed relieved that I'd taken

the task out of her hands. I headed out the door and toward the nurses' station. "I need . . . my daughter needs . . ." I started to cry. "I need a vein whisperer. I want a nurse that can bring my daughter's veins to the surface. Her hands and arms are badly bruised. She just had brain surgery, for God's sake." I took a deep quivering breath. "Can't someone here get the damned IV line in?"

A nurse came from behind the counter. "I'll get someone who's really good, okay?" She put her arm around me and started walking me to Brittany's room. "You keep your daughter company, and I'll find an infusion nurse."

"Britt, they're sending someone good." I pulled a chair to the head of her bed and smiled at her. "I'm not allowing you to bc their pincushion. I told them you need a vein whisperer."

Britt's lips twitched up for a fraction of a second. "I want a shower so bad," she said. "Wonder when that can happen."

"I have a whole package of body wipes. After we get this IV in, I'll help you do a head-to-toe wipe-down. By the time we're finished, you'll feel fresh and sweet."

A different nurse came in with a supply tray. "Hi, I'm the vein whisperer." She smiled. "I'm pretty good at this." She took Britt's arm and gently hung it over the side of the bed, letting the blood drain down. "I'm sorry you've had some misses on this IV. I'm going to get it started."

"I hope so," Brittany said.

"I have to tell you, you're really alert and looking good for having just had a craniotomy forty-eight hours ago." She smiled. "I'm sure you don't feel that great, but I see a lot of patients, and you're bouncing back strong." The nurse was tearing open packages and preparing to start. Seconds later she lifted Britt's arm, released the tourniquet, applied pressure to the vein at the tip of the cannula, and removed the needle. She capped the cannula and disposed of the needle, then carefully taped the IV in place. "Done." She smiled triumphantly.

Brittany moved her arm carefully to rest on her abdomen. "It doesn't hurt, either. I don't feel that pulling sensation. Just a little cold feeling when you started the drip."

"Well, I taped it down like Fort Knox," the nurse said. "Okay, sleep well, you two." The door swished closed.

Brittany and I struggled through a less-than-satisfying cleanup with the body wipes. She used a roll-on deodorant, making me nervous that the motion would loosen the

IV line. Then I got a glass of water, her toothbrush, and toothpaste. She brushed her teeth and spat into a little dish.

"There's nothing I can do with your hair," I told her. "It's stiff with some sort of orange sterilizing soap."

"I feel better. Tired." Brittany settled back as I placed another pillow under the arm with the IV lines. "I need some pain medication, so I can sleep."

I decided to ask at the nurses' station.

"Sure, but let's get her to eat a little something before she takes the pills." The nurse disappeared and came out with some Jell-O and crackers.

"I thought she received her pain meds intravenously?" I asked as we walked back to the room together.

"Not anymore. We try to get patients off of IV-administered meds as soon as possible."

Brittany ate quickly. "My jaw is starting to really hurt." She swigged the pain medication down with water. "Shit, I hurt so bad. Momma, can you get me a clean pair of fuzzy socks? My feet are cold."

I dug around until I found the pink fuzzy socks in the overnight bag. Slipping them on her icy feet, I wondered what had caused her to be so cold. If the IV fluid wasn't kept at a temperature similar to Britt's body temperature, it might have made her feel colder.

I put on clean sweatpants and pulled on my own fuzzy socks. I turned off the lights and padded over to my folding chair bed. The way the beds were arranged, my head was at her feet. Sighing, I slipped between the sheets.

I heard Brittany say something. "What?" I asked.

"Momma, will you get some hearing aids? I need you to hear what I'm saying while I'm dying."

"You're absolutely right. Repeating yourself is a pain in the butt. I'll get my hearing tested." I had been missing a good bit of conversations in restaurants and asking my husband to turn the television up louder and louder, avoiding the painful truth that I had lost some hearing.

"Momma. I'm dying. You know that, right?" Her words hung heavily in the air.

Somehow I'd let myself feel stronger by getting a competent person to start an IV. Somehow I'd let myself believe that I didn't need to think about Brittany dying anymore, because she'd made it through the craniotomy. I was still relishing the fact that she was alive. Now, feeling clean and cozy in

154

her room with her, I didn't want to talk about death. I wanted to believe for a few more hours that she was going to live. I wanted to remain in a place where standing up for her was going to be enough. My heart shrank away from this topic.

My voice came out in a strange froggish croak. "I'm so hopeful, Brittany. You've bounced back from a craniotomy, one of the most feared surgeries. I think Dr. Chang bought some time." I swallowed hard. "Also, Gary is searching everywhere. He's making phone calls to other countries. He's not giving up."

"I can tell that Gary doesn't understand I'm dying, but it's important for me to know that you get it." She sighed. "Dr. Chang may have bought me some time. He's not talking five years anymore. He won't even say *anything* about life expectancy anymore."

"Gary will find someone somewhere." I realized that I'd just made Britt's stepdad sound like Superman.

"I'm not saying I wouldn't love a miracle. But if we just back away and look at this situation very clinically, *no one* has survived this type of cancer. You see that, right? No. One."

There's always a first. But I don't dare say

155

this out loud. *What can I say that's hopeful, but won't provoke her anger?* I wondered.

"You're an extraordinary young woman. We'll take it one day at a time."

"No! No! We will *not* take it one day at a time. Did you see my video? I'm planning for the sure eventuality of my death. I am *not* taking it one day at a time!" Brittany's voice rose.

I've said the wrong thing, I thought. *I've said the worst thing possible. I haven't looked at that video yet. I'm afraid to see it. I'll look tonight after she goes to sleep.*

"Britt." I backpedaled fast. "This is a multipronged strategy. Oregon is the backup plan. I support that. I understand. We need to get all of those details in place, and I'll help." I reached across the chasm between our beds, fumbling for her hand. "And honey, Gary is searching for a plan. He's contacted a guy at Mayo who's looking into the way viruses can be used to attack brain tumors."

I felt the closing of communication. We weren't on the same plane anymore.

"That's all well and good, but you need to think about the fact that Chang only removed about 45 percent of my tumor. My best prospect for extended life was extensive surgical resection — like 95 percent removal. With only 45 percent removed, my life expectancy dropped a lot."

"Forty-five percent," I repeated like an idiot. I envisioned the other 55 percent of the tumor tissue entangled, like the roots of a weed, like the tentacles of an octopus, weaving in and out of healthy, working brain matter — too close to attempt to remove without causing loss of speech, sight, hearing, intelligence, and decision-making.

"Please listen to me, and understand. I am *not* going to let them burn the shit out of my brain. I've read about radiation." I felt her hand ball into a fist beneath mine. "Open sores on my scalp. Hearing loss. Loss of memory and speech. They'd have to do so much burning. I won't. Just so you know."

My mind jumped back to Brittany as a teen. She was leaving the house, and as she closed the door she told me, "I'm spending the night with Kirsten, just so you know." I'd always hated that expression. I'd sat her down a couple of times and reminded her that she still needed to ask me to do things; that "just so you know" wasn't going to cut it. But now she was telling me what she would and would not do to try to live longer. She was defining what type of treatment she would engage in, and what treatments were not acceptable. In this case, "I won't do it, just so you know" *was* going to cut it. She was an adult, and it was her body.

"Okay," I said, gently squeezing her tapered fingers beneath mine. "Is your medicine working? Can you sleep now?"

"Yes," she sighed.

I lay on my bed, unable to fall asleep after our conversation. I fixed my pillow at the other end of the bed, so I could hear Brittany if she awakened. I didn't want her to have to raise her voice to get my help. That night I opened the email she'd sent late the night before the craniotomy, and watched the video. In her email, she said:

> Don't watch the video right now if it's hard, but I am proud of it and very confident in all shared within. While it may not be a legally binding document, it helps make my introduction and intention clear. This YouTube video is only viewable to those with whom the link is directly shared, it is not publicly searchable or anything. Video file size required that I share it this way because it's too big to email.
>
> Hope you both are proud of me for

trying to take care of these things wisely.

All my love always,

Britt

Included in the email was a copy of a letter to the palliative care team at Oregon Health and Science University. Brittany introduced herself as a twenty-nine-year-old woman with a diffuse fatal glioma tumor spanning her frontal lobe, temporal lobe, and insula.

She clearly stated the reasons that she had agreed to a craniotomy. "I am pursuing this surgery in hopes to improve my quality of life and prolong my length of symptom-free survival time." She shared that she would like for the OHSU Palliative Care team to take her on as a patient after her surgery. "When I feel that my quality of life is no longer sufficient or I am in a tremendous amount of physical pain, I am choosing to pursue both palliative care and physician-assisted death through the Death with Dignity Act in Oregon."

Brittany spoke of "being clearheaded," of being "prepared to take all of the necessary steps," and of the full support of her family and friends.

When I watched Brittany speak on the video, I was stunned. She was impressive, calm, cool, and purposeful. I knew that the doctors in Oregon would be blown away by her matter-of-fact tone of voice. Although a video could never have actually been used as a formal request (film isn't provided for by law), I knew that Britt had been worried when she recorded this that things might go wrong in the surgery and she might lose the ability to articulate her wishes. I also knew that no physician could watch this and misunderstand my daughter. Documenting her wishes on film must have brought Brittany some modicum of peace as she prepared for her craniotomy.

I was deeply grateful that I hadn't seen it the night before or the morning of the surgery. That day had been hard enough. I trembled and sobbed quietly as I saw with a new objectivity Brittany's commitment to carrying out her plan, her forethought and focus. It was crystal clear that she was of sound mind and had made a conscious decision. If I was a steel magnolia, then Brittany was a rare titanium orchid. It was all there on film: her ephemeral beauty, the sophistication of her discernment, and her resoluteness of will.

My husband wouldn't even talk about the video. It was that powerful, and he was that moved by it.

That night I had a nightmare. In the dream I was lying on my back, and Brittany was straddled atop my upper legs like a wrestler. In her hand she had a small serrated knife. She would search my chest and stomach for a nonlethal place to stab me and slowly insert the knife. "It won't kill you," she said matter-of-factly.

After about a dozen wounds, I begged her, "Please stab me right in the heart and get it over with." I jerked awake. The room was dimly lit and Britt was sleeping peacefully. I was afraid to go back to sleep for fear the dream would start again.

On her third day after brain surgery, Brittany was allowed to get up and walk around. It boggled my mind that she'd had a craniotomy less than seventy-eight hours ago. She was able to walk to the other end of the hall, where big glass windows looked out over the city. Britt had been circling verbally again for the past forty-eight hours. The ring of conversation began anew each time another person entered the room. Scientific recap of operation. Review of the inability to remove more than 45 percent of tumor, and what this meant in terms of life expectancy. Emotional plea for help in getting to Oregon. Detailed list of symptoms of death that she wanted to avoid by utilizing the Death with Dignity law.

My friend Sherri, and Larry, her husband, came to see Brittany. They spoke briefly with me in the waiting room on the way out. They told me that in their short visit, Britt had told them repeatedly that she was dying and must move to Oregon. I could see that they were in total shock and denial.

"Brittany is the most beautiful and intelligent young woman I've ever met in my life. I've been saying that for years. Volunteering in orphanages. Climbing mountains." Larry waved his hands. "We must hold on to hope. There must be something that can be done."

As I listened to them talk about all the things that they'd seen Brittany do, the feats she'd accomplished, the places she'd been, I realized that I had moved some baby steps on the denial continuum. They were beginners, in full denial. "Brittany's not a quitter. She just has to fight. She can beat this," Larry said.

"No, she's not a quitter." I nodded in agreement. "But the way I understand this is that fighting buys time — not life." In the last thirteen days, to my surprise, I'd made some progress in shaking off denial and accepting reality. Pain deepened in my friends' eyes, and their body language was familiar. Brittany must see the same in me, except my resistance to the ugly and terrifying truth must be even more transparent. I knew there had been times when, like them, I looked conflicted, my hands clutching the chair arms tightly, as I simultaneously angled my body away. Away from her face; from what she was trying to tell me.

I knew that denial distracted me with racing thoughts conceived in a subconscious effort to keep me from hearing the truth. I was still doing it, missing important bits of information because my mind sprinted ahead with self-soothing lies. In watching Larry and Sherri, I was able to see that I had made a tiny move toward accepting the truth. The irony was that for the first time since my daughter's diagnosis, I comprehended the frustration that Britt must feel with nearly everyone she spoke to. Sherri and Larry loved us. They were just beginning to understand Brittany's terminal diagnosis.

As I walked my shocked friends to the front doors of the hospital, for the first time I found myself thinking, *They don't get it. It's only smart to fight when there's some glimmer of hope that you can win.*

When I returned to the eighth floor, there

was an African-American man in a clerical collar sitting near the nurses' station. He stood to introduce himself.

"I just went in to see your daughter," he said as he shook my hand. "She kicked me out in one flat second."

Tears welled up, stinging my eyes. "I'm sorry," I said. "She's just so angry. She was raised as a Christian, but right now she feels that God has deserted her."

"That is perfectly understandable." He looked closely at me. "How are you doing?"

"Not well, I admit. I think I'm losing my mind." I brushed at the tears.

"Can I pray with you?"

I sat and let him hold my hand and say a prayer, but my mind was a million miles away. I quickly forgot my impatience with Sherri and Larry's inability to grasp the truth as I returned to upholding my own version of denial. I sensed that Britt would not win this battle; but I still longed to purchase more time. The minister droned on while in my mind I placed my faith in the hands of science, a second surgery.

My relationship with God had cooled in the last few days. *Forty-five percent, God?*

Brittany repeated the circle of information to each nurse, technician, or guest that

164

came into the room. Gary, Dan, and I had now heard this speech many, many times. The record played over and over again, until I imagined grabbing the needle and scratching it across the vinyl. I imagined stopping the words that hurt so much, hearing the horrible zipping sound as I cut a path across the grooved surface.

I stepped out of the room to escape. I asked a nurse at the station about the broken record syndrome. "She's going round and round, like a hamster on a wheel," I explained.

The nurse said that she'd been in Brittany's room and had witnessed her ruminative thinking. "The medication she's on makes it worse. It's a catch-22. She needs the meds for pain and swelling, but they exacerbate this kind of circular thinking." At least now I knew a possible medical reason for her behavior.

Of the three of us, Gary was the least patient with the circular conversation. He spent all of his waking hours looking for a potential cure or treatment, and he found Britt's negative circling conversations daunting. He was unable to keep a placid face when she started the repetitive loop, and often would excuse himself from the room.

When I told Gary about my dream, he was

deeply disturbed. "Deb, you need to take breaks so you can stay strong. Don't you see?" He rubbed his bloodshot eyes. "This dream is about torture because listening to Brittany's circular repetitive monologue *is* torture." My husband ran his hand across his forehead as if he were erasing the image.

"If we can just buy some time," he kept saying. I searched my husband's kind, tired face. He was committed to finding a solution, never once considering that there might not be one. He was that type of person. Positive. Make it happen. Gary mastered in business at Harvard. He had run Fortune 500 companies, flown all over the world, spoken with leaders in industry. My husband was a big-picture guy who tended not to get mired in the past. Oriented toward advancement, he was firmly rooted in a world of data and research. Gary was blunt and confident, and he loved Brittany and me with his whole heart.

Gary was the one person whose reaction Britt noticed. "If he can't take it, keep him out of the room," she said. So Gary spent a great deal of time in the waiting room, on his computer or phone. My husband was interested in an idea that revolved around administering the treatment of choice, preferably immunotherapy, in conjunction with the individual's own immune system's natural cycle. It had been used effectively with melanoma patients at Mayo. He couldn't get any of the doctors a UCSF to listen for more than a few seconds. As soon as they heard that the tests were on melanoma patients, their attention drifted.

Only three days after her craniotomy, Brittany was deemed healthy enough to go home. The goal was to let her bruised brain settle down and heal for sixty days, and then another MRI would be taken. In the meantime, tissue from her brain was being analyzed. As soon as those reports came in, the oncologist would call Brittany for a consultation. Anytime we asked anything about the surgery, we were told that more would be known after the histology report.

No one would talk about life expectancy or proposed therapy until the report came back from the pathologists, who inspected the slides of tissue culture collected during surgery and delivered diagnostic data based on their analyses. Everything hinged on the histological examination.

So for now, everything we thought we knew about the tumor was set aside as we waited for the findings. Brittany had known this before us. "Momma, this is one of the major reasons I agreed to the craniotomy.

167

Doctors don't really know jack until they have tissue. We don't even know for sure it's an astrocytoma."

I should have known this. Why does my poor sick child have to be the smart one? Why am I moving around in a depressed fog?

Gary flew home to check on my father, our home, and our dogs — all of whom had been taken care of for the last two weeks by our friend Pamela. I returned to Brittany's home with her and Dan.

Brittany was allowed to shower but not to soak, rub, or scrub near her incision. Finally, she would be allowed to rinse her stiff wad of hair. The staples would be removed in eight to ten days. She was given a cream with which to gently massage the incision.

Carmen and I helped Brittany climb into the shower and sit on a stool. Dark orange water ran down the clean white walls, splashing onto the floor. Brittany was careful not to let the spray directly hit her incision area. She used shampoo and conditioner liberally until the water ran clear.

Carmen searched for more conditioner as I helped a towel-wrapped Brittany out of the shower and onto a chair we'd pulled into the bathroom. For the next hour, Carmen and I used multiple bottles of conditioner in an effort to save some of Brittany's long hair. At first we finger-combed, then we used a wide-tooth comb. Eventually, backs aching, we looked across Britt's scarred skull at each other. We had to admit that we couldn't get a portion of the hair below her shoulders untangled. It was a hopeless rat's nest. We could comb through the hair in the back to just below shoulder length, but there was a snarl there that resisted any of our attempts.

"It's okay," Brittany said, weary of the task. "I'll get it cut tomorrow. I guess I should be happy that I have *any* hair."

The new shoulder-grazing haircut was longer in front than in the back. When it was clean and parted on the side, you couldn't see Brittany's scar. But since we were putting the ointment on the incision every night, the hair naturally parted there.

Girlfriends came to visit. I saw the shocked look on their faces. Brittany looked so cute. So healthy. So full of piss and vinegar. I watched her girlfriends laugh and talk normally with her. When Brittany entered the circle-of-death conversation, they nodded as if they totally understood. Who were these strong, resilient young women? How could they do exactly what Brittany needed? How could they listen and not fall apart? I was so grateful that they could be there for Brittany, calm and dry-eyed. We were over two weeks out from the diagnosis, and I was still stumbling around with swollen red-rimmed eyes.

Brittany was charming and funny with her friends, but tired easily. When they left, her charismatic façade slipped away and the Brittany who lashed us with discourses about her plans for death and the fucking unfairness of the situation returned. She was cranky and at times mean-spirited with Dan and me.

If I made the mistake of saying that maybe the surgery had bought enough time for us to look for a cure, my daughter looked at me like I was insane. "Cure? There is no cure. This is a death sentence. Oh my God, Mom, please tell me you aren't still thinking I can survive this? I'm the walking dead."

She also made it clear that she didn't want anyone telling friends or family without her permission that she'd just had a craniotomy.

My sister Sarah had sent some videos for viewing while Britt recuperated. One of them was British comedian Eddie Izzard's *Dress to Kill.* Brittany and I snuggled up on the oversized couches as Bella burrowed under the blanket.

Eddie Izzard, a British comedian, was irreverent as hell. He was wearing high heels, a Japanese pajama tunic, and shiny pleather pants. Izzard began with a few insults about San Francisco. Britt turned to me and said, "His shtick is so smart. He's hilarious."

Eddie did a bit about how the Spanish Inquisition wouldn't have worked well had it been the Church of England, because it would have been all about having tea and cake with the vicar, or you'd be killed. You'd be given a choice: "Cake or death?" As he continued with his riff, I watched Britt's face to see how she'd react to this unexpected turn. Eddie was jumping from one side to the other, playing both the inquisitor and the prisoner.

"Cake or death?" he snapped at the prisoner.

Then, pretending to be the confused prisoner, Eddie turned to field the question, saying, "Eh, cake, please."

Brittany laughed loud and hard, and I joined in. We both grabbed our sides and fell over on our respective couches. Prisoner after prisoner chose "cake" until the Church of England ran out of it, much to the last prisoner's dismay.

I wanted to meet this ridiculous genius. I

171

needed to thank him for giving us our first really good laugh, our first good time — and for all I knew, our last. I would've hugged that silly, satiny, Japanese tunic–clad man so hard, had I been given the chance. I knew that he and Brittany would have loved each other.

12
HIGH SCHOOL HELL

1999–2001, Ages Fourteen to Sixteen

It was only high school after all, definitely one of the most bizarre periods in a person's life. How anyone can come through that time well adjusted on any level is an absolute miracle.

— E. A. Bucchianeri,
Brushstrokes of a Gadfly

Eighth grade graduation. How could I have been so practical in the face of such ludicrous excess? But I grew up in Texas, where there was one graduation. Two, if you were lucky: high school and college. But I wasn't in Texas anymore, and I should have done my homework.

My daughter had insisted she needed a fancy dress. "People are getting really dressed up, like for a dance. They're getting their nails and hair done."

"Well, that's absurd. I won't buy into it. It's middle school graduation, for Pete's sake."

But later, as I watched eighth-graders tromp across the gymnasium floor in full-length gauzy gowns and tiaras (can you believe it?), with fake nails and glitter in their coiffed hair, I realized that I'd made a parenting faux pas. Somewhere between the empire waistline, above-the-knee, sleeveless shift that Brittany wore and the Glenda the Good Witch frothy ensembles that some students glittered in, there might have been a middle ground. As my statuesque daughter slipped a cardigan on over her dress, I regretted drawing such a hard line.

I also knew that the graduation dress argument was the beginning of a long line of such discussions, if my daughter got her way and entered a private Catholic high school that coming fall. It was attended by the children of professional sports heroes, well-to-do attorneys, and doctors. But frankly, I hadn't heard such great things about the school. The student parking lot was full of new Tundra trucks, Beemers, and Benzes, while the teachers' lot was just like any other teachers' lot — filled with buckets of bolts.

Brittany had been in private Episcopal

schools since first grade. I wanted her to attend the local public high school and navigate these difficult years in a more diverse environment. But she'd thrown herself on the bed and cried for hours. "Everybody I know is going there!" she wailed.

My gut instinct told me this environment would be bad for Brittany, and I tried to hold the line. But in the end, I caved. Brittany started ninth grade in 1999 at the forty-two-acre campus. During that first year, I'd get off work at the middle school and drive the one and a half miles to pick her up. Over time, I came to wish I'd held my ground about not going to this school, where there was a significant drug problem in spite of the drug dogs' visits.

Picking Brittany up, I pulled into the small circle near the administration building, parked, and watched high school boys head for the track in the late-afternoon light slanting through stately trees. As a gaggle of girls rounded the corner of the building, I was amazed at the short length of their skirts. The school uniform looked almost pornographic on some of these girls, like an adult Halloween costume.

My heart always fluttered when I first caught sight of Brittany among the plaid skirts, white kneesocks, and oxford shirts. I knew the way her long neck swiveled as she talked to friends; the way she spotted my car but never acknowledged that she knew I was there. I still wanted to talk about our day, maybe go out to eat. I still wanted to be close.

But now we were the furthest thing from "close." Brittany dropped her stack of books in the back of my now-decrepit two-door Saab, flipped the front seat back up, swung her long legs in, and reached for the radio knob. I told myself that I could listen to whatever it was for the short trip up the hill where we still lived in our small home. The music was loud enough that conversation was impossible. I was pretty sure that was the idea.

I'd asked how her day had been. The answer was either "okay" or a long speech about how stupid the teachers were.

"But you wanted to go here," I protested, eliciting a withering glare.

"Dude, if this is how it is at private school, just *think* how bad it is at public."

"I'd appreciate it if you wouldn't call me 'dude.'" For some reason this really bothered me. I wasn't a "dude."

"Dude, chill. I'm cranky 'cause I had to walk all the way to BFE to get my English book. I left it in beeotchy dragon lady's room."

"What's BFE?" I asked.

"You don't really want to know, so don't ask." Brittany had taken off her platform Mary Janes and was rolling down her white kneesocks.

"I do want to know." I waved my hand in the air to indicate that the socks were rank, and cracked both of our windows.

"Buttfucking Egypt."

"Brittany! That's disgusting. Can't you just say 'out where Christ left his sandals' or something that doesn't use the f-word?"

Brittany laughed. "Whatever. I'd probably get in more trouble for disrespecting Jesus than for saying 'fuck.' Mom, you are so lame. You just passed our street."

"Darn it." I saw the street sign fly by.

"No biggie. Just flip a bitch."

"What's that?" It was like she was speaking a foreign language sometimes. I signaled to turn left.

"Just flip a U-turn. *Duuh!*"

A former customer of mine from my semi-conductor sales job called and mentioned that a man I'd met five years ago at a sales luncheon was newly separated and had moved from Florida to California. "Why don't you go out to eat with Gary?" my friend asked. "He's lonely, and such a nice guy, even though he's a bit older."

"I'm never getting married again," I said. "I'm focusing on my teenager and trying to get through these years with as little drama as possible."

"You don't have to marry him. I just think it'd be good for you to have some male companionship, get out once in a while. Besides, it'd be good for Brittany to not feel like she's your sole focus."

Britt and I had seen a counselor on and off during her teens to discuss her resentment toward me, and whatever else was bouncing around in her hormone-fueled brain. The counselor had the same opinion about dating that my friend had. So I accepted a date with Gary, with the caveat that we meet in the parking lot of a local restaurant. He didn't need to come to my house or meet my daughter.

For Southern California it was an unusually cool evening, so I wore a full-length pink wool coat with large shoulder pads. In fact, it was my only coat. As I slipped my arms into it, I realized that it was a leftover from catalog shopping in the late eighties. But what did I care? I wasn't out to impress anyone.

I arrived on time and sat on a bench in front of the restaurant. I'd told Gary that I'd be wearing pink, and that I drove an old Saab.

"Really? I drive an old Saab, too. We have that in common," Gary said.

Ten minutes went by. Even in my coat, I was chilled, so I went inside and sat in the waiting area. Another ten minutes went by. I called home.

"Britt, has a man named Gary called?" I asked.

"Isn't he there yet?" I could hear irritation in her voice.

"No. I wondered if he'd called."

"Mom, you've been stood up. Hang up and come home. Do not wait one more minute," she ordered me.

"Okay." I hung up and headed for my car. As I pulled into the driveway to the main street, I saw a Saab behind me flashing headlights on and off. The driver jumped out of the car and ran to my window.

"I'm just leaving," I told him. "You're a bit late."

"No, I've been sitting right here waiting. I got here early. I never saw a Saab come in the driveway." Gary had the same kind face that I remembered.

"There's a second driveway right over

there." I pointed.

"Oh . . ." Gary seemed at a loss for words. "Can I still take you out for dinner?"

"No, I'm sorry. I've already called my teenaged daughter, and she's expecting me home. She told me I'd been stood up, and to get home immediately." I didn't smile.

Gary looked disappointed as he buttoned his navy blazer against the cold. "Please, let me make it up to you," he said. "You could call your daughter to let her know you weren't stood up." He looked at me hopefully with soft blue eyes.

I thought about how much easier it would be to just go home and grade papers. But part of me didn't want to return with my tail between my legs. "Okay." I rolled up the window and parked the car.

Inside Gary's blue Saab, I called Britt. "He was here all the time," I told her, "just watching the wrong entrance."

My fifteen-year-old daughter showed no mercy. "Mom," she said in her beeotchiest voice, "that's lame. He should've gotten off his ass and looked for you."

I was pretty sure that Gary could hear both sides of the conversation. "Well, we're going out to grab a bite, and then I'll be home."

"Where is he taking you? Does he have a

180

reservation?"

"Um, Gary, where are we going to dinner? Do you have reservations somewhere?"

"Momma, it's seven thirty on a Friday night in Orange County. This better be good."

From the look on Gary's face, I knew the answer. "We're just going to catch as catch can," I told Britt. "I'll be home by ten o'clock."

Gary took me to a posh sushi restaurant in Laguna Beach, where I noticed that he looked young for his age and was dressed immaculately, very old-school East Coast. As we chatted, I thought, *He looks older than me, but not that much older. In fact, his face is so pleasant that after I've had a particularly quarrelsome day with Brittany, he might actually look younger than me.*

Afterward we went for a walk along the bluff, where it was windy and cold. "What do you consider a romantic evening?" he asked over the sound of crashing waves.

I looked out at the starry night and said exactly what I thought, no filter. "Romance doesn't have to be about people. Enchantment can be about life. I think a gorgeous inky-black sky splashed with sparkling stars, a glass of wine, and the sound of birds roosting in the trees can be dreamy." I paused for a beat. "Even when you're all alone."

Gary's facial expression went from surprised to bewildered. His mouth opened and closed. "I see that you and your daughter are very blunt," he said with a smile.

"We prefer the word 'direct,' " I answered. " 'Blunt' carries a negative connotation, as it's often used to describe females who are forthright. 'Direct' carries a positive overtone."

Gary burst out laughing. "Conversation with you is unpredictable. I like you, Deborah Ziegler. It's cold, and I need to get you home to your teenager, but I'd like to take you out again."

I was surprised. I thought I'd done a pretty good job of being disagreeable.

At sixteen, Brittany managed to wangle a yes out of me for a car. Now, that was a time when I should have put my foot down, but saying no would have been the equivalent of World War III. The car was the beginning of the real trouble.

"Just so you know, I'm going to go to a movie with some friends, and then spend the night at Helene's."

"Brittany, you can't just add 'just so you know' in front of anything you want to do.

You have to get permission." This phrase of hers lit me up, as she would say, "like no other."

"Dude, don't go postal. It's not a ginormous deal. Her mom's okay with it. You can call her if you want, but she's kind of a hot mess and you might not enjoy that conversation, especially if she's had a drink or two. Although since you're both single parental units, you might like her — even though she sports a whale's tail sometimes."

"Britt. A: Stop calling me 'dude,' damn it. B: What is a whale's tail? And C: Give me Helene's mom's phone number, so we single parental units can chat."

Britt smirked. "A: I can't help the dude thing. B: Whale's tail is a thong that shows above the waist of someone's pants — though I bet you think that's TMI. And C: Here's the number." She handed me a sticky note and slammed out the door to the garage.

I winced at the thong image and ran into the garage after her. "Buckle up!" I repeatedly motioned the action. "Buckle up!"

Brittany pretended not to see me as she backed out of the garage.

"I'm taking away car privileges if you don't buckle up!" I shouted at the departing car.

■ ■ ■ ■

Gary and I had been dating on Saturday nights for a couple of months when the phone rang at about 8:15 p.m. on a weekday. I was sitting in my pajamas grading papers at the tiny butcher-block bar in the kitchen, and Britt was doing her homework on the couch in front of the television. It was Gary, asking me out for dinner.

"Hi, Gary." Having watched to see who it was, Britt started making kissy faces at me. "Go out to eat? Now?" I said incredulously.

"We're already in our pajamas!" Brittany shouted from the couch.

"I teach school. I can't start a date on a school night at eight thirty." For some reason it irritated me that he didn't get this about my life. "I'm in my pajamas grading papers."

Gary mentioned that he hadn't thought about how late it was before calling.

"Look, I know that you and your management team might go out for dinner and wine at eight or nine o'clock, but middle school teachers don't. We're early to bed and early to rise. Buh-bye."

Brittany thumped her pen on her book. "Holy shit, Mom, you were really rude. Do you not like this Gary dude?"

I sighed. My instinct was to jump on Britt, to chastise her for the cursing. But honestly, this was as close to a good conversation as we'd had in weeks, so I held my tongue and decided to choose my battles.

"I like him well enough, but he doesn't seem to get a teacher's life." I picked up my papers.

"He seems like a nice guy. Maybe you should lighten up a little. When are you going to let him meet your fabulous daughter?"

"I thought you'd rather I keep him out of your life." I watched for a reaction.

"Gawd, Momma. If he's nice, at some point I should meet him, right?" Britt waved her pen at me. "Does he *like* you? Does he think you're *pretty*? Does he want to *marry* you?" Britt called out in a singsong voice.

"Don't be silly. I've already told him I have no intentions of getting serious with anyone until you're out of high school." I banged my stack of graded papers on the butcher block and clipped them together.

Britt was quiet for a minute. "That's okay by me. I don't want a 'dad' in the house getting all up in my grille. But I'm okay meeting the guy."

■ ■ ■ ■

Britt and I had long, drawn-out arguments about curfew. They felt like water torture at the end of a workday. I could see each drop of water coming, but they never came in the same pattern or frequency. After hours of this, I felt like there was a hole in my forehead.

Now instead of picking Brittany up from high school, I drove home to find her car already parked out front. I sighed. I wanted to see her, but I knew that there would be something wrong as soon as I entered the door. I was exhausted, and I felt like I was walking on eggshells.

Heading toward my room, I caught a glimpse of Brittany lying on the floor of her bedroom talking on the phone. Her elegant long, tanned legs were propped high on the wall, her grimy bare feet leaving a dark stain on the paint. Long honey-brown hair fanned out around her face, wadded gum wrappers tipping the halo of hair with glittering sliver. My daughter could chew an inordinately large amount of gum in one phone call. With a condescending glance — a gaze that could wither flowers — my daughter extended her leg toward her door. Flashing white bikini panties beneath her too-short plaid school uniform skirt, she firmly closed the door in my face, giving me no chance to complain about the nail polish stains on the carpet.

Britt was caught up in the Orange County definition of beauty. She attended school with girls who had fake fingernails, expensive blond weaves, and blown-out hair. It wasn't uncommon for these students to get breast implant surgery or a perky new nose for their Sweet Sixteen. There was a heightened anxiety about the appearance of their bodies, rather than their bodies' abilities. This pursuit of physical perfection took more time each day than scholastics required. In spite of this, as always, Brittany brought home straight As.

With the car came a job. Brittany secured a front-desk position at a fancy golf club and restaurant in a nearby gated community. Soon after she began working there, from the smell of her clothing it was clear that she was smoking dope. I suspected that the source of the pot was someone at the golf club. When I asked Britt about the smell, she laughed. "The chair I sit in at the club smells like weed and tobacco, Mom. The daytime employee must be a toker and a smoker. The smell gets all over my clothes."

I called her boss and tried to have a discussion about my concerns. The woman was a fan. "We all just love Brittany. She's so efficient and dependable for her age."

"I know that Britt is working with an older girl and is hanging out with her a lot. Is this girl a good influence? Do you know her well?" I felt like a creepy stalker mother, and I probably sounded like one, too, but I was so worried.

"Oh, you must be talking about Celia. She's wonderful. I think she'll be a good influence. They're both top-notch."

I hung up with the feeling that Brittany and Celia really had this gal snookered.

Gary and I invited Celia and Brittany to join us for a Zingaro Horse Ballet, with horses flown in from France. Zingaro ("Gypsy" in Italian) boasted performers from the internationally known French equestrian theater company in an avant-garde show combining horses and dancers. We took the girls out to eat beforehand. Celia was quite the charmer. She was funny, smart, and whimsically attired. Although I distinctly smelled pot on her clothing when I gave her a light hug, I liked her, in spite of myself.

Inside the enormous tent, the classical

music was so loud and grating that I plugged my ears in some parts. Gary leaned over and asked, "Did you know that the show is largely Stravinsky?"

I had thought Stravinsky was a lovely classical musician whose music would play while women in floating white dresses sat astride their cantering sleek steeds. But the performers weren't riding; instead, they were being dragged along in the dirt behind the horses in a crawling sort of motion. The horses were moving in graceful choreography. It was the performers down in the dirt that I found disturbing. The show was bizarre, and the girls were already giggling. I shot them a look. These were expensive tickets; surely things had to get better.

Then one of the slowly trotting horses lifted its immaculately combed tail and released a load of steaming manure into the carefully raked loam. We all stared in horror, sure that the performer behind the horse would modify his routine to avoid being dragged through the dung.

He did not.

Celia and Brittany doubled over in laughter — loud, attention-getting laughter. I looked around with wild eyes before completely losing control, too. Gary herded us out the door before we were kicked out.

In the car, we lost it again.

"I'm sorry! I completely lost my shit," Celia sputtered from the backseat. She held up her hands in a mea culpa between guffaws.

"The horse lost his shit first, though," said Brittany.

One Saturday morning, after a walk with a friend, I drove up the hill toward our house. Britt's car was parked against the curb, and to my shock it had two spiderweb-like cracks in the front windshield. I checked the house. Not there. My heart thumped and my stomach churned as I dialed her cell phone. No answer. I got in my car and raced over to the emergency room. The front desk told me that Brittany and a friend had been in an accident, and neither had been wearing a seat belt. They were doing a brain scan.

I paced the room until they wheeled her out. Thank God the scan came back normal, with no signs of bleeding. They released her, warning me to watch for loss of memory, confusion, vomiting, or abnormal behavior. Britt said the other girl refused to go to the hospital, insisting she was fine, and had been picked up by a friend.

"Do her parents know?" I asked.

Brittany shook her head no. "Mom, it's not a big deal. I wasn't hurt. Steph wasn't hurt. Don't cause trouble for her. She and her Mom have enough issues."

I could relate to that!

"How did it happen?" I asked.

"My phone rang, and it slipped out of my hand and under the seat. I reached down to get it and plowed into the back of this lady's brand-new Mercedes. The cops came and called an ambulance when I said my head hurt."

"Did the lady in the Mercedes go to the hospital?" I asked.

"No, she was getting her car towed when I left in the ambulance." Britt sighed.

"Brittany, how many times have I begged you to buckle up?" I began to lecture, the volume increasing as I continued. "This has been an ongoing thing. Can't you listen to me about anything? Are you determined to learn everything the hard way?"

"Please don't nag me now, Momma. I can promise you one thing. From now on, I'm always buckling my seat belt. I did learn this one the hard way." Her eyelids fluttered as we drove past her car, as if the sight of the cracked glass made her head hurt. "I won't be fooling around with my cell phone, either."

I was grateful that she only had a head-ache, no other injuries, and I believed her. She would never drive without a seat belt again. She had learned it the hard way.

Gary turned out to be a gentleman worth knowing. I'd told him that I would never marry again, but that if he wanted to hang out, I was fine with that. Magnanimously I mentioned that if he wanted to get married again, since he was older than me, he might want to look elsewhere. I'd also told him that he could never attempt to discipline Brittany.

"You're not her father. I'm not bringing father figures into my daughter's life at this stage in the game. She's kind of spinning right now, and it wouldn't be fair to either party."

"It's hard to hear her disrespect you, or listen to her statements that start with 'just so you know' and end with the door slam-ming," he said. "But I'll abide by your rules. She's your child."

"Yes, she is. I'm in this alone right now. Trust me, if there's any hope of a relation-ship between you and Britt, you've got to bite your tongue and stay out of it."

"Could I see you more than once a week?" Gary changed the subject. We'd been seeing each other for several months, but up until then, I'd limited my time with him to either a Friday or Saturday evening.

I thought for a second, and decided to go for it. "I've always wanted to take ballroom dancing lessons. We could try to take a midweek class." I was chuckling to myself, thinking that no man would ever sign up for that.

"Great. Just let me know where to be and what time," Gary said.

He kept his word, and we started a Wednesday evening class at an Arthur Murray Dance Center.

Brittany summed up her opinion about Gary on a phone call to a friend. "This older guy's really got it bad for my mom," she said, "but I encourage it because it keeps her from watching me like a hawk."

Gary and I were on our way to a dance class when I received a phone call from security at a fancy department store.

"Are you Brittany Maynard's mother?"

"Yes." My heart pounded. "Is my daughter all right?"

"Oh yes, ma'am. She's fine. She and her girlfriend are sitting right here. Perhaps I should let her speak to you."

"Momma." Britt was crying. "We're in

trouble for shoplifting. I need you to come and get me."

For the love of God, what next? "Tell the man I'm on my way."

Gary drove me there and walked me to the security office, but stayed in the background as I handled the situation. My daughter sat alone, her tearstained face humiliated and contrite, her shoulders hunched in embarrassment. I was angry, but when I saw her sitting there, I was also sad. It didn't seem like she thought very much of herself. This was not the confident and bold Brittany of middle school; instead, this was a mixed-up teenager. My daughter was bigger, smarter, and better than this moment in time. I needed to remember that.

I spoke with the security guard, who showed me the clothes Britt and her friend had stolen from several shops at the mall. I told the guard that I wanted Britt to return the items to each of the other businesses they'd shoplifted from, as well. We visited the stores, and at each I had her ask for the manager. Britt told them what she and her friend had done, apologized, and returned the clothing.

Brittany was wrung out when we returned to the department store, but grateful that her apologies had been accepted and no further fines had been inflicted. The guard handed Britt paperwork banning her from shopping in the store for one year. There was a fine, as well, in lieu of filing charges with the police. Brittany and I both signed the papers and found Gary outside, where he'd been patiently waiting.

The ride home was quiet. Brittany repaid me every cent of the fine. She said that she would never shoplift again, and she seemed truly heartbroken about what she'd done. Later, before her death, Brittany told me that making her go to each store and look people in the eye had been the right thing to do, although at the time she thought I was a flaming bitch.

At the beginning of Brittany's junior year in high school, she contracted a bad case of mononucleosis. After seeming to recover, she returned to school, only to relapse again. It was almost impossible for her to keep up because she slept most of the day. I picked up schoolwork and friends dropped it off, but the pile seemed insurmountable. As I tended to Britt and worried that she seemed unable to shake the mono, I began to think about other options for her. I discussed getting her transferred to the public high school, but she seemed overwhelmed by the idea of joining a junior class at a new school. She also seemed overwhelmed by trying to complete all of the work and tests that she'd missed. "Why don't I just get my GED?" she said, falling back into her pillow. "Or sign up for continuation school and get my diploma that way?"

I couldn't believe that my brilliant daughter was talking continuation high school. It shocked me out of complacency. It made me realize that my instincts were right. This high school had been all wrong for my kid.

I got an appointment with our therapist, who was now very familiar with our family dynamics. As I saw it, our mother-daughter war was only in a cease-fire because Brittany was so ill. Brittany seemed depressed and defeated, and I was sure that the private school was just not a good fit. I also knew that when she got past the mono, we were going to be in full-on battle again.

The therapist suggested that I consider allowing Brittany to start college early. Britt could easily pass the General Educational Development test. Once she turned seventeen, she would be eligible for the test if she met certain criteria. "I can help get a request letter from Saddleback College that will allow her to take the GED at age seventeen. If she wishes, she could sign up for University of California–approved courses and transfer to one of the ten campuses in the UC system," she said. "It's been done before."

This course of action went against everything I stood for. I was a teacher, for God's sake, who dreamed of her child graduating from high school and going on to a great college. I wished I could afford a school like Harvard or Yale, because Brittany quite likely could get accepted. I had been thinking along the lines of UCLA, UC Berkeley, or University of Texas at Austin. Community college hadn't ever entered my mind.

Seeing my shocked expression, the therapist said, "Brittany is one of the brightest and most difficult girls I've ever dealt with. You need to think outside of the box." She watched me struggle with this idea.

"Your daughter can get to the same destination by taking a different path. Depending on her class load, she could be entering her sophomore or junior year at a major university when her classmates are just graduating high school."

My countenance must have brightened.

She smiled at me. "Honestly, high school isn't for everyone."

■ ■ ■ ■

Gary was dead set against this idea. He couldn't help but tell me this every time we talked.

Of course everyone I taught with thought it was a terrible idea. Brittany's middle school teachers adored her, and couldn't fathom the idea of her as a high school dropout. I didn't even mention it to Brittany's grandparents. I didn't want to hear the uproar and worry that would inevitably arise from such heresy. I couldn't even talk to my sisters, Sarah and Donna, about the idea. It just wasn't done in our family.

I was the family member who'd already moved to crazy California and divorced twice, and now I was letting my beautiful, smart daughter run amok.

Brittany and I had lunch on the lake. She was feeling well enough to go for a short outing, and I had decided to talk in a neutral environment about what to do. First we thoroughly vetted the idea of her transferring to the local public high school. I'd already called to find out what we'd need to do about transferring midsemester, and had been told that with her straight-A transcript, the incompletes wouldn't be a problem.

Brittany said it would be a difficult move for her. School was in full swing, and finding a group to hang with would be hard. The school was quite a distance from where we lived, and parking was a bear. "Mom, I'd be miserable there."

I knew she was right. It would be tough, even if her health was 100 percent.

I suggested that after she was completely well, she consider working full-time until she could get enrolled at community college. When she enrolled for a full load, she could quit the job and concentrate on getting As in UC-approved courses. Then she could transfer to one of the University of California schools.

Britt met my gaze. "I never thought in a million years you'd agree to this."

Tears flooded my eyes. "I can't believe I am. Everyone thinks I'm nuts. But my instinct tells me that this high school is no good for you." My lip quivered. I had so wanted to get through this meeting without appearing weak or vulnerable. "Please, honey, set your sights on getting into a good university. This is just a different path to arriving at what I'm hoping will be the same place we've always dreamed about."

"Seriously, I'm not going to be a community college dropout. I'm gonna kick ass," Britt said with a smile.

"Look ahead. Image the diploma that will hang on your wall. You want it to be from a top-rated school."

I held my hand out across the table.

Britt grasped it and shook it. "Deal," she said.

13
BAD MOTHER

*January 25–February 16, 2014, During
the First Weeks After the Craniotomy*

I am not a bad mom. I am a good Mom
having a bad day.

— Unknown

I flew home after twenty-five days of either
staying at the hospital, or with Brittany and
Dan at their house. Brittany assured me that
I should go home, take a break, see
Grandpa, and love up on my puppies. Gary
had gone back ten days ago to take care of
things. My daughter talked about having
the second surgery and going after more of
the tumor. She waffled between saying "no
one is getting inside my head again" and
speaking somewhat hopefully about buying
more time by agreeing to an awake craniotomy. If she was operated on while fully
conscious, the surgeons would be able to do

brain mapping. They could find out specifically where brain functions had migrated over the last decade, and this would in turn allow a more aggressive surgery while preserving function.

I found the airport difficult to navigate alone. There were so many people, and they were all so very alive. I found myself looking at young women and thinking truly hateful thoughts, such as *Why do you deserve to live? Why not my daughter?*

Through my tears, the gate numbers blurred. My red-rimmed eyes flicked from one person to another. Seeing so many people coming and going made me angry. *How come my family suffers a living hell, while these people walk around, many of them rude and cranky? You want rude and cranky — try finding out your precious daughter has a brain tumor!*

Gary met me at the airport. He stood there in the blue cotton sweater that matched his eyes and held his arms open. I collapsed into his embrace and drew in his clean smell. "I've missed you so much," he whispered into my hair.

As we walked to the car, it was all I could do not to scream. As soon as he closed the passenger door behind me, I wailed. Gary slid in on the driver's side and held my hand. "Let it all out."

I did. I wailed and sobbed until I couldn't breathe. Gary handed me tissues and when I slowed down, he started the car and we pulled out.

"I didn't want to leave her," I sobbed. "I had an anxiety attack on the way to the airport."

"Honey, she's coming down for a visit in less than two weeks." Gary navigated the entrance to the freeway. "Are you having an anxiety attack now?"

I tried to concentrate on my breathing. "Close," I said. "I'm very close."

"Do you need me to pull over? What can I do?"

"Take me to the ocean. I want to go out on one of the rock jetties and curse and scream until I lose my voice." The answer came from some place deep inside.

"Okay. Carlsbad Beach, here we come."

At the shore, I left Gary on the beach and slowly made my way out onto the boulders. Gray and grim, the ocean waves crashed against the rocks, sending spray flying. I looked back and saw Gary squatting in the sand, never taking his eyes off me. He raised one arm. When I could hear nothing but the roaring of the waves, I let out a primordial wail.

"Fuck you, God!" I screamed into the wind and waves. "I tried to be a good person. I prayed to you. I begged you! I got down and groveled!"

I screamed. I cursed. "Forty-five percent, you bastard! I hate you! If you even fucking exist." I fell on my knees and shook my fist at the sky.

Unremitting gray waves thundered in my ears, complacent and unperturbed by my grief. "Love is never-ending," they said. "A mother's love is an endless ocean."

"The pain is never-ending!" I shrieked. "How could you hurt her like this? How could you hurt me like this?"

I watched the waves and listened. Nothing.

"I want a fucking miracle!" I bowed my head. "I want a miracle." My tears splashed on the rock.

"You already have one," the ocean said. "Brittany is a miracle. Her brain has been miraculously adapting for years."

"I want her to stay here with me," I whispered, because in my deepest heart I already knew that Brittany was leaving me.

"She is not yours to keep." The water hit the rock jetty and pulled sand from the cracks, creating a foamy current dragging detritus out to sea.

I got up and stumbled back to Gary. "I need to sleep," I told him. Once we got home, I slept for twelve hours.

Gary worried about my health. He took me to the doctor, who prescribed a new cream for the hives that had erupted during Britt's surgery and told me to drink more water. Gary took me to a psychologist, who told me to use the mindfulness tapes. "Go ahead and accept any emotion that you feel. They're all valid." He prescribed a tiny, white tablet to be used only when I had a full-on panic attack. Finally, Gary took me to the dermatologist, who confirmed that I did indeed have impetigo and prescribed an antibiotic that made me sick unless I ate a great deal of food.

My friend Pamela took me to church, where a prayer team prayed with me. I saw the horror in their eyes when I told them what Brittany's long-term plan was, but to their credit they did not shrink away. They prayed over me and around me with fierce determination. I told them that I'd cursed God. The oldest gentleman on the team smiled and said in a gentle, amused voice, "At least you're still on speaking terms."

On February 2, Dan, Carmen, Gary, and I

received a detailed email from Brittany. She spelled out specifically what types of resuscitation efforts she forbade anyone to use on her. The list included intubation, mechanical ventilation, chest tube, chest compressions, defibrillation, vasopressor, artificial feeding, and tube feeding. She stressed in the email that she was terminal, and that she wanted us to understand that she was dying. She emphasized that she wanted to finish the planning involved with moving for her disease and death because she was anxious to enjoy the beauty of the world with her family and friends. She also requested that we read an article by the American Hospice Organization that pointed out the problems with artificial feeding.

In a phone call, I asked if she knew what was entailed in each process that she'd asked not to have performed. "As his executor, I went over this list with Grandpa when he moved here," I said. "I had to explain what each procedure involved."

Britt's answer was so detailed and lengthy that I was convinced she thoroughly understood the various processes. She also explained, "Momma, I'm so healthy from the neck down. My death in hospice care would take a long time. I'm not like their elderly patients. I'm not frail. My major organs are healthy; they will fight to stay functioning. My heart will keep beating. I would have a long and difficult road to death."

"I don't want that for you, either," I said in a soothing voice.

"People with brain tumors become restless, confused, they try to get out of bed, they fall, shake, and have hallucinations. They can be delirious, have involuntary jerking and seizures. This can go on for weeks before they finally become semicomatose." Brittany sounded terrified. I was scratching the hives along my hairline in abject terror.

"I'll read every word. I promise," I told her.

"Momma, please, you and Gary cannot try to keep me alive using these heinous processes when I'm going to die anyway. My friend's husband lost his father to a brain tumor. He said his father became enraged and threw his own shit at the family. They have to live with that memory. I don't want to go that way."

"I understand you. I will honor your wishes no matter how hard it is, Brittany." I'd caused the hives to bleed again.

"Promise me. Swear it."

I took a deep breath. "I swear. Now, let's

talk about going to Palm Springs for a few days and getting some sunshine and rest." Before I left, she'd said she'd like to visit me in Southern California and plan a getaway. Brittany chose Palm Springs for our girls' trip because something had changed in her body since the craniotomy and she was cold all the time. "Have you told the doctor that you can't get warm?" I asked.

"He says sometimes your senses reset after brain surgery. I can hear things so clearly now that I want to hit loud people. I just want to smack them."

"Wow. We should bring earplugs, because you never know what the noise is going to be like in a hotel. Also, I'm going to order you a heated mattress pad." I was already searching the Internet, my fingers clicking on the keys.

I picked Britt up at the airport. She got in the car talking very fast, telling me that she was freezing. "Momma, if I get really sick, if for some reason I lose the ability to speak, will you always make sure that I'm warm? It scares me that I'll be unable to tell people how cold I am."

I assured her that I would always make sure she was warm.

208

Brittany pulled an envelope from her purse. "This has my POLST in it. I'll have this with me at all times. If for some reason I have a violent seizure, or pass out, *do not call an ambulance.*" She was showing me a pink form, just like the one I'd filled out for my ninety-two-year-old father: Physician Orders for Life-Sustaining Treatment.

"My POLST says no medical intervention other than comfort-focused treatment. If something happens to me, if we are in a car accident . . . whatever . . . let me go. No intubation. No CPR. No tube feeding. Keep me out of Intensive Care. Momma, I need you to promise me that you will not call an ambulance, because this form won't be honored by EMTs. Ambulances are not legally bound to follow my wishes, and they won't."

"Okay. I didn't know that about ambulances. I understand, honey." I was concentrating on my driving, but nodding that I understood.

"Momma, I need you and Gary to be onboard with this. It worries me that he'll talk you into calling an ambulance." Brittany was talking so fast, it was hard to keep up.

"You have to calm down and have some trust, sweetie. Gary, Dan, and I will support you and take care of you. We are going to follow your wishes."

It was a balmy and beautiful mid-February evening in Palm Springs when we checked into the hotel and went out for dinner. At the restaurant, we saw a family with two children. Brittany frowned. "Stupid little brats. I don't want to eat near them."

"Brittany, you've always loved children! What are you talking about?"

"Well, I don't love them anymore. They remind me of everything that I wanted and can't have." Britt's voice was loud enough that I feared others might hear. "Little kids talk too loud. They hurt my ears."

"Sweetheart. You don't know for sure that you can't have children. Your surgery was successful, and the doctors may be able to resect more of the tumor. What if they buy you more time?"

I tried to comfort us both with hope. This amount of sorrow turned outward in the form of anger was painful on so many levels.

"Listen to me," Britt said. "I'm not bringing a baby into this world. I'm not setting a child up for loss. I'm not having a baby, even if the best-case scenario plays out and I survive this bastard in my brain for three to five years. That dream is over. Done."

I put my hand up. *Stop,* I involuntarily thought. We locked eyes. Hers had shifted from silvery sage to sea-green.

"Momma, get mad. Get angry. God just took away your only hope of grandchildren. You have figured that out, haven't you?"

The words were like a punch in the stomach. They humiliated me, made me feel stupid. I'd been so focused on praying for a miracle for *my* child that I hadn't given enough thought to the fact that Brittany had wanted three children. She had been longing for her own child. These words walloped my solar plexus, my soft spot, and yes, my dreams of being a grandmother.

Just this past Christmas — only seven weeks ago — Brittany had made unmerciful fun of me when I'd said I wanted to be called "Mimi" instead of "Grandma." I'd felt foolish and vain for trying to come up with an alternative name, but I was definitely enjoying the thought of grandchildren. So much loss, so much selfish pain, washed over me at that moment. I'd thought about this. Of course, I'd thought of this, but my overriding emotion had been the inability to accept that I might lose my daughter. For the first time, I took the loss further and thought about the loss of not only my child, but my grandchildren. I thought about the enormous shattering loss of Brittany's dreams of being a mother.

"Let's cross one bridge at a time," I said, desperately wanting to change the subject.

"I can't do that. I will not be the creator of this level of pain for a child."

I kept quiet. My daughter, sitting across from me picking at her food, green foam earplugs peeking out of both ears, head bent, hair falling away exposing a pretty startling craniotomy scar, clearly meant what she said and wanted to be understood.

That night in our hotel room, I set up my rollaway bed at the foot of Brittany's bed. I wanted her to be able to sleep. I didn't want her to feel me move or hear me clearing my throat right next to her sensitive ears. She fell asleep before I did, playing Scrabble on her Kindle. I crept over and took her picture. She looked like an angel sleeping.

The next day, we headed to a street fair. Brittany wouldn't let me take any photos, and grabbed my camera to delete any picture taking I attempted. She allowed me to keep the one I'd taken of her sleeping.

"Dan took a photo of me sleeping, too," she said, her head cocked to one side, her finger hovering over the delete button.

"Because you look like an angel." I breathed the answer like a prayer.

Inside a restaurant, we ordered wine and dinner. Brittany began to talk about death. "I'm going to try to donate organs. I have to get my driver's license in Oregon anyway. I'll register for organ donation then."

I looked across the table at my daughter's huge almond-shaped sea-green eyes and she said, "I'm going to donate my corneas. They have to harvest them within twelve hours of my death, which will be easy to arrange, since I will know pretty precisely when I'm going to die." The waitress set our plates of food down without a word and then retreated hastily. "My corneas will go to someone that is approximately my age."

I looked at Brittany's face, her beautiful eyes. Tears splashed onto my shaking hands.

"Oh for fuck's sake, Mom. Can't you be happy that some good could come from my death?" Brittany took a bite of her pasta.

I couldn't speak. I couldn't move. The noise and activity in the restaurant seemed detached, as though it was part of an old movie scene viewed through wavy old window glass. I felt numb, and I certainly couldn't eat. I wasn't able to search my purse for a tissue, or even wipe tears away with my hand. I could only sit still and feel my heart's thready beat. The image of someone cutting her lovely eyes flashed graphically in my mind.

"Corneal transplants have a very high success rate. Someone might be able to see, thanks to me," she added.

I felt dizzy and clammy.

Brittany continued to eat. "Aren't you going to eat?"

I shook my head no, and the dizziness grew worse.

"This is ridiculous." Brittany motioned to a busboy. "Could you bring us some to-go boxes?"

Brittany scraped the food into the boxes and paid the bill. I sat frozen, tears streaming down my face.

"Let's go." She was out the door before I'd staggered to my feet. When I stepped outside, I tripped and regained my balance. I looked around the crowded street, but I couldn't see Brittany.

I knew the direction to go in. I began weaving around people, still crying. I realized that I wasn't entirely sure how to get to our hotel. I stopped in the middle of the crowd and tried to orient myself, wondering if I'd stumbled too far down the street. The wave of people broke around me as I stood deciding whether to keep going or turn back.

Someone grabbed my arm. "Follow me,"

Brittany said, dragging me forward for a short distance. She dropped my arm and took off at a brisk pace.

I followed, but couldn't keep up. I was trying not to trip again, and by now my vision was blurry from crying. When I finally arrived at the hotel, the room door stood open. Brittany was already in pajamas and coming out of the bathroom. "Pull your shit together, Momma. I can't take care of you when I have a terminal brain tumor." She stuffed the earplugs in her ears and climbed on the bed with her Kindle.

I lay on top of the covers of the rollaway bed fully clothed, and continued crying. This weeping seemed not to be a choice, and it wasn't loud. Usually when we cry, we sort of choose how long we will indulge ourselves. This crying seemed endless. I used the corner of my sweater to wipe my nose now and again. I didn't think of anything, except occasionally I was forced to address how to breathe.

They say you can't think of nothing. But when I recall this crying binge, I can't remember thinking a single thing. Oh yes, I can remember one thing: thinking that I wasn't sure if I'd ever be able to pull my shit together again.

■ ■ ■ ■

The next morning, we went downstairs for massages. There was no mention of last night. When we came out of our much-needed therapy, Brittany slipped on her black bikini and acted like nothing had happened. That took some acting because my eyes were two puffy slits.

I put on my bathing suit, and we staked out chairs by the pool. Brittany took a photograph of our feet and the glittering pool, and posted it on Facebook. We ate a light lunch, saving room for the great dinner we hoped to have later that evening.

We got just a little sun, but it took a lot out of Brittany. After our showers, I asked if she'd like me to go get dinner so we could eat it on the balcony near the outdoor fireplace. I could see she was relieved.

I yelped nearby restaurants and settled on a charming Greek place across the road. We'd brought wine with us, so we uncorked a bottle of red and dined under the stars. That evening remains one of my favorite memories of that trip. We were loosened by massage, sunshine, and wine.

Our last day in Palm Springs was Valentine's Day. We shopped in the part of town that caters to those enamored with midcentury modern décor. It was fun and relaxing, and Brittany found a few things she wanted. She selected a little pair of owls for Dan. "I'm going to write a note with them and leave them for him to open after I die," she said.

I felt the familiar knife of pain in my gut. After lunch, we took the tram up to the top of Mount San Jacinto and hiked a little. Brittany's energy was understandably still low, and I was grateful after my emotional outburst to not be hiking as far as Brittany would normally have insisted on.

A new phobia surfaced as I watched Brittany walk to the edge of the mountain and look out over the valley. I felt like I was going to hyperventilate. The fear that grabbed me was illogical and powerful. I was terrified that Brittany might fall and hit her head. I had suffered from claustrophobia since childhood. It was an embarrassment to me, but a very real physiological reaction to enclosed spaces. Now I felt that same panic rise in my throat. I called out to Brittany, "Come back here, further away from the edge!" and clawed the air as if I could magically pull her close.

"Mom." The exasperation in Brittany's voice was palpable. "There *is* no edge. It's a slope." She moved even closer to what appeared to be an endless abyss.

"I'm serious! It's making me afraid. I feel like you could fall and hurt your head."

Brittany laughed a hard, bitter laugh. "Hurt my head? Geez, Momma. I think my head is about as hurt as it can get."

As we continued to walk around and take photos, I relived this irrational fear several more times. I tried very hard not to show it, but I would grab for her arm or make noise when she got near the edge.

"Momma, I need you to let this go! I'm going to travel between now and the time I die, and I'd like you to travel with me. But this overprotectiveness isn't going to work. I want to go to Alaska. I want to hike on the surface of a glacier. I want to zipline, dogsled, kayak, and in general do anything that strikes my fancy."

"Okay. I just feel protective of your head."

"Well, I don't. If I bashed my head and died doing something I liked doing, it would be a gift. It would save me from having to take things into my own hands, because this precious head and brain of mine are on a steady course to rob me of everything that's important to me. And that, I'm not taking lying down."

It was time to head home. That night I told Gary about Brittany's marked escalation in cursing, the discussion about donating organs, and my horrible reaction. "You were in shock," he said. "It's like Brittany has lost her ability to feel sympathy or compassion."

I wish that I'd thought carefully about what Gary said. I wish I'd done some reading. I didn't, though. I just thought that I'd been weak, that I'd tested her patience.

Much later, I read that victims of traumatic brain injury — and I would say having a chunk of your brain removed would qualify as traumatic brain injury — sometimes exhibit egocentrism and insensitivity to the needs of others, because they have lost emotional empathy and their capacity to understand the facial expressions of others.

Gary and I had several conversations about Brittany's cursing, saying that we needed to de-emotionalize ourselves to it.

What I didn't know then was that scientists had determined that strong swear words are not stored as sounds or phonemes (as other words are). Curse words are stored as whole units in the right hemisphere, and therefore we do not need the left hemisphere's help to process them. There is also ample evidence that swearing affects human perception of pain. Humans are able to tolerate levels of pain longer while swearing than if just using neutral words.

How I wish I'd known this. It would have helped our family to depersonalize some of what Brittany was saying. As it was, my spirits were floundering. I worked as hard as I could to try to help Britt, yet I felt that nothing I did was good enough. None of us did. We were not doctors or clinicians, and we didn't understand the neurocognitive changes that she had been undergoing for years. It would gradually become apparent to us that Britt's impulsivity, her inability to apologize, her desire for adrenaline-pumping activity, all were quite likely a result of her slowly growing brain tumor. Because these behaviors were typical young adult behaviors, we hadn't noticed.

Sunday morning at our house, Brittany stayed immersed in her laptop, sipping a cup of coffee and hopping up and down to do laundry. Gary and I prepared brunch as she sat at the kitchen counter.

As soon as we all sat down to eat, Brittany

pulled her laptop over and asked us to watch something. It was a video of an awake craniotomy in which the patient was being asked questions. Gary, who gets queasy if someone cuts their finger, held up his hand. I looked at my husband's pale face and knew he was nauseous.

"Brittany, stop," I said. "We can't have these kinds of discussions at mealtime. Let's talk about this later. Let's enjoy some downtime together."

Brittany's eyebrows drew together and her eyes widened in a bold stare. "You're telling me that you can't stand to talk about my illness, about my options?"

"Brittany, come on. Anyone would think that talking about, much less watching, a craniotomy at a meal is gross." As soon as I said it, I knew that I'd pressed some irreversible trigger.

"Gross. Now I'm gross? My tumor is gross?" Brittany yelled.

"We're asking to take a break from disturbing conversation while we eat," I said. Gary's face looked ten years older. He had pushed his plate away.

"You think it's disturbing to discuss a brain tumor, to discuss a craniotomy? I'll tell you what is fucking disturbing: *Having* a brain tumor and craniotomy!" Brittany snapped her laptop closed and pushed away from the counter.

"It's not unreasonable to ask that we not discuss surgery or plans for death at the dining table," I said, looking at my husband's washed-out coloring.

"I'll talk about this whenever I damn well please." She opened the dog gate at the kitchen entry.

"Then we'll have to ask you to go back home to Dan. We can't live like this," I said. "There have to be some downtimes where we let the subject rest."

The dog gate slammed shut. "Really? Really? Like 'this subject' ever . . . ever . . . *ever* gives *me* downtime? Like 'this subject' isn't racing through my mind 24/7?" She stormed down the hall and slammed the door to the guest room.

I started toward the gate.

"Let it go, Deb. Let her have some time." Gary scraped his food into the trash can.

Later, working at my computer upstairs, I heard the front door slam. I ran downstairs and saw that all of Brittany's things were gone. I'd been thinking about what she'd said. Of course she was plagued by this subject every waking moment. Were we selfish to ask that it not be discussed at meals?

222

As I stared at the empty room, everything felt wrong. Everything.

14
SPREADING WINGS
2000–2001, Ages Sixteen and Seventeen

But they fly. It is what fledged birds must do, and she's always known that. The nest can't always be full.
— Susan Fletcher, *The Silver Dark Sea*

I sat outside the hair salon, watching Brittany sweep the floor, collect the hair in a dustpan, and empty it in the trash. True to her word, she had gotten a full-time job as the receptionist at a hair salon. Seeing her do these simple tasks tugged at my heart. Her car was in the shop, and thus a great excuse to pick her up and have dinner together. Most of the employees were immigrants from Vietnam, and Britt had gotten to know one woman who'd escaped on a boat with only the clothes on her back. Brittany was learning up close and personal about people who hadn't lived a life of privilege, and her heart and mind were expanding in new ways.

My therapist had kindly walked us through the steps we needed to take in order to get Brittany enrolled at the local community college. Her high school wrote a letter about Brittany's stellar academic career there and sent her incomplete transcript. The community college accepted Brittany, and gave her special permission to take a heavier load of eighteen units. She was anxious to accrue enough credits to transfer. Because Britt was older now, I had left teaching and returned to sales for the much higher pay. This time I represented an engineering company that placed engineers in mostly aerospace environments. Once again, I found that I excelled in the sales environment. Often I didn't come rolling in until eight o'clock at night, since I had a long commute.

Britt and I were squabbling again. Except they weren't really squabbles; they were ugly exchanges that left me tired and feeling bad about myself. One day when we'd had a particularly vitriolic disagreement, I stopped by her room. "Sweet Pea," I said, "all daughters do this angry dance in and out with their mothers. You dance away because you feel you don't need me, and then dance back in because you still *do* need me. This is normal. Let's just try to be a bit kinder to each other. Okay?"

Brittany came to the door and stared into my eyes. "Nothing about our relationship is normal," she said. "I hate you, and when I'm able to move out, I will never speak to you again." She started to close her door, pausing to say, "And for the last time, do *not* call me Sweet Pea!"

This war over absolutely everything went on for weeks. The good thing was that Brittany attended class regularly and was doing extremely well scholastically. Finally, exhausted, I saw the therapist again. "How can I continue to live like this? I'm not getting enough sleep, and every single day I dread coming home. Brittany turns everything into a world war."

"I think you need to think of three rules that would improve your life. Only three. These rules are nonnegotiable. You don't have to justify these rules. You don't have to explain them. These are three rules that are not about Brittany. These rules are about you, and achieving an environment that allows you to work, because you are the breadwinner."

"What do I do if she says no?" I asked.

"If she can't follow these three rules, she

will need to find another place to live."

My mouth opened and closed. "She's only sixteen."

"And you're worn to a frazzle. I'm concerned you're not going to make it to your next birthday." The therapist flipped some pages in her notes and looked up. "Brittany will be seventeen in a few weeks. She's extremely bright, and she is also very sure of your love. You are the target for all her teenage pain and angst. Right now that's toxic for you. I'm quite worried about the situation."

I nodded.

"I've dealt with many troubled teens. Drug addicts. Alcoholics. Cutters. Sniffers. Eating disorders. Brittany is verbally the most detached girl I've ever seen when in conversation with her heartbroken mother. Even all these hard, rough, kick-ass troubled kids would soften around their mother's tears, but Brittany doesn't. She's lost the ability, for the time being, to see you as a separate human being with your own needs and feelings. I hope she will grow out of this stage. Because until she does, your life is pretty much like that of a donkey standing in the rain."

I listened and nodded, thinking of how Brittany raided my closet or read my emails.

I imagined a donkey, ears laid back, with heavy-lidded, limpid brown eyes, stoically standing in the pouring rain.

"When she was a child, you two had no boundaries. You became enmeshed. The teens are a natural pulling-away period for children as they begin to want to separate from parents and establish personal boundaries. However, you are not being allowed to do the same. It isn't healthy for either of you."

I decided to write a kind but firm note. I gave Brittany three rules. They had to do with my being able to sleep and be comfortable in my own home. Britt's curfew was 10 p.m. Sunday through Thursday night, and 12:30 a.m. on Friday and Saturday nights. If I'd fallen asleep, I asked that she wake me up to let me know she was home. She must always ask permission to drive the car; "just so you know" would not cut it. The note explained that none of the rules were about her. The rules were intended to keep me healthy; to allow me uninterrupted rest during the workweek so that I could keep my job and pay the bills, including the bills for her education. I told her that I wanted her to graduate debt-free.

When I woke up the next morning, she was gone.

■ ■ ■ ■

Over the next few weeks, I cleaned Brittany's room and carpet. The grimy places she'd put her feet on the wall disappeared under a new coat of paint. I got a new bedspread for the bed.

She called to let me know where she was. She'd moved into a small apartment with my friend Sherri's son, Tyler. She said she couldn't live with my tyrannical rules.

Tyler was three years older than Brittany. At twenty, he had a job at a liquor store and was drinking too much. Tyler and Brittany had grown up together and had been like brother and sister. I knew that Tyler would never want Brittany to be hurt or in danger. However, he wasn't in a good place to ensure this for himself or Britt.

Coming home from work was lonely but peaceful. Now that Britt had moved out, Gary spent weekends with me. We were closer than ever, but Britt was my main concern. Any plans that Gary and I might have were on the back burner as I struggled to keep my daughter on a purposeful path. My overwhelming worry and tension about Brittany colored everything; even the blossoming love that I felt for the kindest man

I'd ever met.

Gary and I asked Brittany if she'd like to come over for dinner, and she accepted the invitation. We had a pleasant evening. I'd put some bags of Britt's makeup items and more clothing by the door, thinking that she might need them.

As she left my house that evening, I heard her talking on her cell phone. "My mom had some of my shit by the door. I don't think she wants me to come back."

It hurt to hear her say that, but there was some truth in it.

Sherri and I stayed in touch. She told me that Brittany and Tyler were an item now.

"What? No way," I protested. "They're like brother and sister."

"I know, Deb. But you need to be able to hear this. Tyler and Brittany are sleeping together."

I wanted to stick my fingers in my ears. Too much information! Tyler was like a son to me, and I loved Sherri in a forever way. Tyler had been a difficult child to rear. He had learning issues and anger issues, and now he had addiction issues. I loved him, but I did not want our children living together.

Brittany called and wanted to have dinner again.

"Tyler and I saw some really nice apartments right across from the school," she said. "Tyler has a DUI, so he can't drive. The apartment is really nice. I liked it a lot. But Tyler won't keep it nice. We're always arguing about keeping our place tidy."

This was a shock. Brittany had never cleaned up after herself at my house. It was one of the things we'd argued about. I asked Britt if she'd thought about a one-room studio apartment, and she asked me to look at some with her.

The first one we looked at was a second-story studio in a group of apartments built in the 1940s. Tiny. No central air or heat, but lots of light. It was within walking distance to a pretty harbor. "It's like a ghetto Melrose Place." Brittany grinned at me. "I love it!"

These little places were the most affordable housing in Orange County. They went fast, so I signed the lease right away.

Downstairs from Britt's new apartment was an Italian restaurant, and we stopped in to celebrate with some appetizers. Brittany was anxious to begin planning her move. I told her she could have her double bed and the family room love seat. I told her the best way to get furniture was at thrift stores. That evening, one of our greatest common interests began. We became a thrift-shopping team extraordinaire.

My daughter made that rudimentary studio into a warm and inviting little home. We found all kinds of awesome deals at second-hand stores, and she reveled in the ability to decorate on a budget. The smell of bread baking and Italian food cooking wafted up from below. Soon Brittany knew everyone at the restaurant. Girlfriends were invited to spend the night and make dinner. Often Gary and I met her at the restaurant. Her microbiology class was a killer, but so interesting. Every meal we shared with her, she informed us of new cutting-edge science. She said her instructor was unbelievably good, and she'd joined a microbiology study group. "Two guys are vying for my attention." She smiled. "Geeks."

My daughter was healthier and happier than she'd been recently, and we were getting along better than we had in years. Brittany made dinner, and Gary and I brought wine. We sat talking and laughing in the warmth of the plug-in heater. Gary agreed that with her newfound autonomy, Brittany seemed to flourish.

15

It Can Always Get Worse

February and March 2014,
Ten Weeks Out from Craniotomy

The human person cannot face up to a
bad outcome, that's just the deal.
— Barbara Kingsolver, *Flight Behavior*

It took many emails and conversations to
mend the rift over graphic conversation
while dining. I called Britt to apologize and
told her that I would try to listen to whatever she needed to say, whenever she needed
to say it.

I spent eight to ten hours a day researching astrocytoma tumors. Gary was in his office doing much the same through phone
calls. We were planning to visit Britt in her
home in a week. I filled a cardboard file box
with printed material. I learned a great deal
about brain tumors, specifically glial astrocytoma tumors. The standard treatment was

to cut, burn, and poison. Surgery first, then radiation to kill as many leftover tumor cells as possible, often done concurrently with chemotherapy.

However, radiotherapy did not cure massive diffuse brain tumors The goal was to slow the cancer down. Unfortunately, radiation kills healthy brain tissue along with tumor tissue. Because Brittany's tumor was large and they'd resected less than 50 percent of the tumor tissue, radiation would have to be done on a large area of her brain. The side effects for whole-brain radiation included hair loss, nausea, vomiting, extreme fatigue, hearing loss, memory loss, problems with speech, and skin and scalp burns. The radiation would also cause brain swelling and possibly seizures.

Chemotherapy interfered with cancer cells' ability to reproduce. The problem was that chemotherapy didn't discriminate between healthy and diseased brain cells, either. Many adverse side effects accompanied it, although some patients seemed to tolerate chemo for the brain better than others.

The prognosis was poor, especially for those who had only part of their tumor removed in surgery. As I read, I began to understand why Dr. Chang had completely stopped talking about a five-year survival. The extent of surgical removal of tumor matter was clearly related to prognosis. Brittany's tumor resection had been hampered by the infiltrating fingers of the tumor entwined in her brain. We would definitely know more when the histology report came back. A neuropathologist was reviewing frozen tissue from Brittany's craniotomy.

I read one very disturbing article written in December of 2013, printed only weeks before Brittany was diagnosed. It indicated that when treated by chemotherapy (temozolomide), some gliomas actually transformed from low-grade gliomas into deadly glioblastomas. Glioblastoma patients had a median survival rate of twelve to fifteen months. Alarm bells rang in my brain. I couldn't believe what I'd just read. It was terribly disturbing to find out that chemotherapy might make the tumor jump to a higher grade and grow faster. Another article pointed out a growing body of evidence that cancer surgery itself can increase the risk of metastasis. It would appear that cut, burn, and poison — the "gold standard" treatment that doctors had to offer — was fraught with perils that weren't fully discussed with the patient. As I read, I felt that what we knew about treating brain cancer had not changed much since the days of wagon trains. I felt that we were in the wilderness with only rudimentary tools to assist with survival.

With radiation and chemotherapy both looking like terrible treatment choices, I started looking for other types of approaches. The most promising seemed to be at Duke, UCLA, the Mayo Clinic, and UC San Diego. They ranged from using the polio virus to experimental vaccines, immunotherapy, and even cannabis and the patient's own urine.

I read about what MRI scans could tell doctors about brain tumors. I found a lot of things that no one had mentioned to us. Soon thereafter, Brittany wrote a strong email to Dan and me. She indicated that Gary's search for a miracle cure and his suggestions of things we might try had not been helpful in the least. She also stated that she loved Gary, but that he was no longer free to weigh in on decisions having to do with her disease or death *at all.*

In the email, she told Dan and me that Plan A was to go to Oregon and die peacefully. If for some reason she lost her ability to speak and there needed to be a Plan B, she asked for no feeding or fluids and for intravenous painkillers. She said that if she was taken care of by a hospice, to do all we could to make sure that the hospice upped the morphine as fast as possible to not keep her lingering. She also requested that both Gary and I watch a movie entitled *How to Die in Oregon.* In the email were two articles, one from brainhospice.com, and the other titled "End of Life Signs for Brain Cancer." Both were detailed accounts of what happened when the brain tumor metastasized out of control and swelling could no longer be controlled. It was grim reading.

I responded with one line: *"I have read and saved this information. I understand and support Plan A and Plan B."*

Brittany wrote back that the move would protect her medical wishes, and that at some point, it would become necessary to live in Oregon for her end-of-life plan. She said that Dan couldn't move, with his job and needing insurance, but that of course he would visit her in Portland often. She also wrote again about her anger with Gary and me for not discussing what she needed to discuss at the table. *"I won't be punished for protecting my patient rights, legal privacy, or just being a scared, terminally ill young woman, who needs to talk about the very real ramifications of my hideous cancer, especially 1 month post craniotomy and only weeks after diagnosis. . . . I am just very sick and totally frightened and doing the dang best I can."*

As I read this, I realized that we were going to have to buck up and hear whatever graphic information that Brittany wanted to share. We might need to just push the food away and listen. Over the following nine months, there were many meals that we pushed aside and didn't finish, but we never again tried to restrict mealtime topics.

In the meantime, Dan's mother, Carmen, had taken Brittany to speak with her oncologist. "Some of my histology is back," Britt said on the phone. "I don't have a good marker on MGMT. This means that if they tried to use chemo on my cancer tumor cells, the chemo would not be able to knock the cancer back. Also, a combined chromosomal loss of 1p and 19q is associated with a more favorable prognosis for use of chemotherapy. Of course I don't have the combined loss, and therefore that is another reason I'm *not* a good candidate for chemo." Brittany spoke fast, and the terminology wasn't familiar.

"I don't understand. Did you understand what they were telling you?" I felt like a non-swimmer grabbing, clutching, and grasping at nothing, just air, as I sank thrashing and kicking into murky water.

238

"What's not to understand? I've already been given a death sentence. They can't cut the monster out. It's like an octopus with tentacles embedded in my brain. So now they're looking at the exact genetic tissue for clues about whether the tumor can be slowed with chemo poison. Lo and behold, that option sucks, too! So next they'll be dragging me in and telling me I need to sign up for radiation five days a week for six weeks. Now they'll want to burn it."

"I thought they'd already agreed that radiation wasn't a good option for a tumor as diffuse as yours."

"They got nothin', Momma." This time I heard her voice crack, but she quickly recovered. "That's the cold hard truth. They don't know what causes brain cancer, and they don't know how to cure it. Brain cancer is such a red-headed stepchild. There's no money in it. Shit, if I had breast cancer, lung cancer, colon cancer, or even leukemia, I'd be better off. Those cancers get more money for research."

"Then we'll leave UCSF. We'll go somewhere else." I tried to sound positive and strong.

"It's the same everywhere. Cut. Poison. Burn. Everywhere we go. This is what they will say — in nicer terminology."

I realized that Brittany and I had been reading the same information. We'd both been researching, and we knew the cut, poison, burn drill.

I started to say something, but she interrupted. "It was nice of Carmen to go with me. I want you to be here when I go for my meeting with Dr. Berger and when I get my MRI. If the meetings go poorly, promise me you won't try to blow smoke up my ass."

"I promise I'll do my best."

"No one is going to burn my brain. I'm never allowing them to do it. The therapy is worse than the disease. I'm not going to allow them to damage my cognitive ability. I'm not letting them destroy the quality of the little life I have left." Britt's voice rang strong, with no hint of self-pity.

I, on the other hand, was crying silently on the phone, trying to make sure she couldn't hear me. "I'll stand behind you, and I'll defend your right to choose," I said in a strained voice.

In late February, Gary and I flew up to Dan and Brittany's. We had a pleasant weekend with them, and tried not to think about our appointment with Dr. Berger. In our hearts, Gary and I hoped that the doctor would be telling us about a second surgery that would remove much more of the tumor, buying more time. Gary was still looking at other countries for a potential cure or promising treatment. In other words, we were *still* in denial.

On Sunday, Brittany and I made plans for a trip to Alaska. We were focusing on her desire to see and do as much as she could before she died. I decided to be an active part of this agenda, because with or without me, she was going to do her thing. I desperately wanted to be with my girl.

On Monday we drove to San Francisco to meet Dr. Berger, the surgeon who'd advised her to have the first craniotomy with his colleague Dr. Chang. We thought the plan was that Dr. Berger would do an awake craniotomy when he returned from overseas. Gary and I felt like the scarecrow and Dorothy in *The Wizard of Oz* preparing to meet the wizard. Dr. Berger stepped into the examination room. He seemed surprised at how beautiful Brittany looked so soon after surgery, and how intelligently she presented herself. My daughter wore her newly cut hair softly curled, her incision concealed.

As the discussion deepened, it became clear that he had no intention of operating on Brittany. In fact, he was recommending that she begin a course of chemotherapy.

He said that he wouldn't operate until chemotherapy had shrunk the tumor's tentacles. We didn't understand this statement at all. We hadn't read or heard of the tentacles of astrocytomas retracting. All we could think was that the "two surgery plan" had just been an effort to get Britt to have surgery with Dr. Chang. We wondered if Dr. Berger had known that he'd be pushing chemo before a second surgery.

Brittany informed him that she was very aware of her genetic markers. "Even my oncologist hasn't recommended chemotherapy," she told him. "In fact, UCSF has an article published that indicates that temozolomide, the chemotherapy agent most often used with gliomas like mine, actually causes the tumor to transform from low-grade to highly malignant glioblastoma more than half the time."

The doctor stood his ground, saying that despite her genetic markers, a wait-and-watch approach was not wise.

"Roughly what percent chance do you think that I have of the chemo shrinking my tumor?" Britt asked. He replied that there was less than a 30 percent chance that chemo would be beneficial in any way. However, he still recommended trying it.

"And what would you guess is the percent

chance that chemo will shrink the tumor enough, wither the tentacles sufficiently, that you would consider doing an awake surgery?" Brittany's chin jutted forward in a way I knew well.

He replied that if the chemo did anything, the chance of it being so effective that he would consider an awake craniotomy to resect more of the tumor would be quite low, a single-digit percentage. He added that there were unknown factors.

"Have you ever recommended that a patient consider seeking end-of-life care in Oregon?" Brittany's dark eyebrows arched upward and she watched him intently.

I thought the doctor seemed uncomfortable when he said that he had never advised that, and that he didn't believe it was a viable course of action.

Britt straightened in her chair. She smoothed a hand over the leg of her black pencil slacks. "Have you ever stayed with a patient all the way? After you guys have opened up the patient's skull and done a partial resection?" Brittany's eyes were green lasers.

The doctor said that he prescribed pain medication, and that he didn't leave a patient to suffer.

"No, I mean: Have you been there when

243

they can't talk anymore? When they become belligerent or violent? When they can't remember their family? When they moan and grimace in their sleep?" Brittany paused and drew in a big breath. "When they go blind? When they are partially paralyzed? Where are you then? Operating on another patient, right?"

Dr. Berger began to say that he referred patients to hospice care, and then he trailed off. He said that he would like to focus on the benefit of treatment, and that it was premature to be talking about this.

"Is it?" Brittany said. "I have terminal brain cancer, and no one wants to talk to me about how I will die. Well, I can tell you one thing for sure. I'm not dying in California. And I can tell you I'm not spending the last days of my life sick on chemotherapy that hasn't got a hope in hell of saving my life — or even of buying me a significant amount of time."

In the car on the way home, my husband said something completely inane about Dr. Berger's being proactive. *Oh my God,* I thought, *he really isn't present. He's shutting out what is happening, and concentrating on what he wishes was happening.* I wanted to wring his neck.

I sat thinking of the hopes that were

dashed by the great and powerful wizard of brain surgery. Brittany had pulled the curtain back to reveal a man who seemed to be grasping at straws.

Brittany's last bit of confidence in medicine (and I hadn't thought she had any) slipped away that day. I could feel her hopefulness crashing over a waterfall and dashing on the rocks below. She never admitted it out loud, but it was obvious that she had pinned some trust in Dr. Berger's plan for doing an awake craniotomy. After that day, her go-to emotion became anger, which I knew was to cover her fear. The great Oz had spoken. Like Dorothy, my first instinct was to tell him that he was a very bad man. Maybe, like the Wizard of Oz, Dr. Berger was a very good man; just not a great wizard. We felt that the meeting couldn't have gone much worse.

Gary's niece, Erica, who was about ten years older than Brittany, was diagnosed with stage four colon cancer the same week Brittany was diagnosed with a brain tumor. Erica and Brittany had only met once, but through Facebook they were comparing notes on their journey.

Erica was teaching elementary school when she was diagnosed. She wrote to tell Brittany that they had found cancer in her lungs, as well. The two young women couldn't have been any more different in their approach to their diagnoses, but they both thought the world of each other. Their long-distance relationship bloomed over their shared enemy.

Brittany and I confirmed our plans for our Alaska trip in May. We also wrote to several doctors at UCLA, Johns Hopkins, and the Mayo Clinic, sending them information from Brittany's file and asking if they had a different approach they'd like to discuss. We offered to travel to each place for a second opinion. My plan was to fly home with Gary and to cover our responsibilities in Southern California, and also try to find some alternative therapies that would interest Brittany.

I struggled to care for my ninety-two-year-old father, who was ill with the flu. I asked our dear friend Pamela to think about leasing her town home so that she could eventually move in with us to help with my elderly father and care for the dogs while we were gone. Erica had a biopsy of her lungs, which confirmed adenocarcinoma, a cancer that forms in mucus-secreting glands throughout the body. Meanwhile, Gary's brother was on a waiting list for a heart transplant. What else could possibly happen to one family?

I wrote an email to Carmen four days after

our disastrous appointment with Dr. Berger, saying in part:

I'm striving to plan some trips with Brittany that we can have some fun on. During those times, I hope Dan will avail himself of the freedom he has after work and weekends to have some fun with his brothers and family. He desperately needs some time to think of something else for a while. I worry about Dan as well as Brittany. This is a HUGE blow to such a newlywed couple. Gary and I love them both so much.

I believe that Brittany is very bright. Gary and I are realizing that she understood what she faced much better than any of the rest of us — from the start. She immediately skipped the "denial" phase and jumped to anger and planning. It left me in the dust of denial. I'm slowly understanding the limited options that she has — and thus I can embrace her desire to seek more dignified ways to die when that time comes.

I planned to fly back up to Britt's because on March 26, she would get her first postop scan. Ten weeks postop, we avoided the subject, and our tension built.

Gary and I discussed the possibility of needing to take Brittany to Switzerland, which had a death with dignity act, if the tumor progressed rapidly and her wishes to qualify for legal residency in Oregon were thwarted. There were some pretty rigorous qualifications to meet in Oregon, and Brittany worried that with one bizarre move of the tumor, she would be left with no options. We felt that a backup plan to the backup plan was prudent. We were beginning to go through the motions of understanding her wish. Though neither of us was 100 percent there, we were forcing ourselves to take tangible steps forward in formulating her plans.

When I flew up for the MRI consult appointment, I took some of the most promising files from my box of documents on experimental treatments that Britt might pursue. No one had told us that if you hadn't pursued chemo and radiation, clinical studies wouldn't accept you. This was my box of false hope.

I prepared a lengthy list of questions about the MRI results. Since these scans were all we had, since we were in a "watch and wait" mode, I wanted to be sure that we got a thorough review from the MRI.

Most of the questions that I'd written

down I didn't even understand. I hoped that by asking and getting answers, I would be helping Brittany get more information about her tumor. My list included detailed questions about the information to be obtained from the MRIs, queries about astrocytoma growth indicators, and possible therapies outside of chemo and radiation.

The bad news was that Brittany's oncologist at UCSF was on medical leave, and therefore a doctor whom she'd never met before would discuss the MRI with us. When the doctor came into the room, he made some light chitchat as he opened up the MRI files. However, his chatting came to an abrupt halt when the files had downloaded. He quickly excused himself to find a colleague to join him. "Fuck," Brittany said. "This does not bode well."

The doctor came back alone, looking stressed. He opened the files and pointed to an image of Brittany's brain. "I've never seen anything like this," he said.

I could see that the empty space that had been created was full of a brightly lit-up substance. My slow, uninformed, stubborn mind thought, *Is that blood? Is her brain bleeding?*

"The tumor has grown 20 percent larger in ten weeks," the doctor said.

Pain knifed through my heart. It was so sharp and real that I gasped for air as tears stung my eyes.

This . . . I was not ready for.

I looked over at Brittany's face. She maintained a cool mask of indifference. There were no tears in her eyes. I glanced down at my questions. There was a raging monster tumor in my daughter's head, and none of these questions mattered. Death was coming for her.

As we walked out of the hospital, we passed a large glass window looking down on a busy street. I wanted to crack the thick, dirty glass with my boot. I wanted to jump and fall eight floors. The desire to do damage, to run away from life, to jump, the image calling to me of my body falling through space — I can recall that desire so clearly, I can taste it.

Brittany Diaz

On New Year's Day, I was diagnosed with a fatal Grade 2 Astrocytoma Glioma brain tumor, spanning 3 lobes of my brain, crossing hemispheres. I spent weeks in the ICU/hospital supported by my wonderful family and close friends. I had a partial resection craniotomy at UCSF on Jan

10th. They removed a fist size chunk of my left frontal lobe, and I healed super fast. Felt great. Body is healthy, just my computer is sick. Now 2.5 months later post-op, it has changed to "High Grade" and I have been told I have roughly 1 year to live. I am so sorry Dan, my dear husband. So sorry that I am sick. For months, I kept this information to a very tight circle. I felt ready to share now but don't worry, not too frequently. In the next few weeks, I will go to Mayo Clinic, UCLA, and OHSU to explore options and clinical trials but also to discuss palliative care and ways to die peacefully rather than painfully. Right now I feel physically great, suffering no seizures or deficits. This photo represents to me, the body's amazing capacity for healing. There are many painful things on the horizon for me at just 29 years old, but it is important to LIVE WELL, SEIZE THE DAY. The world is SO beautiful. So many beautiful places and people, kind hearts. If I can still make it to Alaska in May with my dear friend Maudie and my mom, Deborah, I will be there. You are both stars. LOVE TO ALL. Truly, just love.

On March 31, Brittany posted her diagnosis on Facebook. This was how Brittany told her wider network of friends where she was in life. Up until the MRI review, she'd kept the circle of people who knew about her brain tumor small. She had guarded her heart. I was shocked when I saw the posting and the photos. I don't know why. My daughter had nothing to lose anymore.

Nothing at all.

Twelve-year-old Brittany on a rafting trip with me in Oregon. (*Courtesy of Deborah Ziegler*)

Middle school Brittany with me at a friend's house in Mission Viejo, California. (*Courtesy of Keira Connors*)

The two of us on a family vacation in Florida. (*Courtesy of Charles Allison*)

Brittany (*far right*) poses with two friends before a middle school dance. (*Courtesy of Deborah Ziegler*)

Brittany comforts her grandfather O. T. Ziegler at a Thanksgiving dinner after he spoke about the shooting death of his jeep driver and his subsequent capture by the German forces in France during WWII. (*Courtesy of Deborah Ziegler*)

Brittany smiles her megawatt smile prior to a high school dance. (*Courtesy of Gary Holmes*)

Cousins Brittany and Mary Iris sit on their respective mothers'
(Deborah and Sarah Ziegler) laps in 2004.
(*Courtesy of Charles Allison*)

Brittany, Gary, and I celebrate Gary's birthday in July 2004.
(*Courtesy of Gary Holmes*)

Brittany posing in my hat in Dieulefit, France, on a family trip in 2008. (*Courtesy of Gary Holmes*)

Berkeley buddy Jade Wood and Brittany pose at Machu Picchu in 2009 with Huayna Picchu peak in the background. (*Courtesy of Jade Wood*)

Brittany laughs (my favorite sound in the world) at her wedding in Sonoma, California, 2012. (*Courtesy of Charles Allison*)

Gary and I visit Machu Picchu on the one-year anniversary of Brittany's death, as Brittany requested of us. (© *by Gary Holmes and Carmen Solis*)

■ ■ ■ ■

THREE:
EPIPHANY

■ ■ ■ ■

"I cannot live with myself any longer." This was the thought that kept repeating itself in my mind. Then suddenly I became aware of what a peculiar thought it was. "Am I one or two? If I cannot live with myself there must be two of me: the 'I' and the 'self' that 'I' cannot live with. Maybe," I thought, "only one of them is real."

— Eckhart Tolle, *The Power of Now*

16
FIRST LOVE

Fall 2002–Summer 2004,
Ages Seventeen to Nineteen

The magic of first love is our ignorance
that it can ever end.

— Benjamin Disraeli

My daughter and I often met for happy
hour at the Italian restaurant down the
stairs from Britt's studio apartment. Britt
wasn't legally old enough to drink. However,
she knew all the servers and they adored
her. How could the funny, wicked smart,
hot girl who ran up and down the stairs not
be a favorite?

During these halcyon days, my heart
quickened in anticipation of dinner with
Britt, much as my heart had fluttered when
picking her up from school when she was
younger. Our conversations were lively and
interesting. We no longer bickered and

fought. We both loved science, and often discussed topics from her courses. I even allowed myself to think she might want to go into a science-related career. Brittany had stolen my favorite T-shirt, which said, "Talk nerdy to me." I pretended that I was deeply offended and wanted it back, while secretly I smiled.

One evening I drove to meet her for dinner and found Britt sipping cabernet and nibbling an eggplant Parmesan appetizer. There was a gleaming glass of cabernet waiting for me. Gary and I didn't nag her about wine, and had allowed Brittany to have a small glass with us at dinner. When she fixed us dinner in her little studio, we brought a bottle of wine to share with her. Part of me wanted to protest that she shouldn't order alcohol in a public place, and the other part of me felt that she had demystified alcohol. She never, ever drove when she'd been drinking. She took a taxi. She didn't drink to excess in front of me. She seemed to be developing a taste for good wine, savoring it, not just throwing it back in great gulps. I worried about a lot of things with Brittany, but alcohol wasn't one of them.

Clearly, Brittany was thriving in an environment where she felt independent. Gary and I paid half her monthly rent; her biological father paid the other half and provided a car and car insurance. I provided health insurance and money for groceries and utilities. Brittany was taking a fifteen- to eighteen-unit load of University of California–approved courses each semester, and making straight As.

My rebellious daughter had blossomed. She looked healthy, strong, and happy. "I'm in a kickass study group," she told me as she forked another piece of eggplant into her mouth. "We're acing everything."

"I guess it doesn't hurt to have two guys in the group with crushes on you, either."

Britt threw back her long, slender neck and let out a natural, uncontrived laugh. It sprang from a well inside, a source she'd nurtured and fed. A place of feeling motivated and self-assured. A place where laughter could just bubble up and spill all over the listener, bathing him or her in vicarious delight. Where laughter was liquid and bright.

It was the kind of laugh that people want to be the cause of; laughter that washed over people in the restaurant. They half-turned to see who'd expressed joy in such a charming way. Male customers' eyes lingered on her silhouette, especially several men at a long table near us. Women smiled, perhaps remembering earlier times when they, too, had thrown their own heads back in unabashed laughter.

"I've let one guy down gently. I like him sooo much as a friend. But I'm dating the other one now. His name is Ellis." Color rose to her cheeks, which she didn't cover with heavy makeup anymore. "I really like him, Momma."

I smiled. "Ellis, huh? So tell me about this Ellis." I motioned for the waiter, and we ordered. Britt tilted the glass and watched the legs of the wine form on its side. "He's older than me. He worked for a while after he graduated, and then he traveled around for a while."

Trying to do the math, I was coming up with midtwenties.

"Ellis is premed." Britt smiled.

"Well, Gary and I would be delighted to meet him. Are you and Ellis nerds, like Gary and me?"

"Oh my god, Mom. We *so* are. We talk about science *all* the time."

We continued chatting until we finished our meal. I definitely wanted to meet this new guy whose name alone caused my daughter to blush.

■ ■ ■ ■

During her two years at the community college, Ellis and Brittany were a hoot to watch. Ellis was tall, with a handsome boyish face. They were boisterous and roughhoused like siblings, but were clearly in love. First love, perhaps for both; a thing of beauty. Gary and I could see that they probably wouldn't wind up at the same school, so it was bittersweet to watch. We worried about the physicality of their romping, feeling that Brittany was slugging Ellis a bit too hard. I didn't think hitting of any kind, even in fun, was a good idea in a romantic relationship. I suggested to Britt that it wasn't ladylike. But the two of them were like a comedy team popping out and walloping each other, scaring each other, grabbing each other. Perhaps worrying about Brittany had become my de facto position, those worry grooves so deeply embedded in my brain.

The two ate meals at our house quite a bit. Ellis was polite, kind, and funny. He and Gary got along very well. Conversation at dinner was spirited and fascinating. Brittany and Ellis explained to us that scientists had mapped all the genes of our species. They sparked conversation about stem cells and the possibility of curing debilitating diseases like Parkinson's. My daughter spent her eighteenth year enjoying a playful yet cerebral relationship with Ellis.

In her second year at the community college, Brittany was in love and academically on fire. Life was good. She and Ellis were jogging in Dana Point, acing their classes at the college, and more in love than ever as Britt began contemplating transferring.

Brittany applied to seven of the ten UC campuses. UC Irvine offered her the Regents' Scholarship, the most prestigious scholarship for transfer students entering from a California community college. It was a full ride with priority registration, travel abroad, and other benefits. She was delighted, and we visited the Irvine campus.

Britt was also accepted to Berkeley, the number one public university in the United States. It looked like she was going to accept the Irvine scholarship and stay close to Ellis while he finished up his premed work. However, we toured the Berkeley campus in the San Francisco Bay Area. How could she be accepted there and not even go look at the campus? I argued. I expected to see hippies, tie-dye, and lots of Birkenstocks. But what I saw was a dignified urban campus

260

with some elegant old buildings. We took a serene stroll under the canopy of oaks, redwoods, and eucalyptus. At Berkeley, there seemed to be room for experimentation without ostracism. I saw lots of vintage clothing and some pretty interesting hair colors. Later, I laughed with Brittany about how strong my Texas stereotype of the hippie nation at Berkeley had been.

Gary and I discussed Brittany going to Berkeley (no scholarship) versus UC Irvine (full ride). I regretted not going to a better school. I did have great professors at Stephen F. Austin State University, who infused me with a passion for teaching. I got what I needed for my chosen profession, but I wanted more for my daughter. Don't we all?

Berkeley was rated by *U.S. News & World Report* as the number one national public university. I couldn't afford to give Brittany a private college education, but I could give her Berkeley. She could go there for two years and graduate with zero debt. This I could do. This was why I had worked so hard as a single mom.

In the beginning, I wanted it more than she did. But then we stumbled upon an apartment in a storybook-like complex with French Normandy–style towers and arched doorways and windows. The problem was that the rental began in summer, and she had already committed to volunteering on a women-owned banana farm in Costa Rica.

"Brittany, look at this place! It's whimsical. It's charming." I scrambled out of the car. "It looks like little gnomes will come down the path any minute."

"Hobbits, Momma, like *The Lord of the Rings.* This has to be housing for professors or something. It looks like a fairy-tale château. But Costa Rica's not negotiable," Brittany said. "I'll just take the scholarship to UC Irvine and stay in my studio."

"I'm not suggesting you give up Costa Rica. I'm asking what diploma do you want on the wall of your place of business one day? If you become a psychologist, or get your master's and doctorate in another field altogether? I'm saying if this is the right school and this is the right apartment, I'll pay for it for the summer, even though you won't be here."

Brittany looked at me. "Really, Momma? Can we do this? What does Gary think?"

"Gary thinks that you should look at the two schools and choose based on where you want to go, not on whether you got a scholarship or not. He called Berkeley 'public Ivy League.' "

"Are you kidding me?" Britt's voice rose.

"Harvard-educated Gary said that?"

"I've worked all of your life for you to be able to go to a great school. It's why I worked so hard. So, I agree — it should be all about where you really want to go."

Ultimately Brittany decided to take the apartment and attend Berkeley. She had made one of the biggest decisions of her life.

I thought it was the right decision — not in the fluttery-heart, nervous-stomach, God-help-me-if-I'm-wrong way that I'd accepted her decision to drop out of high school, but in a chest-puffing, lung-expanding proud momma way.

Ellis loaned Brittany his extreme, internal-frame backpack for her six-week trip to Costa Rica, and she stuffed it to the max. Gary and I shopped for a rain poncho, mosquito netting, and other supplies. I caught Brittany taking some of those items out and adding a large makcup bag. Gary and I couldn't convince her that makeup was the last thing she would need on a banana farm in Costa Rica.

Luckily, Brittany had taken Spanish in school, and I hoped that if she truly needed something she could buy it when she got there. The volunteer/adventure tour entailed working alongside farmers who were learning new organic and sustainable farming practices. The volunteers stayed with a host family on a farm. There was electricity but no television, computer, or telephone. Britt would receive academic credit for participating in the program.

I was concerned, but I also thought the experience would be very good for Brittany. She had attended school with affluent kids, and this trip would be an eye-opener. The only contact would be from a public phone booth, which would be a forty-five-minute walk away. The brochure emphasized that volunteers would be working hands-on to increase the productivity of the farm.

After a few days there, Brittany called from the phone booth. She'd walked three miles down a dirt road to get to it. "Momma, I wear rubber boots that come up above my knee because the mud is so deep here. I tie a rope around my waist and pull banana trees down, like a mule."

"Don't hurt your back! I can't believe they expect young women to topple trees."

"Don't worry, these suckers would blow over in a strong wind — of which there is none. God, it's so hot and muggy here!" She described the mosquitoes and the snakes, but I could tell she loved it.

"So, you're liking it? I'm so relieved."

"I love this family, Momma. This brave, strong Costa Rican woman and her beautiful, happy children. Her no-good husband abandoned her, just walked out. She's trying to make a go of it on her own. Kind of like you, Momma."

At the end of one month on the farm, Brittany joined other volunteers for a two-week tour of Costa Rica that included whitewater rafting on an eighteen-mile stretch of the Pacuare River with class-three and -four rapids. Britt's favorite part was hiking through the Gandoca Wildlife Refuge, where she crossed rivers on rickety suspension bridges and saw adorable white-faced capuchin monkeys, toucans, and tiny poisonous frogs.

When Ellis brought our suntanned daughter home from the airport, she was happy and relaxed. "People were stoked that I was going to Berkeley," she told us as she wolfed down a late-night snack.

I thought I saw Ellis flinch, but to his credit he was elated that she'd had such a good experience. I looked at Ellis and felt a twinge in my heart. His boyish face belied a maturity he'd shown by not getting in Brittany's way when she wanted to travel, and even helping her get prepared for the trip. He wasn't trying to hold this butterfly back, catch her in a net, or pin her down as a specimen. He loved her enough to wish grand experiences for her. He loved her enough to freely let her go to Berkeley. He, like Brittany, would probably choose the best school that accepted him. Pain lay ahead for these two, and I couldn't protect either of them.

Her glorious trip to Costa Rica stirred something beautiful inside my daughter. She'd been bitten by wanderlust, and as Britt regaled us with stories of the trip, her face softened with kindness. "The children are so happy, Momma, and they have nothing. A new pencil makes them dance around in delight."

My daughter's mind had broadened. Exposure to a different way of living — leaving the comfortable bubble of affluent Orange County — had already changed her in ways I couldn't begin to define. She had matured more in Costa Rica than in the previous five years of growing up. Travel had done something wonderful for Brittany's soul.

17
No Cake for You

March–May 2014,
Ten to Sixteen Weeks Postsurgery

While I thought that I was learning how to
live, I have been learning how to die.
— Leonardo da Vinci,
The Notebooks of Leonardo da Vinci,
trans. Edward MacCurdy

I texted my sister Sarah, who'd sent us the
Eddie Izzard CD.

We asked for cake, but the MRI said no
cake for you! Death within a year — the
sonofabitch has grown 20 percent in 10
weeks — it ain't stage 2 no more! I am so
very afraid, and sad hardly captures the
pain. I am indulging in why . . . why us . . .
right now.
We fly Britt to Oregon to meet with Death
with Dignity doctors on April 8. Will know

more after that trip if we need to go to Switzerland.

Every cell in my body hurts, every bone and joint screams at me, I think I'm getting stomach ulcers. What lies ahead — I must pull enormous reserves of strength from some deep reserve that I haven't even tapped yet.

She typed back at 12:35 p.m.:

Let me know if you want someone else to go with you to any of this.

My sister Sarah, who worked with counselors and psychiatrists, had asked her colleagues what could help us wrap our heads around what was happening. She sent a CD called *When Things Fall Apart: Heart Advice for Difficult Times*.

Gary and I sat in our family room, our two Cavapoo pups at our feet, and listened. Pema Chödrön's voice crawled under our skin. It was all I could do to sit still. Gary actually stood up and said he couldn't listen.

"We need to listen," I answered, looking up at him and locking eyes. "I need you to listen with me."

My husband, his expression perturbed, sat down again.

Pema said provocative things. She suggested that we may feel like shit, but we had to take a long hard look at things. She submitted that sometimes things fall apart and we must accept that. She advised us to accept not knowing, told us we couldn't run from fear, and claimed it was helpful to lean toward what made us anxious.

It was the phrase "leaning toward" that burrowed deep in my mind.

We listened to the entire CD. "Let's think about it," I said. I left my husband in the family room. His body language told me that nothing about this type of thinking sat well with him.

I thought about Brittany being the beautiful sand castle that Pema described, a glistening creation of sand turrets, shell, and colored glass. I thought of how the tide inevitably came in, and no matter how attached we were to the castle, we watched it melt back into the sea. Was my child going to be a part of something bigger than her life? Was she struggling to stop us from clinging and clawing at her in her last moments of regal, palacelike glory?

I thought about the panic that gripped my heart each morning when I woke up and realized again that the nightmare was true. Pema said something about fear being close to truth. Was that why I was terrified? Was I teetering on the edge of truth? I realized I needed to breathe in worry, and breathe out comfort. Since I couldn't ward off death, I needed to just sit and be still with fear, anger, and the tumor.

Some of what I heard settled in dark, frightening corners of my heart, shedding light and chasing away panic.

Some of what Pema said still frightened me, made me want to shut the message out of my brain. Sooner or later, people experience something in life that they can't control. We can't be good enough human beings, or do enough research, or buy enough stuff, to be secure. Security is an illusion. Natural occurrences in life happen randomly to all kinds of people. Sad, horrible, senseless tragedy strikes for apparently no reason. Every journey begins without hope. It just begins.

The next day, I stopped Gary in the kitchen and laid my hands on his shoulders. "Gary, I need you to turn toward Brittany. I need you to lean toward her. I need you to be able to say that you will not let her die in a terrible way. Because she *is* dying, and come hell or high water, I'm going to support her in a gentle death."

Gary started to object, but I didn't allow him to.

"If you don't believe this, then I ask you to do it anyway. For me. I need you to tell Brittany that you will keep looking and hoping, but that you are going to make damned sure that she has a place to live in Oregon. I need you, a loving man, to take her in your arms and tell her you understand."

We stood looking at each other. Tears filled his eyes. I felt the rigidness of his body.

"Gary. She needs to feel safe. She needs to know that you have her back." Tears were running down my face. "I'm going to go to Oregon with her. I'm going to rent a house. I'm putting this plan in place — with or without you. But it would feel safer to Brittany if you stepped up. Can you do this?"

My husband wrapped his arms around me and pulled me in. His voice was choked. "Yes. I will do this."

"She needs your physical presence. She needs your arm around her. She needs you to touch her, tell her she's brave and beautiful." I sobbed this into his ear. "We have to lean toward the truth. We have to embrace the truth. No matter what that truth is. We can't run anymore."

"We won't." Gary held me tight.

I had become obsessed with these warm sweatshirts and hoodies that had positive expressions on the front. With a little research I found the company, Peace Love World. I ordered a soft pink sweatshirt that was perfect. It said "I Am Loved" in big white letters on the front. Instead, they shipped me a purple sweatshirt that said "Love Is in the Air." I called the company and explained that my daughter was wrestling with a terminal diagnosis. I told them that "Love Is in the Air" couldn't be substituted for the one I ordered.

They sent the correct sweatshirt in white with red letters and told me to just keep the wrong one. This sweatshirt was my way of telling Brittany she was loved. This was my way of saying, "We've got your back." It was ridiculous how much I hung on that sweatshirt. It became a symbol to me. I was leaning in. My daughter was loved.

I asked Gary to photograph Brittany and me in front of the pool and fireplace at Dan and Britt's house. I was wearing "Love Is in the Air," and she was in "I Am Loved." This was a turning point. On this trip, with these sweatshirts, my daughter and my husband

and I planned to go to Oregon. There, we would meet with the palliative care doctors.

Everything had changed since the visit with the Wiz. The Wiz wanted Brittany to undergo chemo to try to shrink the remaining tumor. But, days later, an MRI showed that the tumor had other ideas. The tumor said, "F-you! Guess what, I'm growing like gangbusters!"

Britt and I tried to spend time taking walks, baking a tart with fruit from her backyard, going to local nature areas with the dogs. I returned home to take care of Grandpa for a couple of weeks, and then came back up to retrieve my daughter for our initial visit to Oregon.

Brittany met with Dr. Chang, the young surgeon who had done her craniotomy. She told UCSF to note on her chart that she never wanted to see the Wiz again. Chang talked to Britt about a second craniotomy, an awake craniotomy. He disagreed with Dr. Berger. He thought that given the tumor's growth, a second awake surgery was the best plan. He would propose a plan to the tumor board to remove more of the tumor mass with her awake to answer questions, so that he could be sure he wasn't jeopardizing her speech or other eloquent skills.

He would take more tissue to ascertain

what grade the tumor was, because even though he saw this swirly-looking spot that everyone thought was stage four, he couldn't say for sure unless he had tissue samples analyzed. Dr. Chang understood that Brittany had scheduled a trip to Alaska, and he supported that. The only thing he worried about was the pressure in Brittany's head. She was off the steroids and wanted to stay off until she got back from Alaska, but we wouldn't return from Alaska until the end of May.

Brittany agreed to schedule the surgery for June 2. It meant she would go in for her second craniotomy almost immediately upon returning from Alaska. Britt posted the news on Facebook on April 2:

Just scheduled my full day awake craniotomy today at UCSF for June 2nd. I postponed just long enough to make it to my big Alaska adventure with Maudie and my Mom. Feeling love, feeling strong . . . T-shirts courtesy of my cool Mom.

However, Britt told me that she probably wouldn't have the surgery. "I'm giving myself the option. I'll think about it."

Gary and I hoped that Brittany would go through with the second surgery. We also hoped we would find some cutting-edge treatment. We still hadn't figured out that none of the experimental treatment studies took patients who hadn't already been through the cut, burn, and poison regimen. We were still taking our little girl to Oregon. We were meeting with the doctors there at OHSU. We would sit beside Brittany and support her while she applied for Death with Dignity.

We had turned a corner. We understood that Dan needed to remain gainfully employed in California, and that he would fly up often to visit Britt. We understood that this corner was a hard one to turn. Gary and I had reached that critical point in a complex situation where we were ready to make a relatively small move that would produce a large change. On April 3, I posted on Facebook a summary of where I was.

During the last three months my beautiful daughter, Brittany Diaz, has taught me a great deal about bravery and facing fear. Somehow, even on pain medication she mentally raced past everyone else in her life . . . leaving us fumbling in a cloud of denial. All of her family members and friends had to play catch-up. She was the first to ask difficult and pointed questions of the doctors. Even now, months later, waking up in those first sleep-fogged moments of morning I sometimes struggle for a microsecond — thinking that Brittany's brain tumor is just a bad dream. First comes denial — then anger. I know I'm moving through the stages of grief because this week I felt like breaking the plate glass window at the hospital. I was one deep breath away from making a bad situation worse. They say that anger is a necessary stage of grief. I'm trying not to let anger scare me. My life has taught me more about suppressing anger than feeling it. Although, it was good to suppress the urge to break the window, somehow I have to be OK with feeling the anger.

Britt gave the green Honda Element that I'd given her when she was a part-time nanny during her last year at Berkeley to her friend Maudie. Now a doctor, Maudie was able to talk to Brittany about medical issues. Britt was divesting herself of her possessions, giving away her clothes and rings that no longer fit because the steroids had made her body swell.

On April 8, Gary and I scooped up our girl and took her to Oregon. We booked a hotel suite with a view of a tree-lined bend on the Willamette River. It was raining, which we understood was the norm. After a massage, Britt and I joined Gary for a delicious dinner.

Britt was nervous the morning of the meeting. We found the parking structure at SW Moody and Gibbs and parked our rental car. We took the aerial tram to the main Oregon Health and Science University campus. The tram ride lasted three spectacular minutes. Gary pulled Brittany to his side, and I snapped a photo of her ponytailed head as she snuggled in. My two loves looked down at the Willamette River, and Gary pointed at snow-covered Mount Hood in the distance. This photo is one of my favorite pictures ever, my daughter gaining strength and support from her stepdad. It speaks volumes to me about our difficult journey. The back of Britt's precious vulnerable head makes me tear up every time I look at it.

We met with a team of doctors at OHSU, along with a social worker. They had already received Brittany's file from the University of California San Francisco Medical Center and had reserved a conference room. The physicians and the social worker were kind but inquisitive about how Brittany would become a legal resident of Oregon. Gary and I said that we would be helping Brittany financially so that she could get established in Oregon, and that we would move with her. The doctors said that their top neurosurgeon would like to meet with her and consult on her case. He also described comfort care, hospice care, and pain control.

We listened to the options, other than physician aid in death. Brittany asked questions. She shared with the doctors what she'd already researched about death from a brain tumor, and the process that she understood she would go through if she died with hospice care. I could tell that they were impressed with her calm, cool demeanor and the amount of information that she had about her illness.

"I'd be happy to meet with your neurosurgeon," Brittany told them. "However, the two neurosurgeons that I've already consulted with at UCSF have had more experience with brain tumors than your top surgeon. You do understand that I am moving to Oregon in order to be legally eligible to use the Death with Dignity law, right? I wouldn't move here for surgery or treatment. If those were viable options, I would stay in California."

The doctors referred to the video that

she'd sent them prior to her surgery. "We knew when we saw the video that you'd done a great deal of research and thought deeply about how you wished to live the rest of your life." I saw tears in both of the men's eyes. Gary and I were swiping at our cheeks. The social worker's face was full of empathy, and I'd seen her wipe a tear or two away. The only dry eyes in the room were Brittany's huge, luminous ones.

Brittany agreed to come back in less than two weeks for a series of MRIs that the Oregon neurosurgeon wanted to do over the course of three evenings. They would administer iron oxide to Brittany intra-arterially. The doctor maintained that the gadolinium used in other MRIs leaked out of the blood vessels, whereas the iron (feru-moxytol) stayed intravascular, allowing for a more accurate scan of the brain.

"Three MRIs, Britt?" I asked as we trudged back to the tram.

"It's okay, Momma. This guy is going to see the same big-ass tumor with swirls of stage four, only he'll see it with iron, and then he'll be on board. I don't want him screwing this up by creating doubt."

It was cold on the tram. It had been a long day. We had accomplished a lot.

On Friday, April 11, Gary and I flew

home, and Brittany flew home to Dan. Brittany's beloved college friend Mina had written and offered a free stay at a lodge in Yellowstone Park. This perked Brittany up after so many awful doctor visits.

Brittany's beautiful blond friend Leni stayed very active with Britt. They took their dogs to the local dog park. Leni's little pup wasn't old enough to be afraid of Charley the giant.

Before we knew it, it was time to go back up to OHSU. I flew on Easter day, eating an airport hot dog for my Easter meal. Brittany and I were off together on our second trip to Portland. On this trip we had a very full agenda. We were going to the hospital on three different evenings, getting Brittany's Oregon driver's license, and looking for a place to live. I stayed in Oregon with Brittany, ten days in total, until we found a house to rent. Gary and I were giving her some feeling of independence, even if it meant that she was totally dependent on us.

The weather was miserable. It rained and/or hailed every single day. We stayed at the same riverside hotel, but the gray days and endless rain made the view a moot point. Brittany was using terrible-tasting, tarlike medical marijuana in the evening. I prayed that the cannibis would slow tumor growth. I prayed every night looking at the endless rain. "Please God, if you are there, show us the way. I'm so lost, in every way possible."

I'd bought Brittany more sweatshirts with sayings. I pulled the tissue-wrapped package out of my suitcase and held the red sweatshirt up. "Ta-da. To cheer you up," I said.

Brittany stared at the white lettering and started laughing. "No way in hell," she said. "Momma, I am not walking around Portland in a sweatshirt that says 'I am adored.' Add to that, it's freakin' hard to tell what it says."

"Well, I'll wear it," I said.

The next day I was waiting outside the MRI area, when a woman sitting near me said, "I love your sweatshirt. I'm adopted, too!"

I quickly crossed my arms across my chest, and we had a conversation about how great adoption was.

When Brittany came out after hours in the MRI area, I had to tell her. My humiliation was complete when she laughed her head off. "I told you! I can't believe that happened the first time you wore it."

I heard her regaling a friend with the story

281

on the phone that night. It was worth the embarrassment to hear Brittany's magical laugh again.

I wanted to find a house for Britt, rather than an apartment. I wanted my girl to live in a neighborhood and have a backyard. I hoped we could bring her beloved dogs up. The housing rental market was different than in California. Realtors seemed uninterested or unable to show us rental homes, but finally one told us about a website with some listings.

After visiting several houses, we saw one that was up a steep hill with gracious, older homes on winding tree-lined streets. The rental was a darling two-story yellow home about a hundred years old. We loved the hardwood floors, the wavy old glass in the windows, the large three bedrooms upstairs, and the bedroom/office downstairs. There were so many windows, looking out at enormous trees and a garden. Brick steps led to a front door adorned with an old-fashioned knocker.

We didn't know it, but we'd just stumbled onto a rental in one of the most exclusive neighborhoods in Oregon. All I knew was that it felt right.

As Brittany looked around in the backyard, I walked across the street to a little glass display on a post. Under the glass was a sheet of white paper with a printed poem.

Upon closer inspection I saw that the poem was titled "When Death Comes," by Mary Oliver, who would become Britt's favorite poet. I shuddered and read about death like a bear, or an iceberg, or a man taking coins from his pocket to buy our lives.

I shivered again. It had begun to mist. Had this been foreordained somehow? I walked back across the street to our house. In my mind, it was already our house.

"It's really beautiful here," Brittany sighed, "and I just know that Dan and Gary would hate it."

"They won't like the age of the house, the age of the plumbing, the tiny bathrooms." I smiled at her.

"I'm going to see what that is." She pointed at the little glass display across the street.

"It's a poem, Britt. It might . . ." I walked with her, thinking the poem might upset or hurt her.

"What?" Britt arched her eyebrows.

"Nothing. It's very beautiful." I watched her read the poem, gobbling it up, eyes moving swiftly left to right. I saw her start over and read it again, more slowly. Her lips mouthed the words about stepping through a door. She turned to me, eyes glistening. "Don't you think this is a little bit of kismet?"

My voice was stuck behind the lump in my throat. "Fate," I croaked. "The first good thing that's happened to us in a long time."

"What do you think? I know the house isn't modern or sensible, but I love it."

"I think we should rent it. Right now," I said. We got in the car and drove to the property management office.

Before we went inside, Britt said, "Gary and Dan can fix almost anything that needs fixing. We'll just tell them up front, this is where I want to die."

"Then the house is ours."

About forty-five minutes later, we walked out of the office with a lease that took effect on May 1. We wouldn't move until around June 1, but we had signed, and we were faxing it to Gary for his signature.

This felt like it was meant to be. If my daughter was going to die in rainy Oregon, it was going to be in a charming old house with lots of personality, just like her. Brittany and I explored the area near the house. Our new street dead-ended in a beautiful park with walking trails. Up one trail was a panoramic view of downtown Portland. This vista was just a short hike from the house. We also liked a historic area called Nob Hill, which had eclectic restaurants, homey pubs, and charming shops.

Dan joined Brittany and me in Portland for the weekend. We showed him the house though the rental was a done deal, signed by Britt, my husband, and me. The weather cleared, and we drove to Multnomah Falls and to the Columbia River Gorge to watch steelhead trout jump the ladders of the dam.

Britt left with Dan to take her friend Mina's offer of the lodge in Yellowstone. By May 1 they would be marveling at geothermal features, subalpine forests, buffalo and elk above a super volcano. Back home, I combed the local thrift stores and consignment stores for furniture. I found a beautiful four-poster king bed with a headboard, two cherry nightstands, and a double dresser. It was important to me that Britt love the bed, because if a miracle didn't come along, my child would die in this bed. I purchased all the things we'd need to furnish the house and make it homey. I also spent time with my elderly father, who was confused by my many comings and goings in the past four months. I told him Brittany was sick and that she needed my help, but nothing more than that.

In mid-May, the gardener banged on the front door of Gary's and my home. "Fire!" he said, pointing across the street. I could see a large cloud of smoke. The phone rang with a reverse 911 call telling our neighborhood to evacuate.

Pamela called from Dad's assisted living care to say they were evacuating the elderly population. "I'll go with him and get him settled in for the night," she said. "You won't be able to get here, because the main thoroughfare is blocked by the police." What would I do without her?

I tried to get to Dad's and was turned back by police. So I went home and packed Brittany's baby albums, my jewelry, and an overnight bag. We watched helicopters pull water from the local golf course pond and dump it on the hill nearest our house. "Are you ready?" Gary asked.

"I am. Daddy has been evacuated. Can you believe this? What else can go wrong?"

"Don't ask that question, Deb. Life is teaching us that just when we think it's over, another blow can try to slap us down. Our beloved daughter with terminal brain cancer; Erica, our sweet niece, with stage four colon cancer; my brother needing a heart transplant; and now fire threatening our home. There can be more. There *might* be more. Never tempt fate by asking 'what else?' But know this: together we will be all right."

Arms wrapped around each other, we stood and watched the firefighters, who saved hundreds of homes. One person died, eighteen apartments were destroyed, and eight single-family homes were left either gutted or gone. Although we were thankful we didn't lose our home, in the grander scheme of things, it just wasn't important to either of us. We were in the midst of losing something much more sacred.

18
BERKELEY GIRL

*Summer 2004–Summer 2006,
Ages Nineteen to Twenty-One*

Your playing small does not serve the
world. There is nothing enlightened about
shrinking so that other people will not feel
insecure around you.

> — Marianne Williamson,
> *A Return to Love: Reflections on the
> Principles of* A Course in Miracles

While Brittany was in Costa Rica, Gary
helped me move furniture into her rental
apartment in Berkeley, and I cleaned everything. We had decided to sublet one of the
bedrooms in the place, and I interviewed
and found a nice young woman to live there
and pay part of the rent.

At first when Britt returned from Costa
Rica, she suffered a bit of culture shock.
The weather was so rainy and dark in

Berkeley. Sometimes when she called, she sobbed on the phone, and it broke my heart. She shocked me by saying that her professors at the community college had been more engaging than the ones at Berkeley. I flew up several times during her first semester to hang out and see how she was doing.

We went to the Scharffen Berger chocolate factory and took the tour. I bought a T-shirt that said "(Extra) Bitter" across the front. I thought it was hilarious in view of my decision to never marry again. The first time I wore it, I joked that my two former marriages had made me (extra) bitter. Brittany said something extraordinary.

"You aren't bitter, Momma. That's the thing. You have this eternal hopey-ness. Like you think if you're just a good enough person, things are bound to get better. I'm more logical than you are." She popped a piece of sample chocolate in her mouth. "I think Gary's the best thing that's ever happened to you."

"But honey, he's fourteen years older than me."

"So what? Take the happiness. Grab it, Mom. He is a wonderful man, and he's been following you around like a puppy for almost five years now."

"You want me to marry again? You told

289

me to *never* marry again."

"Oh for God's sake, I was eleven years old then!" Brittany cocked her head to the side. "Is that why you keep telling Gary 'no marriage'? Because of something I said when I was a little girl?"

"Kind of. I didn't want you to ever have to . . ." My voice choked.

"This is different. *He's* different." Brittany squeezed my hand. "He's a keeper. I love him. He's been more of a father to me than anyone."

"I've turned him down so many times." I felt a twinge. "What if he doesn't want to get married anymore?"

"Momma, that man adores you. Anyone can see that. It's written all over his face. My girlfriends all want a man like Gary."

I smiled. I'd actually heard one of her friends saying that she wanted a man who treated her like Gary treated me.

Gary and I announced to our family and friends in a New Year's card that we would be getting married in the coming year. Some family members seemed surprised that, since we'd both tried and failed at marriage twice already, we were willing to take a walk to the altar again. We got mixed reviews on our happy decision. Nothing fazed us. Our relationship was stable, our love unwavering. Brittany's approval had cinched the deal for me. We were in no hurry but Gary and I were going to be husband and wife.

In Berkeley, Britt haunted the open-air farmers' markets. She wasn't afraid to grab ugly tomatoes, beets, globe eggplant, and even figs, and use them all in one fabulous dinner. She was the girl you see touching all the fruit, laughing with farmers, selecting gigantic bouquets of flowers, and stuffing organic goat cheese and fresh-baked bread in her backpack.

Brittany was the girl who walked home popping fresh strawberries in her mouth or dripping peach juice on the sidewalk. Watching my daughter at a farmers' market always made me think, *Where did this lovely foodie creature come from?* My mother was a typical World War II British rationing cook. I was a single mom cook. Not a lot of organic or farm-fresh veggies, though I refused to use canned.

Ellis went up to visit a few times, and that cheered Britt immensely. She had volunteered to work at a suicide hotline and caught the bus to get there. She would call either Ellis or me to talk all the way to Oakland, because the area was rough. She found the work rewarding and challenging.

Brittany kept her apartment for the second year in Berkeley. If she took summer courses, she could graduate by the following December. She stayed there for the summer, and Ellis moved up to be with her. He had applied to medical schools throughout the country. They knew that the relationship might be tested soon, and they lived as if there were no tomorrow.

There were no more sad phone calls; in fact, there were almost no phone calls. The summer of love in Berkeley flew by. That June, Gary and I flew to Italy for a pre-honeymoon trip, as we'd decided to get married in November. While my twenty-year-old daughter experienced love in Berkeley, I let my guard down and fell deeply in love with Gary. Brittany was in the spring of life, while Gary and I were in the fall of our lives. I was forty-nine, Gary sixty-three. The summer of '05, Britt and I joked that we were like the Gilmore girls — both in love.

Summer drew to an end, and Ellis decided to go to med school on the East Coast. Exactly what Gary and I had worried about happened. It was painful to watch. Brittany toggled back and forth between anger and sorrow. I flew up to Berkeley and helped her "de-Ellis" her home. Pictures were taken down, and new photos put in the frames. My brokenhearted daughter stormed about her apartment, bitter and angry. Though her wrath wasn't rational, Britt somehow thought that if Ellis had valued their relationship enough, he could have found a good med school closer than the opposite side of the country. I knew that being angry was easier than being sad. I also knew that it would be good for Brittany to meet other men, try out different relationships. She was only twenty, and Ellis had been her first true love.

In her second year at Berkeley, Brittany became closer friends with a young woman who advised her not to graduate early. "Why would you graduate in December? Just because you can? Slow down, enjoy college life. Don't be in such a hurry to get in the rat race." Brittany slowed down in some ways, and sped up in others. She decided she would remain at Berkeley the full second year and not take a heavy load to graduate early. This enabled her to participate in other activities. She volunteered to visit the local state penitentiary and provide socialization by playing board games with felons as part of her psychology program. She also took an afternoon job as a nanny for three young children. Brittany picked them up from preschool and watched them until their parents got home.

I flew up to visit for a couple of days. I watched in pleased amazement as Brittany met the children, loaded them in their stroller, and collected their belongings. Brittany's charge didn't have a coat on and the day had turned cold. Brittany unzipped her jacket, swept the girl up into her arms, and zipped her into the jacket. The child clung to Brittany's neck, and was asleep within minutes.

Her brother threw himself around Brittany's leg. Britt walked with him clinging to her until she could load him into a stroller. She tucked him in, and we exited onto a neighborhood street. It began to rain and Brittany rolled her charges up onto someone's porch.

"You need a car," I said, watching the sleeping child inside Britt's jacket.

"We're doing okay. No worries." Brittany swayed back and forth.

Who was this creature? I thought. This young woman who took Berkeley, prisoners, lost love, rainstorms, and children in stride? Who was this lovely nanny, whom mothers and teachers fawned over at the preschool? My daughter was capable, full of common sense, and probably someone who could give Mary Poppins a run for her money. I was impressed.

When I got home, I discussed the situation with Gary. "Did she ask for a car?" he said.

"No. She walks to their house, then from there at least eight blocks to the school. It's a lot of walking in inclement weather, and winter is coming."

"What if we get you a new Honda Element and take the one you're driving up to Britt?" Gary grinned. "I'm so proud of her for getting on with life — without a car and without a boyfriend."

We couldn't wait to give the car to her. I picked out a red Element, and Gary and I drove up to Britt's the next weekend in the green one. No more dragging the children around in the rain. Britt called to say that now on clear days she loaded the kids up in the car and took them to the park.

On November 12, 2005, Gary and I were married. Brittany, Gary, and I flew to Dallas, Texas, so that my parents could attend our wedding. My sister Donna and her husband lived nearby. Sarah and her family, my sister-in-law Renda and her two girls, and both of Gary's brothers and their families flew in to witness our union. My niece, Mary Iris, was my flower girl, and

Brittany my maid of honor. It would be a small and intimate ceremony at the Baptist church I grew up attending.

Then, my British mum threw one of her holier-than-thou, world-class hissy fits. She said she wouldn't attend my third wedding. I was a tainted woman. It was a sacrilege. She simply wouldn't condone it. God would not bless such an abomination. Then she began lecturing my nearly blind father and harassing him until he called me. "There will be hell to pay if I come to the wedding," he said.

"It's okay," I told him. "The amount of grief that Mum would cause isn't worth it. I understand."

At our wedding Brittany read a poem by e. e. cummings, "I Carry Your Heart with Me." When my daughter said the words, "root of the root," I started crying. I knew that for the rest of my life anytime I heard or read this poem, I would always see my daughter, her green eyes shining, reading a poem about love, even when her own heart still ached from losing Ellis.

Brittany went to visit Ellis out east that winter. They had a tender visit and agreed that they still loved each other, but that they must move on and date others. On her last day there, Britt looked out the upper-floor window to see that Ellis had written "I Love Brittany" on the top of his car in the snow.

Brittany graduated from Berkeley in May 2006. Gary and I drove to the Bay Area and stayed at a hotel. We treated Britt and one of her girlfriends to a lovely dinner the night before the ceremony. Brittany looked radiant the day of graduation. She pinned her graduation cap at a jaunty angle. I met one of her friends outside the Greek Theater. He touched my arm and said, "Brittany speaks very highly of you, and I must say that you raised one of the finest human beings I've ever met." I felt grateful for the compliment.

Brittany graduated with a BA in psychology. She wore a different color stole because she graduated with honors. Her hair was almost waist-length, red and copper tints glinting in the sun. Her dazzling white smile made her easy to spot in the crowd. As soon as the ceremony was over, we hugged her and left her to party with friends. I had offered to take Brittany to France for her graduation gift, but she'd accepted an entry-level sales position with an insurance company. I'd lived the life of a saleswoman and wondered if it was right for her. She would work out of a beautiful office building in upscale Walnut Creek. It appealed to her because she could remain in the Bay Area without having to drive to downtown San Francisco. It was a plum job for a fresh-out-of-college kid. France would have to wait.

19
LIVING IN THE MOMENT
IN ALASKA

May 2014, Fourth Month After Craniotomy

Death twitches my ear; "Live," he says . . .
"I'm coming."

— Virgil, *Copa*

Brittany and her college bud Maudie were immersed in getting the details of their portion of the Alaska trip lined up. Brittany had twisted her ankle in Yellowstone, and it wasn't completely healed. Her plan was to ignore it. I was meeting Britt in Juneau on May 21, when Maudie flew home.

On May 15, Brittany and Maudie did a moderately strenuous hike to Mount Healy Overlook in Denali National Park, starting along the Nenana River near the Denali Princess Wilderness Lodge. The climb ascended seventeen hundred feet in 2.5 miles, the trail twisting back and forth using switchbacks. As they climbed, they left behind spruce, alder, and aspen, and entered alpine tundra, consisting of moss, lichen, and wildflowers. They saw moose, caribou, and big-horned sheep. They kept a close eye out for bears and wolves.

Outside Denali, Britt and Maudie went ATV riding in bush country. Splashing through mountain-fed creek beds and driving over tree root–rutted trails, they watched for moose, fox, and Dall sheep. They also saw a mother black bear and her cubs. "Nature is my happiness," Brittany wrote on Facebook.

Days seemed to never end, with the sun shining brightly until eleven o'clock at night. In the evening, the girls sat on their cabin's deck and clinked beer bottles as a pair of bald eagles soared in a thermal over the lake.

Because Maudie had a medical degree, she and Brittany were able to talk about the brain tumor and death openly and scientifically. These days in nature shared with someone not afraid to discuss death and what it would look like were exactly what Brittany needed.

The next adventure was the 8.2-mile round-trip Harding Icefield Trail. Starting on the valley floor, the toe of Exit Glacier was visible before the trail wound through cottonwoods and alders. Finally, they broke into heather-filled Marmot Meadows. Here they saw chubby marmot squirrels popping their heads out of burrows. Britt said they had to fight the urge to yell "Riiiiiicooool-laaaaaah!" at the top of their lungs.

The climb got much steeper, and there were patches of snow and ice. Brittany said, "This hike at one thousand feet of incline per mile is not for candy-asses like you, Momma." I could hear the pride in her voice. "Not too shabby for having 'less than 6 months,' " she wrote.

The girls kayaked Kenai Fjords National Park. Paddling through ice-cold, turquoise water, they saw sea otters, gray whales, and a pod of orca whales eating a seal. On the rocky shore, Brittany posed with ice chunks that looked like they'd been carved into sculpture by wind and sun.

The evening of the twenty-first, Brittany and I relaxed at our no-frills B and B. Our first morning together we drove to the Mendenhall Glacier Visitor Center and took a mile trail called the Trail of Time. We felt that we were indeed walking through time as we trudged past willows, alders, and cottonwoods on what used to be barren glacially carved terrain. The trail dumped us on a sand spit where Nugget Waterfall thundered in an icy veil near the toe of the glacier.

The next morning, we drove into Juneau to catch a helicopter ride up to Mendenhall Glacier. Soon we were lost in the view as we choppered over the rain forest, along alpine ridges, then past rock sentinels that soared thousands of feet in the air. Our first glimpse of the deep blue rock crevasses elicited gasps. We descended and made a gentle landing on the glacier. At the mushers' camp, the dogs' names were painted on their doghouses. Brittany laughed and pointed at dogs named Viagra, Levitra, and Cialis.

I wanted to be in the moment with Brittany. I wanted to feel the thrill of knowing that we were moving in a sled pulled by dogs, on top of a huge moving chunk of ice pulled by gravity, on top of a huge ball of rock and water called Earth that was also spinning and moving through space.

I wanted to feel unadulterated joy as my daughter insisted that I be the driver. I wanted to burn this moment into my brain, freeze it in time. In fact, I wanted to stop time. I was able, for seconds, maybe minutes, to forget that my daughter was dying and there wasn't a damned thing I could do about it. I wasn't able to manage my terror for long, though. I felt anxious in all my waking hours and many of my sleeping ones. There was a never-ending feeling of ultimate loss. I was on a glacier trying to pretend I was happy, when fate was stealing the person I was most attached to. The fact that Brittany was the child and I was the parent made it the ultimate injustice.

During the helicopter ride back, I found myself daydreaming that it would go down and explode in a fiery crash. This seemed better than trying to live without her. I wanted to go with her instantaneously.

I had just spent one of the best and worst days of my life with my daughter.

For our last adventure in Alaska, I'd signed us up for a Tracy Arm fjord boat ride captained by Steve, a Merchant Marine officer. The notes I read about Captain Steve made him seem like the ideal guy for Brittany. He was skilled, highly rated, and viewed as a bit of a risk-taker. His boat trip was aptly named *Adventure Bound.*

Steve took his passengers right up to the face of Sawyer Glacier, past the research boat that was anchored there for observation. He bumped through floating chunks of ice until we were tantalizingly close to the glacier.

On the floating ice, we saw bald eagles,

harbor seals, leopard seals, and seabirds. The captain turned off the engine and we floated in silence. "This is an active tidewater glacier, folks. So keep watching the half-mile face of the glacier for movement." We watched up and down the blue ice. "This phenomenon is known as 'calving.' Pieces of ice anywhere from the size of a Volkswagen to the size of a cruise ship fall off."

I heard a buzz as someone spotted ice movement. A thunderous roar sounded as a chunk of ice hit the water. I had imagined the ice breaking and quietly floating away, so the deafening roar made me scream. Brittany thought it was hilarious that I hadn't factored in noise. We watched giant hunks of ice float past our boat. Farther up Sawyer Glacier, the ice was a lighter robin's egg blue.

It was icy cold, and I began to shiver uncontrollably. Brittany took off her orange climbing jacket and gave it to me to wear. We were two of the few people who stayed on the deck rather than go below to the warm compartment.

When we came inside, people were interested in seeing Brittany's close-ups of the glacier calving. We passed the camera around as we chugged away from the glacier. Without even thinking, my daughter and I were holding hands across the table.

A lady next to us asked where we lived. "I'm from Southern California," I said.

"I live in the San Francisco Bay Area," Brittany told her.

"Oh. I thought you were a couple," the woman said, looking pointedly at our hands.

Brittany and I started laughing. "Um . . . no. This is my mother," Brittany said. "She's taking me on a bucket list trip. I've always wanted to go to Alaska."

"Bucket list?" The woman looked confused.

"I have a brain tumor and less than six months to live," Brittany said in a conversational tone of voice.

I saw the woman's husband flinch, and tears sprang to my eyes. He looked at me and tears welled in his eyes, too.

Someone overheard the conversation, and the next thing we knew, the dozen or so passengers on the boat all knew Brittany's story. Later, the captain came down to meet everyone. Apparently the news had gotten to him.

"Heard this is a special trip for you." He nodded his head at Brittany. "Trip's not over. Not by a long shot," he told her. "We're on our way to a waterfall and a spot where we usually see bears. So keep that camera ready."

"It's been a magical trip for everyone," Brittany said, as he turned to climb the stairs. "It is without a doubt my favorite day in Alaska. In fact, of all the traveling I've ever done, this day is epic."

"More to come," he said gruffly, as though there was a catch in his throat.

Brittany and I conversed with various people on the boat. It turned out quite a few of them had thought we were a couple. We all became friends as Brittany shared herself with this captive group of intrepid voyagers. There was a back-and-forth of humanity at a level that people don't usually reach. Brittany spoke of her impending death, of her plans to move to Oregon, with clear eyes and not a quiver in her voice. I saw complete strangers gazing at her lovely face, their heads nodding in understanding, their watering eyes giving away their instant feeling of intimacy with her.

Brittany shared herself although her head was beginning to pound from the sound of the engine. I think that death, whispering in her ear as he did, gave Brittany the potential for immediate intimacy with strangers. She let down the barriers and allowed people to see her without her normal defenses. At precisely the same time, the tumor, death and his infernal murmuring, was making it hard for her to remain intimate with those she was closest to. She had started distancing herself from me. She was even less able to tolerate my sadness, my tears, my feeling of loss. It was easier to be open with people who would go their way in a little while, who didn't cling or cry.

The engine throttled down, and suddenly we heard a loud crashing noise and water splashing the observation windows. "We've arrived at the waterfall," Captain Steve said in his understated way. People were on their knees looking out the window. I took off running, Brittany close on my heels with the camera. The water pounded the front deck of the boat. We were so close to the rock wall, it was terrifying. Anyone who has ever stood under a waterfall knows that rocks often come with the water. Our captain was definitely bringing on the adventure.

Brittany and I were laughing and screaming. "Who does this crazy shit?" she yelled over the noise.

"Captain Steve does!" I shouted back.

We had barely sat down when the engines throttled up and we were off again. Captain Steve showed us black bears eating mussels and a pod of orcas. Something about the

307

rhythmic huffing of the whales soothed me at a moment when I'd have taken anything I could get.

As the boat pulled into Juneau, Britt laid her head on my shoulder. "This was the best day ever," she said. "I know you're looking forward to seeing Victoria, but nothing will beat this day."

"No, sweetie, there will never be another day in my life as exquisitely beautiful as this one."

As Britt dozed on my shoulder, I thought about the myriad emotions that I'd just experienced. I'd never found more kindness in strangers, more love in their faces. I'd never seen sadness etch faces faster as fellow travelers comprehended that my vivacious young daughter was going to move to Oregon to die, so that she would not suffer the indignities her brain tumor held in store. I'd never seen Mother Nature in a more overflowing exhibition of her wonder, wildness, and power. I'd never felt such disappointment and sadness in the face of overwhelming evidence that mankind had altered the ebb and flow of ice on our planet. I'd never felt such oneness and love for my child as a part of creation. I'd never felt time and fate pull her away from me more certainly than I did as I watched

Brittany talk about the path she planned to walk toward death. I had never felt such joy and anguish about our little lives. I'd never seen such a sharing of love and sorrow, hope and despair.

On this beautiful day, on this brave little boat, I'd felt the highest highs and the lowest lows a mother could feel. Now my child, weary and with an aching head, seemed to disappear into her sickness on my shoulder. Passengers caught my eyes above her precious head, and spoke volumes with nods or the dashing away of a tear. No one left the boat unscathed by the beauty of our day.

The next morning, we flew via Seattle to Victoria, British Columbia, where I had reservations at the Villa Marco Polo Inn. We unpacked, had tea, and went to bed early.

Our first day-trip was to the gorgeous Butchart Gardens, a National Historic Site of Canada. Each year, more than a million plants in nine hundred varieties bloom there uninterrupted from March to October.

Although Brittany was getting more and more reluctant to have her photograph taken, I was able to get one photo approved. It was of her under a tree with profusely dripping yellow blossoms above her head.

On the way back to the inn, Brittany told me that she needed to make a phone call to a film company in London. "One of the physicians in Oregon was contacted by them. Parliament's House of Lords is debating a bill to permit physician-assisted death," she explained.

"I know that 20 percent of the people who use the law at clinics in Switzerland are British." I hadn't talked to Brittany at great length about Switzerland, except to say that if she couldn't meet the criteria in Oregon, Gary and I would get her to Switzerland, no matter what.

"The British are interested in doing a program that shows the lives of at least three people who are going to use physician-assisted death — except they call it 'suicide,' which drives me crazy."

"Physician-assisted death should not be confused with suicide," I said.

"Well, they tell me 70 percent of Britons want the law to change, should they become terminally ill. But Parliament is stodgy and adversarial."

"Brittany, please make sure this is a reliable crew and that the news program is a really good one. The British press has an awful reputation. I wouldn't want to see you get hurt or your words twisted." I pulled our rental up to the curb.

Britt promised that she would be careful,

and our hostess gave her the best room for Skype service, closed the double doors for privacy, and the phone call took place. The British crew would meet Brittany at our new home in Portland and film there. We needed to get moved in beforehand.

The next day we drove the forty-five minutes out into the countryside and along the coastline. We parked in Sooke Potholes Regional Park and hiked the trails. Brittany bent to examine every flower, insect, and creature. "Momma!" she would call, and I'd run to see what she'd found next.

On that morning, late in May, the light shone down on us with just the right amount of warmth. We felt calm and bonded. If I could have bottled that day, I would have. Never before or since have I felt such blissful peace with my child.

Next we drove to Adrena LINE, Vancouver Island's only canopy ziplining tour. I had booked this activity to please Brittany since I knew she loved adrenaline-pumping activities. At one point on the two-hour adventure, we would zipline a thousand feet and walk across two suspension bridges 150 feet above the forest floor.

Brittany had ziplined in Costa Rica and Southeast Asia, so this would be child's play for her. Atop the first tower, I hugged the tree while listening to the instructions. One by one, we were clipped to the cable by a harness that attached to a movable trolley pulley. It was thrilling and nerve-wracking at first, but after a while I relaxed.

Brittany was subdued on the way to the car. "I was nervous up there," she said quietly. "I started thinking how easy it would be for me to get dizzy and fall."

I stopped and took both her hands. "Oh baby, why didn't you tell me? I did it for you."

"It's okay. I really wanted to go with you. The fear came out of nowhere."

I looked into her stricken face and hugged her, but she pulled away.

"I don't want to mollycoddle fear. I've got too damned much to be afraid of."

We got into the car and pulled onto the road. Only a few minutes had passed when Britt touched my arm. "Something's happening. I don't feel good."

I pulled off the narrow highway, dirt swirling.

"It tastes like metal in my mouth. I'm tingling."

One of her eyelids listed and fluttered wildly like a trapped butterfly. Her face on that side rippled beneath the skin.

"I'm right here, Britt. It's okay."

312

"I'm trying to talk while it's happening. I'm so scared."

I saw her hand curled inward at an awkward angle. "I'm right here. You're doing fine."

"Ummmm . . . uhhhh . . . feels so bad." Britt's head lay back on the headrest.

I said, "It will pass in a minute. You're all right."

Time is hard to monitor when you're witnessing suffering. I would estimate that Britt's eye was fluttering for a minute. It felt like forever.

Eventually she said, "We can go now."

I started the car and pulled back onto the road. I blamed this on the ziplining. What kind of mother ziplines with a child that has a brain tumor? How stupid could I be?

"I've had some little weird incidents before. But this was like an electrical malfunction. So much for taking antiseizure meds," she said.

I thought, *What would it have been like without the meds? Would it have been worse?* "Just lay back and relax, sweetie. Sleep if you can."

"I'm so fucked," said Brittany. "I'm getting sicker every day. I can feel it. I'm actively in the process of dying now. Let's get moved up to Oregon, Momma."

20
CHANGING HER MIND
(A WOMAN'S PREROGATIVE)

End of 2006–2008,
Ages Twenty-Two to Twenty-Four

A woman's mind is cleaner than a man's:
she changes it more often.
— Oliver Herford,
Saturday Review of Literature, Volume 26

After six months of working in sales, Brittany decided it wasn't for her and went back to nannying. In early 2007, she became the sitter for twins, a boy and a girl. The boy had mild Asperger's syndrome. The mother was absolutely devoted to her children. Britt was a natural at working with both kids, and enjoyed thinking about better ways to communicate with the boy, who had social limitations in interacting with peers that led to loneliness. He was very bright yet intense, and Britt was adept at encouraging him to explore ways to calm himself down. Over the next year and a half, Brittany became deeply attached to the family. She truly was their Mary Poppins and to the kids it felt like the wind snatched her away for a while after Britt left. However, the family stayed in touch and remained friends. They attended Britt's wedding and were in touch with her until her death.

In the spring, before she left the Bay Area, Brittany dated an older guy named Dan for a few months. Although she'd dated quite a few guys since Ellis left, this was the most attention she'd paid to another man. I met Dan once when I visited. He took Brittany and me to eat at a lovely restaurant.

"I liked the way he talked about his family," I told Brittany after dinner. "He spoke of them with great pride and respect. It was refreshing." Though they only dated a short while before Brittany moved back to Southern California, it was the start of a very important relationship in her life.

I had planned Britt's graduation trip to France for the summer of 2006. Now I was determined that we would take the belated graduation trip in the summer of 2008. But a couple of months before our scheduled departure I became very ill. I went to the doctor multiple times and was put on various antibiotics. I felt as wobbly as a ninety-year-old, at the age of fifty-two.

Finally Gary arranged for me to see an internal medicine doctor, who discovered that I had polymyalgia rheumatica, an inflammatory disorder that causes muscle pain and stiffness. She put me on a low dose of oral prednisone, and within two days, I felt better. The trip to France was on.

Britt and Dan broke up before she moved out of her apartment in Berkeley and in with us. We were going to take Britt's friend Helene with us on our trip. We would cover her room and board, and she paid for her airfare. Gary and I flew with the girls to London for a couple of days, and then we all took the Chunnel to Paris, where we rented a car for our French adventures.

Gary and I headed for Utah Beach, where my father landed in 1944. Utah Beach was eerie. I remembered my father talking about the smell. He said that there were so many bodies still unburied, that you could smell death for miles. I imagined my father, young, green, from the dusty fields of Oklahoma, landing in the stench of the dead bodies. I imagined his thumping heart when six days after landing, he was ordered to command a jeep and go into the French countryside on reconnaissance. Britt and

Helene were more interested in attending a lunch that the mayor of Villaines-la-Juhel had invited us to. We were being honored because this was the town where Dad had been captured by the Germans and his jeep driver killed. My father had jumped up to pull the driver, Corporal Baker, out of the jeep, and got hit four times in the leg and groin. Dad rolled back into the ditch just as the Nazis tossed a grenade.

We stopped in Saint-Lô and bought flowers to put on the memorial of Corporal Baker. Brittany had comforted my father one Thanksgiving when he'd broken down and cried in telling this story. Now we were here on the very road where the attack occurred. The local press met us at the memorial in honor of Colonel Baker. The next day we drove to Dieulcfit, a peaceful village on the banks of a river surrounded by lush hills. The small homes were painted in pastel pink, blue, and green. Each day we set off to explore something different: vineyards and wine caves, medieval towns, a twelfth-century castle, and the Pont du Gard, an ancient Roman bridge.

Next we headed to the Loire River Valley. For the next few days, we explored the surrounding countryside. "Brittany doesn't seem to be able to see the beauty," Helene said in a wistful voice one afternoon. "She's so miserable about Dan."

"Isn't it strange how women can long for a relationship that *we* ended?" I said. That night I watched Brittany and Helene, their sweet young profiles against the yellowing hazy twilight as a summer evening fell on the river. I wondered why my daughter seemed so unable to settle down, so inherently unhappy, involved in a search for love when what I felt she needed was to love herself. She had everything a girl could ask for: beauty, brains, and a strong work ethic. Brittany could pursue any subject in school and do well. She could choose any career and succeed. By now, she had to know that meeting guys wasn't going to be an issue. Yet she seemed unable to be in this moment, here in France where the rest of us were utterly hypnotized by the country's beauty. She seemed incapable of seeing how gifted she was, how blessed she was. Perhaps that was the problem: all the choices one had to make when met by success no matter which way one turned. Was life actually more stressful when there was no natural paring down? When all of life lay open and available to you?

Our last stop was Paris. We toured several

landmarks and had some amazing meals. Brittany and Helene went out on the town one evening. My daughter seemed to forget her latest breakup and just enjoy the "City of Light."

Gary and I left the girls and flew back home. They were heading off for Bruges, Amsterdam, Luxembourg, Bern, Milan, and finally several days at Cinque Terre National Park. Cinque Terre was Brittany's favorite part of the trip. She loved the beach, the cliffs, and the lack of hustle and bustle. The turquoise water and the locals hand weaving fishing nets intrigued her. She loved the feeling of being transported back in time. After the frenetic pace, this was a much-needed slowdown.

By the time the girls flew to London, Britt was ready for change. She had a salon cut her hair shoulder-length and dye it a glossy reddish-brown. For Britt, there was something cathartic about the post-breakup dramatic crop and color change.

When Brittany returned to California, we took her house hunting in downtown San Diego and found her an apartment in an old house with character. She and I had so much fun combing the thrift stores for furnishings. Within weeks, Brittany adopted a small beagle named Bella from the local shelter. The dog never outgrew her neediness. She would climb fences, dig, or howl when left alone, but she was Britt's baby.

Brittany started an audiology program when she returned from Europe. Her decision to go into this field had surprised me. I'd asked her if she was prepared to spend the better part of each day looking in people's ears. She wanted to get her AuD at a joint program offered through San Diego State University and UCSD. Brittany talked about working in pediatric audiology. She liked the idea of a less stressful schedule, compared to other medical practices. She felt it was a career that she could handle along with being a mother, which she definitely wanted to be one day. There were ten openings for the program, and Brittany was accepted and granted a partial-tuition scholarship,

Though Gary and I couldn't imagine Brittany in the role of an audiologist, we knew that hearing loss was going to be a huge problem for a generation of young people who were listening to personal audio devices at unsafe volumes. It seemed like a very practical, if somewhat boring, choice. We agreed to financially support her while she acquired her doctor of audiology.

Toward the end of her first semester in the AuD program, Brittany called me, very upset. "I hate the program. I don't want to be an audiologist. I'll finish the semester, but I can't do this for the rest of my life." She knew we'd paid her rent, car insurance, health insurance, and expenses, and she'd just signed a one-year lease.

"If this isn't for you, then withdraw now. What do you plan on doing? Have you thought it through?"

"I'd like to tutor part-time and study for the LSAT."

"I always thought you'd make a great attorney. You can argue with a wooden stump. You're on a roll: new hair, new house, new pet, and new career goals," I said.

"You're taking this a lot better than I thought. I guess I might as well tell you: I also have a new boyfriend. I'd like you to meet him. His name is Mark."

"Well, bring Mark over for dinner Saturday night. What does he do?"

"He works in high tech — a senior position — and he wants to take me to Paris for Christmas and New Year's!" She sounded excited. "Imagine ringing in 2009 in Paris."

"Wow. Isn't he kind of moving fast? How do you feel about going to Paris with someone you've only just started dating?"

"Well, we have a couple of months to figure it out."

When I hung up, I thought of the money Gary and I had wasted on Britt pursuing a degree that she ultimately didn't want. However, I also thought about the wisdom of Brittany cutting her losses before she was in too deep. My daughter was changing gears yet again, but she sounded focused and happy.

I've always believed that when students graduate, they embark on a journey to eventually find the field of work they want to be in. It isn't always a first–fit situation. People unwittingly put a great deal of pressure on new grads by assuming that their first job will be their career.

When Britt graduated from Berkeley, I said that if people asked her what she wanted to be, she should answer simply, "I want to be happy."

21
MAKING A NEST TO DIE IN

*June–July 2014, Sixth and Seventh Months
After Craniotomy*

Love should not cause suffocation and
death if it is truly love. Don't bundle
someone into an uncomfortable cage just
because you want to ensure their safety in
your life. The bird knows where it belongs,
and will never fly to a wrong nest.
— Michael Bassey Johnson

The first thing Brittany did when she returned from Alaska was cancel her second
craniotomy, stating that she was exhausted,
and might reconsider the surgery in a
month or so.

The doctors at UCSF seemed displeased.
They began talking about treatment. "I'm
not doing chemo, and I'm not doing radiation," I heard her say on the phone. "No,
I'm not having another surgery right now.

323

The last craniotomy just aggravated the tumor and made it grow faster along the cut line." There was silence while whoever she was speaking to argued their case. "I know what I'm doing," she said. "I'm moving to Portland to die."

June in Oregon was beautiful. It got warmer as the month went on, with daily temps in the seventies, and the sun set at around 9 p.m. June was also when Portlanders affirmed their "Keep Portland Weird" slogan by having the Naked Bike Ride. We didn't plan to join in, although we liked the "keep it weird" mentality. If Portland's traditional progressive stance in protecting our civil liberties was part of being weird, we were in.

We started the month in a moving-in frenzy. Creating a warm, cozy environment had been important to me as a single mother, and Brittany shared that characteristic. Though her energy wasn't what it used to be, she threw herself into making a new home. Dan and Gary were in charge of hanging the pictures, which took extra time because they had to be hung from the quaint picture rails. But Brittany was impatient and rude. More and more she harshly criticized the three of us, although Dan and I bore the brunt of it.

Even though I told myself over and over again that my daughter had a tumor and that she didn't mean to sound so harsh, it began to wear on me. Unfortunately, at no time did any doctor or social worker say, "We need to discuss how her brain tumor and the medication she is taking might affect daily life." Although it is well known that steroids can cause " 'roid rage," this was something I associated with bodybuilders, and unfortunately I didn't carry that knowledge into my relationship with my dying child. Dilaudid, Britt's painkiller, was a medicine that caused agitation, constipation, changes in behavior, and trouble sleeping. The problem was layered. The tumor, stress about a terminal diagnosis, and medication all came together in a crescendo of moodiness and eruptions of anger.

Dilaudid is opiate-based and leads to drug tolerance, which means the patient needs more of the medicine to achieve pain relief. Were the times that Brittany's anger was most out of control those hours when she didn't take the Dilaudid on a structured timetable? It's counterintuitive. Once a patient is dependent on the drug, *not* taking the drug causes extreme irritability, anxiety, and muscle pain. Sometimes Britt's speech was slurred from the medication. Other times her speech was sharp, clear, and harsh. It seemed there was no place in the cycle of medication that was calm and safe.

I knew that my physical and emotional health had been impacted by the high level of stress, and that my coping skills were being stretched to their limit. I'd talked to Dan briefly about this, explaining that he, Gary, and I might have to spell each other. What confused me and Gary was that Brittany seemed to be able to control her temper around friends. This made her callous remarks to us more hurtful.

Dan, Gary, and I were still in shock about Brittany's diagnosis. We drifted in and out of that shocklike state. Financial strain didn't help the situation as Gary tried to keep his business moving forward and Dan worked hard at his job. However, what we didn't factor in was that Brittany viewed leaving her as abandonment. Brittany expected us all to be there, 24/7.

I dove into my cleaning mania. Again, there was a feeling of making things well. If I cleaned this old house, Brittany would be pleased with me. If I could clean it perfectly, there would be world peace . . . or at least peace in our home.

In early June, Britt filmed a piece for the UK. The British media sent a man to interview Brittany and Dan about her decision to move to Portland. The piece included interviews with British doctors and politicians who were against Britons having the right to doctor assistance in ending life for someone with terminal disease.

They filmed Brittany, Dan, and me in our spit-spot-clean little yellow house. Flowers from my sister Sarah were used in the background. Brittany looked beautiful and composed.

She was outspoken, and her words flowed articulately. She seemed to be crystal clear about everything. I, on the other hand, felt conflicted, slow, and overwhelmed. Nothing was built into the process for the caregivers. There was nothing to help us cope with the angry, impulsive, and frightened woman we loved as she faced death. I hoped that Brittany's young, smart friends could fill in all the holes where I was so clearly failing.

On June 13, Brittany gave me a huge compliment on Facebook.

I have never met anyone in my life who works as hard as my mother, Deborah Ziegler. Sometimes I can hold a candle to it, but no one else really even compares.

I read this in my bedroom at ten o'clock

when I turned in after mopping the down-stairs floors. As I sat in bed, just down the hall from Britt's closed bedroom door, fat hot tears rolled down my face. I wrote back, "Hard work feels good. Sometimes. For you, I would move mountains."

On June 16, I was awakened by an early morning phone call. It took a while to orient myself and realize that I was talking to a friend calling from Los Angeles. "Deb, it's Rachel. I'm sorry to call at this hour but it's about Tyler. Sherri's coming, but she'll never get there in time. I know she won't call you . . ."

Befuddled, I tried to understand. "Sherri's coming to Portland?" I sat up in bed. Sherri was my best friend. Why wouldn't she call me?

"Tyler is dying. He's at Providence St. Vincent. An ambulance brought him in. He's not going to make it. His heart is failing, and also his kidneys." I knew that Sherri's son had been battling a drug addiction that had weakened his heart. "Sherri doesn't want to burden you with anything else . . . but Deb, it's our Tyler boy."

"I know that hospital. It's only a few minutes away from our house. I'm leaving now." I hung up, woke Gary, and told him to quietly get ready. "I don't think we should wake Brittany," I whispered.

As we crossed the landing at the top of the stairs, Britt stepped out of her room and asked what was happening. I told her, and she insisted on coming with us.

Gary started the car and Britt climbed into the backseat. "Did he have a heart problem?" Gary asked.

"He had a murmur, even as a child. But the drugs probably caused cardiovascular inflammation. It damages their blood vessels." I sighed and blinked back tears.

"I knew this phone call would come one day. I just didn't think it would be before I died," Britt said quietly.

"Poor Sherri. This is going to break her heart." I wiped my eyes.

Only Britt and I went into the hospital room. Tyler was tangled in a mass of IVs and tubes. The worst part was that he had a large piece of plastic in his mouth, part of endotracheal intubation, and couldn't talk to us. His eyes didn't follow movement, but he seemed to recognize who I was.

"Tyler, honey, it's Debbie. Brittany is here, too." I leaned over and spoke into his ear. "You are loved, Tyler. I know it has been hard. We are here, and you are loved. Your momma is on her way. She loves you so much." I backed away and let Brittany have some time with Tyler.

He still looked much like the big, handsome, good-natured boy I'd tutored in high school. As Britt whispered in Tyler's ear that she loved him like a brother, I watched his eyes staring ahead, unmoving. The hospital chaplain arrived and offered to have a harpist play soft music.

I got on the phone with both my dear friend Sherri and her ex-husband. I told them that we were doing the best we could, and that we were relaying their love. The harpist played as we stood near Tyler, telling him repeatedly that he was loved. Eventually the nurse told us he was gone.

We met Gary in the lobby. I wrapped an arm around Britt and pulled her close.

"Momma, he was only thirty-two. We grew up like brother and sister, and now we're dying in the same year," she said.

When we got home, Brittany said, "I can't stay here for a funeral. I just can't. Today . . . what happened . . . it's exactly what I don't want to happen to me." Her voice rose in panic. "I don't want to be on a gurney. I don't want to be intubated. I don't want people trying to keep my organs going with machines. Promise me."

Scenes from Tyler's life flew through my head like an old-fashioned sprocket 8mm film on a rickety old projector. A grinning little boy holding up a fish. Easter egg hunts. Tyler singing Sinatra on his karaoke machine. A lanky kid riding my saddle-shaped purse through the airport, pretending he was on a horse. Whitewater rafting. Faster. Faster. The film chattered in my brain. A tattooed back. A cigarette dangling. A sheepish grin. Tyler looking up at me as I told him, "You are loved." A fleeting movement in those brown-flecked eyes, letting me know "I'm listening. I hear you. I'm dying."

Britt and I took showers, and she went first. While I was in the shower, we had our first really big thunderstorm since we'd been in Portland — angry, loud cracks that immediately followed bright flashes. I shut off the water and ran to Brittany's room dripping wet, a towel wrapped around me. She was combing her long hair.

Crack! We both started.

"Tyler," we said simultaneously. Brittany's slight smile was forlorn. "He was always so naughty, even when he was little."

"It sounds like he's enjoying some new power in the beyond." I smiled, thinking that he had been given thunder privileges pretty early in his new place.

331

"Momma, if there is anything after this life . . ." Britt paused. "If you're right about that. Go to Machu Picchu — I'll meet you there." She reached for my hand and squeezed it.

"I'll meet you there, darling," I whispered.

Gary had made an appointment for Brittany with a doctor in Texas. Once again, we were still clinging to hope. This persistence on our part was painful. It was our way of covering up the nakedness and helplessness.

"I'm not going to Texas," Britt said the day Tyler died. "I was only doing it for you."

It was discouraging to know that hope could still hurt me so badly. I couldn't even begin to imagine how much my hope hurt Brittany. And yet a little voice inside of me asked, *What will it look like when we've beaten hope into submission?*

Would that place be acceptance? I couldn't imagine what that would feel like. I didn't *want* to know what that would feel like. I was starting to feel submission, which seemed like a passive, reserved word for what I was experiencing. "Submission" was a word with room for bitterness. I was not ready for "acceptance."

On June 17, Dan and Brittany flew back to the Bay Area, and Gary and I flew home.

We offered Sherri and her husband the yellow house in Portland. We knew we couldn't stay or help them, so we offered them our refuge. From there, she and Larry would plan Tyler's funeral.

In Southern California, I problem-solved with the staff where my father lived. He didn't understand why I wasn't there to see him regularly anymore, and his dementia was worsening.

I continued to work on acceptance. Not just bitter acquiescence; I was trying to do better than that. I wrote Brittany the following letter in an email.

My Darling Daughter,

Today your grandpa asked about my mountain climbing girl, and I told him stories of Alaska. There was so much joy in the telling . . . the boom of calving icebergs, the bear's glossy hair parting in the wind, our wild and wonderful boat captain . . . Dad sat spellbound. At the end he said, "You know what you've got there? A slice of the best of life." We talked about how you'd inspired me to take that adventure. He said that there are three kinds of people. People that explore and find beauty in all the wild places in the world. People who can't imagine going anywhere or seeing anything more wonderful than their own backyard. And people who can't see beauty, no matter where they are.

I want you to know that I will go to Machu Picchu with Gary. We will sit and think big thoughts. . . . I still fight denial every single day. This morning I told myself that two very educated doctors in Portland have looked at your files and agreed with you — that you might want to plan things. How much more tangible can the evidence be? But my heart just won't accept this. Even as I type this note to tell you that I will explore the world more because of the impact you've had on me, I resist saying that I'll be waiting for you to join me in the silent wonder of Machu Picchu. I'd rather have you fly there with me.

But, that is not likely to happen is it, baby girl? This is me trying to say that I'm going to do a better job of staring death in the face. . . . Brittany, I'm trying to be present. I'm trying to feel what it is like to be hiking in the woods with you, to be cleaning and decorating a house with you, to be shopping for minutiae, to be watching a comedian, to be eating a meal — but my worries and my fears keep pulling me out of this moment into the fear of a moment that might happen tomorrow or next week. I am going to try to be in each moment with you. This is what we have. The rain. The hail. The sunshine. A cup of cocoa. Holding your hand and having people think we are a couple. These are the moments that we have. We have to live in them. I want to be "with" you.

I hope you know that I love you as much as a human being can love another human being. That is what mothering is. You would've been a good mother. I would've been a good Mimmi — or whatever the hell we settled on as my grandma name. I am cut to the core that this is not in the cards for us. I don't know who I will be on the other side of this. Everything I ever identified myself with was so wrapped up in being your Mom. Who will I be when you are gone?

Will this new woman be bitter and angry? I hope not. I want to still be full of the love that fills me every day when I think of you. Like the feeling I woke up with today. I want to still feel love and kindness. I want to take on a new role because the one I planned is evaporating before my very eyes. My promise to you is that I will find purpose. I promise you that you will be proud that I evolved into a new and purposeful woman. I will not curl up in a ball and become bitter, angry, and so wrapped up in my loss that I can't empathize and help others. I don't know if I'll have accomplished all of this by the time I meet you in Machu Picchu, but I'll be working toward it. Because you make me want to live a bigger life — not a smaller one. You make me want to help others. You make me want to be brave and fierce. Fierce in a good way — not an angry, resentful way. Fierce in a way that advocates for what is good, right, and fair.

I don't know who you will meet in Machu Picchu. But you'll recognize her. You'll be proud of her. I know that you don't like it when I talk about a Divine Spirit or Supreme Being. But I can't end this missive without saying that with all that I am — I know that God loves you more than I do. And that thought always floors me. Because I can't imagine a love bigger than the love I feel for you. A love that big. Eternal love.

That is why I know I'll meet you in Machu Picchu. A love bigger than anything our feeble minds can conceive will get us through whatever comes tomorrow. Today I just need to be present with you — in this moment. And though at present we are miles apart, I am with you. Loving you. Doing the best I know how to show it.

I also want to apologize for the wrongheaded things I've done throughout my life as your mother. I can't undo dumb things I've said and done over the years. And unfortunately, there is a great likelihood that I'll make more mistakes. But I can tell you that you turned out wonderfully in spite of my insufficiencies or maybe even because of them. I am in awe of you sometimes. I am proud of you. Most of all — I love you eternally. I will be there. I will be present. I will be available. All of me.

Love,
Momma

On June 30, Brittany came to visit us for a few weeks. She had given Gary and me a sail on a private boat for Christmas as a gift. Ironically, I gave Brittany an aerobatic ride in an open biplane over the vineyards of Sonoma. We had laughed at our similar lines of thought.

As Britt, Gary, Pamela, and I lounged on the boat, enjoying the sound and smells of the bay, it was impossible to comprehend that when I had received this gift six short months ago, we didn't know Brittany had a brain tumor.

On July 5, we celebrated Gary's birthday, and Brittany made him her famous home-made fudge. Britt's high school friend Colette came over for a barbeque and swim in our backyard. The presence of someone who had known and loved her for so long was calming for all of us.

Brittany also visited her grandpa for an unofficial goodbye. We took him on a long walk and he played his harmonica for us. When Brittany leaned over to kiss him goodbye, I heard her whisper, "See you soon, Grandpa." Britt and I shoved sun-glasses on to disguise our sorrow, and headed out as he fell asleep.

Brittany met two friends at the beach. Both were now married and had babies. "I love them and I wanted to say goodbye, but Momma, it's so hard to be around chil-dren." Tears rolled down her face. "I wanted to be a mother."

My slow, stubborn mind finally grasped that my beautiful daughter was saying goodbye to many people. She was preparing to die in Portland. She was doing what one does when one is leaving and won't come back. This realization struck me hard as I pulled her into my arms. "I know, darling. I wanted that for you. For me." My voice shook.

I tried to plan fun things to do, to keep everything clean and comfortable. But I was aware that I needed skills I simply didn't have. No matter how hard I tried, I was failing at being upbeat.

Maudie met Brittany at home in the Bay Area, and was with Brittany when she experienced another seizure. They seemed cyclical in the beginning, coming in a somewhat predictable pattern, but the in-between periods were getting shorter and the seizures were growing stronger. Clearly they were changing, getting worse in every way. Brittany had officially switched her medicine management to her palliative care doctor in Oregon. He recommended that she increase her antiseizure medication, explaining that the metallic taste was indicative of temporal lobe seizures.

Brittany also met with the mom she used to nanny for, and got to see her former charges, now high schoolers. Brittany said it was "emotional but good." The entire family made Brittany feel appreciated and loved.

I flew up to be with Brittany at her and Dan's house for a few days. From there, we would meet Gary in Carmel for Maudie's wedding. The weather crept into the hundreds. Brittany was taking antibiotics for bronchitis. She was miserable, but determined not to miss her dear friend's special day.

Brittany was also having difficulty sleeping. When people with large brain tumors lie prone, the pressure builds inside their cranium and pain wakes them up. Brittany was also unhappy with the corticosteroid side effects, as anyone would be. Suddenly she had acne again, and the medicine caused her to gain weight. It was heartbreaking to watch her struggle to try to take long walks in an attempt to control her weight and keep endorphins flowing to help with the sadness. But outdoor temperatures in the hundreds and a case of bronchitis meant that she couldn't go on walks. It was important for her to feel some sense of control of little things, like exercise and diet, because the big things were completely out of her hands.

In addition, Brittany was covered in bruises and was retaining water. Her hands and feet were swollen. It hurt to wear her wedding ring. She would be taking the meds for the last months of her life, so the side effects would only get worse. She tried to keep a good attitude, telling me to order her Spanx for the wedding. "Get one that I can cram all of this fat in," she joked.

But when we got to the location on the coastline, Britt was inconsolable about the dress she'd picked out to wear. She didn't like the way she looked in it, feeling that the dress emphasized the weight gain from the drugs. She decided not to be a part of the bridesmaid photos. She wanted to wear something comfortable, and "no photos."

At the reception, in the glow of the setting sun, her mood changed, and my daughter whirled and danced with her dear friend Amber. They spun around like children on the grassy lawn. I was washed with happiness and relief as Brittany's Berkeley buddy loved her, danced with her, and hugged her so hard she spilled champagne. Watching them, Gary's arm around me, I felt incredibly old. I said a prayer that Britt's friends would still care for me, share with me, when my only child was gone. I felt selfish thinking about this. At the same time, I realized that acceptance was what I'd been working toward for so long. *So this is what it feels like?* I thought. *Lonely.*

In contrast to my premature loneliness, Brittany flitted from person to person, mingling and talking. She met a young woman who worked in the media industry in New York. She was blown away by Brittany's clarity, coherence, and eloquence in articulating the reasons she was proceeding with her course of action. This young woman insisted that Brittany must tell her story. She must write an article. Her parting words were that she would be putting Britt in touch with various people.

Brittany and I flew to Portland immediately after the wedding. She had an appointment with her palliative doctor on July 23. He adjusted her medications, answered all of her questions, and took time with her, something we hadn't experienced in California. He also referred her to a therapist who specialized in working with terminally ill patients. In order to stop thinking about when she would need to plan to die, the therapist suggested that she pencil in a date. Just a flexible date that could be pulled in or pushed out. Something to stop circular thinking about *that* day. Britt chose November 1, 2014 — after Dan's birthday, and before her thirtieth birthday.

My sister Sarah, her husband, and their daughter came from their home in Georgia to Portland to be with Brittany for a week and to support us. Two of Britt's friends, Mina and Darcy, also flew in at the same time.

The girls tromped around in the woods exploring Wildwood Trail and Forest Park in Portland. Brittany was happiest when walking on these trails, and her friends indulged her in a very long hike. Afterward, Britt took a shower and I hovered nearby as I usually did, worrying that she would fall or have another seizure. Brittany had documented every experience since they started in April. There had been a dozen, and over time they had gone from tingling and eye fluttering to full-on seizures.

"Momma." With that one word, I knew she needed help. Britt was naked, save for a towel, and her hair was dripping wet.

"What is it, baby?" I touched her wet shoulder.

"Don't feel good. . . . It's happening."

I pulled the bedcovers back. "Lie on your side."

"I don't want to lie down." She sat on the edge of the bed, shivering, her eye fluttering.

"Brittany, please lie down on your side." I'd read the protocol for helping a person experiencing a seizure. For me, the seizures

343

were terrifying. The surge of electrical activity in Britt's brain caused the muscles under her facial skin to tremble and her hands to curl inward. There was a short period while her body tensed and then the violent jerking began. Sometimes people had difficulty swallowing during a seizure and they drooled. I'd read that it was best to lie on one's side so that fluids could drain out of the mouth. Some people thought you were supposed to put a spoon in the mouth of people who were seizing to keep them from biting their tongue. This was *not* true. You could cause a person to break teeth, even swallow teeth. In light of all this, why wouldn't she ever do as asked? "It's safer if you're going to have a seizure." My heart was pounding as I watched the left side of Brittany's face ripple like the surface of water under hard wind.

"Bad one coming . . ." Her body stiffened.

"Baby, lie down. Don't fight it. I'm right here." Before the words left my mouth, I was busy trying to keep Britt's flailing, jerking body from falling to the floor as all the muscles in her body contracted at the same time. Even the muscles of her chest wall contracted hard, forcefully pushing air out of her throat in the most frightening sound I had ever heard. The moan sounded as

344

though Brittany was deeply sad and afraid.

Blood flew because she had bitten her tongue. The towel, bedspread, and sheets were splattered. It seemed like such a lot of blood because she was jerking and convulsing. One of the girls handed me something to put on her. Water ran down Britt's back as I pulled a T-shirt over her head and helped her lie down. Someone handed me a pair of Brittany's panties, and I worked them up her legs and asked her to lift her pelvis. I was given a cold washcloth to place on her punctured tongue.

Brittany talked gibberish. The three of us spoke in soothing tones. I gave my phone to Mina and asked her to call my sister, who was staying in a hotel nearby; my hands were shaking too badly. When I heard Sarah's voice, I just said, "Come now. Brittany's had a bad seizure."

Britt's first words that made sense were about pain. "Head. Eyes. Hurt." We placed a cool cloth on her eyes.

When Sarah arrived and clattered up the stairs, she felt Brittany's pulse and spoke gently to her. Darcy and Mina looked how I felt. Shaken to the core. Gutted. Hollowed out. I gave them my credit card and told them, "Take the car and go to Zupan's Market."

They looked at me wide-eyed. I continued, "If you need to pull the car over and talk and just process this . . . it might be a good idea. Take your time. Pick out some fresh foods." I tried to be the adult in the room, when I wanted to fall apart.

When the girls left, Sarah and I kept cool washcloths on Brittany's eyes. "How did I get clothes on?" Britt asked.

"I dressed you," I said softly.

"Oh." I suspected she hoped that she didn't flail about in the nude in front of her friends.

For some reason, not remembering how she was dressed disturbed Brittany a great deal. "I lost consciousness. I bit my tongue. I could feel it was going to be a bad one."

Brittany was still wiped out when Darcy and Mina flew home. Sarah, Charles, and Mary Iris moved into the little yellow house with us. Sarah found a massage place to soothe Britt's aching muscles.

Britt also began an email dialogue with the young woman in New York whom she'd met at Maudie's wedding, who introduced her to another up-and-coming New Yorker, a video producer interested in coming to make a film about Brittany's decision to die in Oregon.

Mina sent a homemade book of moments

from Brittany's life. Brittany looked at the book over and over again, eking joy from adventures of the past. There was one photo in the book that gave me chills. It was taken in 2009 in Nepal when Brittany did a tandem paragliding trip over the valley of Kathmandu, taking off from a spot 6,500 feet above sea level.

Doctors said Brittany had been living with the tumor for approximately a decade. I tried to think back. It was as though Brittany's brain became hardwired to ignore risk; in fact, to desire it. The part of her brain that regulated behavior had still been maturing when she took that trip, since key portions of the brain involved in regulating impulsive and risky behavior didn't mature until around age twenty-five. A tumor had been tampering with her brain since she was about eighteen. That was when doctors believed that astrocyte cells began to multiply and take over brain tissue. The astrocyte cells directly destroyed brain cells at a slow enough pace that the functions of the temporal lobe moved elsewhere. Functions like speech, emotional stability, and boldness were handled in this part of the brain. What was the likelihood that those functions moved seamlessly to another location in the brain?

I wondered if, when Gary and I once said that Brittany seemed to be "the oldest teenager on earth," that was what we were unwittingly noticing. Was some of the devil-may-care attitude she had about engaging in risk-taking activity a product of the tumor?

I had planned what I hoped was going to be an extraordinary trip to Washington State. I'd rented a home with a spectacular view of Port Angeles. From the kitchen and dining room windows, we would be able to see the Strait of Juan de Fuca, the twinkling lights of downtown Victoria, B.C., and the mysterious lights of huge merchant ships and cruise ships silently moving in the dark of night. I wanted to re-create our experience in Alaska. I wanted to watch Brittany's eyes light up with the wonder of nature's beauty; to see her face relax for hours at a time as she was transported from her medical reality into nature's arms. I longed to see her bent over a new insect or flower.

I was also pleading with the universe: *Is there someone/something out there pulling any strings? Could we catch a break? Could you just let this be a week where I'm doing and saying the right things? Could you guide me this week? Show me the way. Can we have this glorious week? Can I see my child's radiant face as she finds a starfish? Can I memorize her that way? Face uplifted, arms outstretched, slender hands waving me over. "Come see this, Momma. It's so beautiful!"*

22
PLAYING HOUSE

2009–2010,
Ages Twenty-Five and Twenty-Six

Few things we can do in this world are so
well worth doing as the making of a beautiful and happy home.

— James Russell Miller

The new year of 2009 started with Brittany,
Bella, and I bumping north on the freeway
in a moving truck. Brittany was moving into
our little ocean-view condo rental in San
Clemente, California. She was excited to be
living near the ocean again, and she was
glad she'd dropped out of the audiology
program. She had not gone to Paris with
Mark and they had parted amicably. Britt
was anxious to move on, although not sure
yet what she wanted to do.

After settling in at the condo, Britt took a
temporary job teaching gymnastics. I knew

she loved kids, but to my utter shock she said she wanted to become a teacher. I smiled, thinking of the time when she was little and she said she didn't want to be like me when she grew up. She had tried sales and now was going into education; my field of work.

Britt filled out applications forms and was accepted to the UCI master's program. During this time she dated a few guys, but I knew she still missed Ellis because she posted a nostalgic old photo of him with his arms wrapped around her, saying it was one of the best times in her life. She started jogging, and worked up to running seven to ten miles a day.

Britt called me one afternoon, hysterical. She suspected that she'd broken her leg doing back handsprings in the yard with a friend. I told her to get to the local ER and I'd meet her there.

It was a bad break, a spiral fracture of the tibia. I brought her south to our Carlsbad home in a cast and with pain medication. She was not to put weight on the leg for at least a month and I thought the condo stairs were too much to negotiate. We set alarms through the night to make sure she got her meds every four hours. Britt screamed in pain on each bathroom trip. We took Brittany to an orthopedic surgeon, who recast her leg and reminded her that it was a serious break that would require surgery if she didn't follow instructions and stay off of it. The pain didn't diminish, so we went back again. Another cast. More pain meds.

Britt posted on Facebook that I was a saint for taking care of her, but that sentiment didn't last long. Five days later, she blew up at Gary for not giving her pain medication before it was due.

I heard an earful about Gary's insensitivity when I took meds to her at o-dark-thirty. The next day, a friend of Britt's arrived to pick her up. "I don't like the way I was treated last night," Brittany said over her shoulder as she hobbled out to the car on her crutches.

After that, I had to drive an hour to pick Britt up in San Clemente for her orthopedic appointments near my home, then drive her back. She managed to find a collection of friends to help with errands. She suffered from cabin fever, and did a great deal of self-reflection. In mid-April, I brought Britt to our house for dinner, where she announced that she and her friend Amber had planned a trip to Machu Picchu in a month.

I argued with her, saying she'd be lucky to have her cast off by then. "Tickets are purchased. Done deal." Britt balanced on her crutches. "I want to go home."

"Relax, Brittany. Have some dessert," Gary suggested.

"I've had quite enough, thank you." Britt hobbled down the hall.

"Would you like to drive Her Highness home?" I asked Gary.

When he returned from the two-hour round trip to take Britt to her condo, we discussed her behavior.

I defended her. "Have you read about a spiral fracture?" I asked him. "It's one of the most painful breaks. I think she truly is in a great deal of pain."

"Then taking a hiking trip to Machu Picchu is, as you said earlier this evening, nuts!"

"I know. None of this makes sense, does it?" I shook my head. "I'm worried."

The cast came off May 1, and Britt left for Peru on the 15th. The girls had the time of their lives, and the photos they posted were hilarious. Ten days of ceviche, finger puppets, crazy taxi and train rides, llama hats, beer, whitewater rafting, and of course Machu Picchu itself.

Gary and I picked up Britt at LAX and took her to dinner. She was exhausted but radiant. "I thought big thoughts there. I stretched my mind and my life's goals.

Traveling is in my soul now, part of my DNA. You two have to go, Momma."

Soon after her return, Britt had orientation for her fifteen-month master's program in education. In June, she started classes. She complained of insomnia, which had set in since she broke her leg. (Later, I read that insomnia is one of the first signs of a brain tumor.) Britt worked hard at her master's program that summer and came down to our house every so often. We didn't push her to get a job while pursuing her degree, as it would have been difficult to do well at both. The teaching job market was very impacted by the recession, so it was important that she graduate at the top of her class.

Brittany had started seeing Dan again. By the end of August, she told us that he was moving into the condominium with her . . . "just so you know." Dan's parents traveled to So Cal for a friend's wedding, and we invited them over for dinner. I liked Carmen and Barry a great deal.

"Gary, why do you think Britt is so harsh with us?" I asked one night.

"Because she can be, dear. Britt knows that you and I are forever parents. She vents with us because she knows when all is said and done, we will be there for her, no matter what."

"Don't you think she's a bit over the line sometimes? I feel like we haven't made that much progress since her teens."

Gary laughed. "Then you can't see the forest for the trees. Remember, I was there, on the outside looking in during her teens. She *has* made progress since then."

After they had been together a few months, Britt told Dan to move out, in a scorching breakup scene that set neighbors' tongues wagging. She even helped move things along by tossing Dan's mattress and clothing off the one-story roof of the garage.

Britt planned a Christmas trip with her neighbor, who had also just broken up with her boyfriend. The two young women took their dogs to a rented cabin in the mountains. They built a snowman, had a fire in the fireplace, soaked in an outdoor Jacuzzi, and walked their dogs along country roads. Britt told me there was nothing like being in nature to help one move on.

A new young man sought Britt's companionship in January of 2010. He was the climbing, jumping, bicycling, adventurous type. Cash enjoyed the thrill of outdoor activity and hard work. One of their first dates was skydiving. Brittany admired the fact that Cash was a self-made man. He was intelligent, loyal, exuded energy, and enjoyed living in the moment.

When Gary and I met Cash and Brittany for sushi, it was obvious that they were physically very connected. I liked the fact that he met our eyes when he spoke. He and Gary were both from the Midwest, and Gary thought Cash's admirable work ethic came from those roots.

At spring break, Britt took off for Los Cabos with a girlfriend because they were so burned out from their grad program. Mina and Britt cemented a forever friendship while kayaking and Jet Skiing.

Returning from Mexico, Britt and Cash went hiking, took dance lessons, and attended music festivals. While Britt finished up her master's degree, she moved in with Cash and seemed content but was increasingly harsh with me. When we met them for dinner one night, Britt embarrassed me with a cruel critique of work I'd done on a website for Gary. I left in tears, and we didn't speak for weeks. On the other hand, Cash and Brittany's relationship was on fire. Gary and I privately called them "Brash."

In June, Britt graduated at the top of her class with a master's in education. She had worked hard and thoroughly enjoyed student teaching. I wasn't invited to the ceremony, as we were still avoiding each other. Perhaps because she'd paid for her master's, she felt all the more entitled to celebrate it with Cash and friends instead of her parents. Unfortunately, it soon became obvious that with the latest round of budget cutbacks, there were no teaching jobs. So Brittany took a job preparing students to take SAT exams, and also did tutoring on the side. She had met some fine young women in her master's program. Their love and loyalty would be the most valuable gift from the experience because some of those relationships carried her through some tough days.

Brash went to Hawaii to celebrate Britt's graduation. Things looked pretty serious at the six-month mark. With time Britt and I resumed communication, and one day she and I did a smack-down house-and-yard cleaning of Cash's two-story home in Orange County. Cash loved it — or at least he had sense enough to act like he loved it.

The adventure continued. In July, Britt and Cash started a vegetable garden, went deep-sea diving, entertained, and were joined at the hip when not working. Cash seemed content to let Britt travel without him, because I saw no resistance to her plan to climb Mount Whitney or travel to Kathmandu.

Cash began preparing for a big road trip that would last for almost two months. Britt planned to go along, but after a few days on the road, she concluded she wasn't cut out for touring with a hard rock festival.

When Cash returned in October, they threw a big Halloween bash before leaving for a tropical island vacation. When they returned, they sent out invitations to two dozen people to have Thanksgiving at their house. Then "Brash" hopped on a jet and visited London, Stockholm, and Berlin. Brittany sent photos of the two toasting drinks in an ice hotel.

At Thanksgiving, Brittany told us that she was planning a spectacular Christmas. She wanted Gary and me to stay with them in a rented house in Colorado. Gary and I drove there with our Cavapoo puppies, for the best Christmas ever.

There were signs, and I missed them. Isn't that what every mother thinks when their child ends up in trouble? If only I'd . . . done something sooner, stronger, better, my child wouldn't be sick or dying. Mankind's powerful, instantaneous, primitive amygdala response. The animal mind seeks links between our parenting and the well-being of our child, looking to assign fault. What did we do wrong? How can we avoid doing it again? This is human nature; protecting our species. When push comes to shove, we revert to animal instinctual behavior. For mothers, this is self-blame; an instinctual response that leads to guilt, sorrow, and endless pain. It is perfectly normal, and absolutely useless.

Cash and Brittany took us sledding, snowmobiling, cross-country skiing, snow-shoeing, and on a horse-drawn sleigh ride. We mixed cocktails at night, played games, and engaged in lively discussions. Bella curled up on Cash's jeans in the laundry pile, having accepted him as the alpha dog in her life. The couple wore matching Christmas onesies on Christmas Eve.

It was on this wonderful, memorable Christmas trip that I mentioned two things to Gary. I asked if he thought Brittany's frenetic level of activity seemed strange.

"Gary, think of this past year. It's crazy! She parachuted from a plane at fifteen thousand feet. Scuba diving lessons, trips to Los Cabos. Dance lessons with Cash." I raised my eyebrows. "Their main problem was that she led!"

I started ticking things off on my fingers. "Hiking Muir Woods, ziplining, scuba diving." I took in more air. "Wine tours. Las Vegas. Maui. Del Mar races. Could it be Cash's influence?"

Gary laughed. "If anyone is influencing the other, I'd guess *she* influences him. Our girl is a whirling dervish."

I felt myself winding up. "London, Stockholm, and Berlin. Now she's planning a solo trip to Nepal. Doesn't the pace seem frenzied? It's like she can't stop. I get tired just thinking of all she packs in." I sat down on the bed. "It's like she can't stay busy enough. She's impulsive and volatile. She's taking too many risks."

"She's young and in love!" Gary drew me into his arms. "She's thinking about marriage, sewing her oats, going for the gusto."

I pushed away. "What about her eye?"

"What *about* her eye?"

"When we were discussing healthcare reform, and she started lecturing us. One eye was heavier. Didn't you see it?"

Gary thought back to our discussion. "I know what you're talking about. I think it's an affectation she gets when she's on her high horse about something." He hugged me again. "I can assure you, she won't appreciate you pointing it out."

We put it out of our minds and went to bed. I had been worried about Brittany all year. But I was a worrywart. I came by it naturally. There were a long line of worry-warts in my family. Non-risk-taking, careful, penny-pinching people who didn't kayak, zipline, or scuba dive their way through life.

There is no way to know if in December 2010, three years before Brittany's diagnosis, her six-year-old astrocytoma was causing personality changes, or causing one eyelid to droop infinitesimally when she got worked up. But there were two red flags, two mournful blasts of a foghorn, two yellow flashing lights. And I missed them.

23
LOVE YOU HATE YOU

August 2014,
Seven Months After Craniotomy

The opposite of love is not hate; it's indif-
ference.
— Elie Wiesel, *U.S. News & World Report,*
October 27, 1986

In early August, Brittany and I settled into
the yellow house while Dan and Gary both
returned to work for a while. Friends sent
flowers, candy, and food. Brittany loved
answering the door to a package from
friends and family. It meant someone was
thinking of her, supporting her, rooting for
her. Every week my sister Sarah and her
husband sent an exquisite bouquet from a
nearby boutique florist.

Britt's friends began to stagger visits.
Sometimes I felt like I was running a bed-
and-breakfast. My compulsive cleaning

never ended, as the only thing in my life that I felt I could control was dirt. Brittany posted many wise sayings on Facebook. She was in a reflective period in her online persona, while at home and about town she carried a huge Ziploc bag of pain medicines that she self-administered. God forbid if anyone asked how much time had elapsed between pills.

"What? Is someone afraid I'll become addicted? Who gives a rat's ass! I'm dying in a couple of months. So what if I'm addicted to pain meds?"

She had a point.

Dan and Gary returned, and I planned a road trip to Washington State. In daily life, conversations got pretty rough. Britt continued to take most of her wrath and frustration out on Dan and me. We packed the Jeep and headed for the ocean-view home Gary and I had rented in Port Angeles.

Britt's childhood friend Jen joined us. She arrived carrying a homemade bouquet, a delicate jumble of fragile beauty in a simple glass jar, along with fresh-picked berries. We hadn't seen Jen since her early teens, and I took a moment to take in the blond beauty radiating goodness and love.

Our first night in Washington, we watched the lit-up ships gliding through the strait.

The next day, we all went to Crescent Lake for lunch and a short hike to a waterfall.

That evening Britt and Jen were sitting on the couch chatting while I started dinner. Gary and Dan had gone to get some ice cream to eat with the berries.

"Momma," I heard Britt call out. "It's happening again."

"Lie down on your side." I tried to urge her to use the seizure protocol.

"Stop telling me to do that. I don't want to." Her eyelid fluttered, and fear ran through the two of us, much like the uncontrolled electrical brain activity causing Britt's convulsion. We were terrified of what a seizure might suddenly take away. Speech? Choice?

Jen and I knelt beside her as the fluttering eye was followed by rippling facial muscles, the tensing of her body and curling of her hands. Thankfully, this time it was a mild seizure. Jen sat talking with Britt as I finished preparing the meal.

We had a quiet dinner, and everyone headed to bed early. The next day, Britt and Jen were like children again, hiking through a peaceful rain forest to tide pools filled with purple and ocher starfish. Brittany called out, just as I'd hoped, for us to come. Come see the forest of delicate pink and green sea anemones!

Our week in Washington turned out to be a time of beauty and acceptance. Each evening, I went outside and collected raspberries, listened to the birds, and felt grateful for these peaceful days with my child.

The young video director from New York arrived soon after we returned from our trip. Her small crew filmed Brittany, Dan, and me talking about Brittany's choice. The filmmaker seemed to have her heart in the right place. She wanted to find a nonprofit organization to finance the film. Britt and I thought she was spunky and bright, and might put together a film that could educate Americans about the need for terminally ill citizens to have choices.

The next thing we knew, *People* magazine wanted to do an article. They sent a photo crew and did the interviews by phone. The photographer was gentle with Brittany, who now abhorred having her photograph taken. When Brittany broke down in tears, telling them she didn't look like herself, that she felt fat and ugly, he told her that he, too, avoided being photographed. There was only one photo that he allowed his wife to post, of half of him — the other half behind a column.

The photographer stood Brittany in the doorway. She was composed, and stared directly into the camera. He also took pictures upstairs near Brittany's beautiful bed, sun streaming in. He photographed the four of us in the backyard. The day seemed endless, but Brittany felt the article would help to educate readers and policymakers.

In mid-August, Brittany had another MRI. The Portland doctors expressed some good news (if you could call it that): Britt still had space in her cranium. Severe intracranial pressure was not yet an issue.

Britt asked why her symptoms were steadily getting worse, her seizures more frequent and debilitating. She pointed out that she'd lost intelligible speech for over half an hour after a recent seizure, and she'd feared her speech would never return.

"What if I lose the ability to self-administer the medication? What if, after a bad seizure, I have difficulty swallowing? I need to be careful not to wait too long, or I'll lose what I've fought so hard for." She looked around the room. "My right to die peacefully."

She pressed her eyes to emphasize the excruciating ocular pain. "I can't sleep because of pressure and pain at night. I'm an insomniac."

Britt looked at the doctor. "If pressure isn't an issue, why are my symptoms getting worse?"

There was silence in the doctor's office while everyone thought about the dichotomy. My heart squeezed into a hard ball of fear and pain.

"I know, right here," Britt tapped her heart, "that I'm getting sicker with each passing day. I am actively dying. I'm staying with the date to die that I penciled in with my therapist. November 1."

This visit to the doctor unleashed a steady flow of rage when we got home. Brittany became verbally abusive. The anger could be about who ate the last yogurt, or something someone said on Facebook. It could be over how long it took me to do a simple task. "I could do that faster, and I have a brain tumor," Brittany said. "Do I have to think of everything?" she asked me. My slow, grieving brain irritated both of us. Although I knew the anger was at the universe, often my name was attached to it. She didn't rage at friends; generally the anger was directed at her husband and mother. Didn't that mean she could control it, that she was choosing to punish us? Only in researching this book did I find out that aggression, agitation, and combative behavior can be side effects of antiseizure medications.

One of Britt's girlfriends from middle school was coming, so I booked massages for them. I'd ordered heavier curtains for the kitchen to block the August sun. I continued to order T-shirts that said things like "I Am Love" and "I Am Peaceful," hoping that if we wore these messages, we would somehow feel these feelings. I was trying.

I kept the house clean, did the laundry, cooked meals, and suggested outings to amuse Brittany. But in the heat, window fans whirring, nothing appealed to her. Britt spent her time writing and rewriting her obituary and finalizing detailed plans for her funeral. She kept handing me new versions to read.

I was hurting, and it was hard to keep standing like a donkey in the rain of insults. It seemed I could never do anything right, say anything right. It was as though my very appearance sickened Brittany. And damn it, there was still unhelpful, godforsaken hope pushing at the edges of my consciousness. *What if the tumor is slowing?* It was as though Brittany could read my mind, and it infuriated her.

Gary, who'd flown home to check on

things, called to say I was needed. Daddy was transitioning again. He now needed an electric hospital bed. He was so weak he couldn't stand, and he was getting combative. I needed to put new resources in place. Gary had booked a ticket for me to go home on August 14. However, Carmen, Dan's mother, fell in the night while caring for the dogs at Dan and Brittany's house. She was taken by ambulance to the hospital, and they were checking her out. Dan felt that he needed to go home and check on his mother, and I agreed with him.

At breakfast I said, "Go. I'll change my flight and stay with Britt."

Brittany launched into a tirade. The things she said to Dan turned my stomach. I thought, *Caring for Brittany, which in part means being her punching bag, is hard. We all need breaks.*

Finally, I couldn't take any more. I stood up. "Stop it, Brittany. I will *not* listen to you talk to your husband this way for another minute." I held out my hands. "Carmen is his mother, and she's in the hospital. Let him go." I turned on my heel and left.

"Stay out of it!" she shouted. "It's none of your goddamn business!"

Gary spoke with Dan on the phone and encouraged him to go see his family. "Breaks are important. Take a few days. I'm going to be driving up a second car. That will give us more freedom. I'll drive to Oregon while you're visiting your mother."

Dan flew back to visit his mom in the hospital. We thought we had a good plan. Everyone was sure that Britt would come around.

But Britt refused to budge. To her, one of us taking a break was the equivalent of abandonment. On the phone, I heard her giving Dan hell. "Why do you need to stay an extra day to take care of things? I'm dying! Why isn't being here with me your first priority?"

When she hung up, I said, "Brittany, right now you're very angry. But you have little time left on this earth. Don't use it up in this destructive way."

"I want you to take me to an attorney. I want a divorce," Britt said while working on her laptop. "Momma, I don't want to die married to Dan."

"You don't mean that, Britt." I sighed.

"I'm so fucking tired of you taking his side on things." She stormed up the stairs.

I contacted the social worker at Oregon Health and Science University and described the level of animus that Britt was showing toward me and Dan. She wanted to set me up with a therapist. Now, in hindsight, I wish that a doctor, any doctor, had explained the many ways that a brain tumor can alter a person's behavior.

We live in a world where medical care is rushed. Death is not something most physicians are comfortable discussing, much less the journey the patient will take between diagnosis and death. In fairness, everyone's passage from life to death is different. Doctors, even brain specialists, are trying to spend a minimal amount of time with each patient because there are more patients waiting in the lobby. Sometimes a complex health issue can't be explained in a series of fifteen- to thirty-minute appointments. I found myself wishing that the doctors had more time, or that they had at least handed us literature about brain tumors, a CD to view on the basics about the treatments available, and a video about the possible side effects of common medications and how to best deal with them.

Shouldn't some sort of counseling and training be recommended and made available to families that are caregiving for a loved one who is terminally ill? In the medical model that we have now, the limited time that doctors have is focused on the patient, as it should be. However, this leaves families untrained and unprepared for their caregiving role. Our whole family was ill, not just Brittany. We all tried to care for Brittany to the best of our abilities. But neurocognitive changes are tricky. Brittany experienced negativity, depression, and anger, along with aggressive and impulsive behavior. In many ways, emotional changes in both Britt and those who loved and cared for her were the most difficult things to deal with. Seizures were frightening, but so were the emotional outbursts.

In the end, it seemed to me that each family was left to deal with death essentially on their own — no matter how their loved one was dying. My father was on hospice care for a year, and I felt just as alone and in the dark with him — though in a completely different way. It occurred to me that no matter how we die in the American medical system, not enough is being done to educate us on that process.

If I'd spoken up to Brittany's doctors, she would have shut me out of attending any future medical appointments. If I'd dared to say anything about her rage, it would have been viewed as the ultimate betrayal. Of course, doctors were not really at liberty to speak to parents of adult patients in secretive phone calls. And there was little on the Internet about the behavior of brain tumor patients as their tumors grew. Those who knew probably didn't want to relive it by writing about it. Gary and I did a great deal of reading, but we were still ill-equipped to deal with our daughter's complicated health problem.

After Brittany's death, I read an article written by the husband of a cancer patient who described his wife's behavior near the end of her life when Dilaudid, the medicine Brittany was taking, many times stronger than morphine, interrupted signals between his wife's mind and her body. I wept as I read his open and honest account of lying down next to his wife and having her tear into him for hours, her rage fueled by fear, drugs, and disease. He wrote of how she only wanted to eat mayonnaise, of how he feared he would end up worn-out and dying himself while she screamed at him for more mayonnaise. I cried for him, his wife, and their devoted friend; but I also cried because it was the first account I'd read that captured some of the chaos and pain I'd experienced in caring for Britt. My tears were an odd combination of sorrow and relief. I wasn't alone (http://www.esquire.com/lifestyle/ a34905/matthew-teague-wife-cancer-essay/).

Before I could set up an appointment with the therapist, Britt's friend Maudie flew in. It would be a quick visit, as she needed to get back to her urology practice post-honeymoon. I was happy to have her company. Perhaps Brittany would stop cursing at me for a few days.

Britt rode shotgun. Maudie sat in the backseat when we picked her up. The two girls chatted away.

Britt jabbed my arm. "Mom, where the hell are you going?"

I pointed at a sign telling us we could get on the highway.

"Make a damn U-turn. After all this time of going back and forth to the airport, you still don't know where you're fucking going?"

"But the sign says . . ."

"Fucking turn around!" Brittany shouted at me. "Fucking turn now!"

Tears burned my eyes. I was so humiliated. "Welcome to Portland, Maudie," I said, looking over my shoulder. I drove home without saying another word.

Although I needed to stay in Portland to look after my daughter, I decided to take a break while Maudie was there.

When we got to the house, the girls wanted to go out to eat. I told Brittany,

"Here are the keys. Maudie can drive." I added, "I won't tolerate being cursed out anymore. From now on, if it happens, I will remove myself from that environment."

"Oh yeah, let's make this all about you, Momma. That's a good one," Britt yelled at me as I climbed the stairs.

While the girls were gone, I moved my desk upstairs to my bedroom. That way, I could email without crossing paths with Brittany. I was hiding from the rapier-sharp edge of my daughter's tongue, at least until her friend had to leave.

The next morning, the girls took a hike on nearby trails. That afternoon they invited me to join them for dinner, but I passed. I stayed out of sight, giving them the run of the house.

On the morning of August 16, the girls went to Trillium Lake. The news was all about Robin Williams, who had committed suicide five days earlier. I couldn't imagine a person who brought so much laughter into the world being so very sad.

I had no car, but I had a quiet house to myself. I decided to do all the laundry. When I went to get clothes from the dryer, I found myself studying the huge beams in the basement. I thought about how they'd been there for almost a hundred years; how perfect they were for someone to hang herself from. The thought just popped into my mind, along with wondering what kind of wood they were made from. Just an ordinary thought.

Each time I made a trip to the basement, I thought a little more about the beams. They weren't that high, but high enough. I looked at some rough rope that was stored in the basement. What about leather? These thoughts arrived without my feeling a faster heartbeat, without sweat beading on my upper lip. When I put the clothes away, I looked in Gary's closet at his belts. Gary called. I told him that I was letting Britt have time with Maudie, and that I was staying in my room when they were at the house.

"I'm on my way, sweetheart. Hang in there," he said.

I hung up, thinking how funny his statement was, given what I'd been thinking about. I decided to take my little CD player outside to listen to music while lying on the picnic table bench. Sunshine might do me good.

I didn't hear them arrive.

Above the music, I heard Britt's voice yelling at me. I turned the volume down and sat up. She was standing on the back porch with a glass in her hand.

She started telling me what a psychotic bitch I was. How embarrassed for me she was that I wouldn't join in meals or activities with Maudie. "My friends think you are completely losing your shit," she told me, now pacing the length of the porch. I let her rant for a while, and then I spoke loud enough to be heard over her grinding insults.

"The truth of the matter is that I'm your mother and I love you, will always love you, but I won't tolerate your abuse."

Brittany stopped walking back and forth, and looked at me as though I was the vilest creature she'd ever set eyes on. "Well, yes, *motherhood.* We all know you didn't knock *that* one out of the ballpark."

Wow. That was a knife to the gut. I lay down again, my face turned up to the sun.

"Get out! Get out! You cannot come to my death! You will not be on the list for my funeral!" I heard her screaming, but I could no longer see her angry face. Tears rolled into my ears, creating a horrible sensation. Strangely, all I could think of was my ninety-two-year-old father singing a country song about "lyin' on my back, cryin' over you."

"I don't want to see you until October —

if ever again at all!" Brittany raged on. "My friends think you're psychotic. And by the way, you are *never* allowed to correspond with my friends. Get your own fucking friends!"

Gary would arrive later that night. I told myself I could make it until then.

Gary had no sooner stepped in the front door than Britt jumped on him.

"Why haven't you been answering my texts?" she snapped.

My husband held up his hand. "That tone of voice may work with everyone else in your life, but it will not work with me, young lady." He went to find me upstairs.

"Why didn't you answer my texts?" she asked again more loudly.

Gary stopped and turned around. "I don't ask how high when you say jump, Brittany."

"You're just a frickin' enabler!" she shouted at Gary's back.

After listening to me recount the last few days, Gary got out his laptop and booked me a flight home the next day. "You've got to get out of here. I'll take Maudie to the airport and stay here with Brittany."

My husband's expression was grim. I touched the side of his face, looking into his blue eyes.

"Honey, I think Britt would like you to get so depressed that you decide to go with her," he said.

I bent my head and sobbed. I admitted my thoughts about the rafters.

Gary pinched his nose, and his eyes watered. "Look. I'm not a psychiatrist, but it seems to me that the people she loves the most are also the ones she hurts the most. Maybe it's a way of detaching from you. If she's angry with you, it won't be so hard for her to leave you."

That night, I wrote my two sisters the following email:

I have been kicked out. Told to "get out" repeatedly. I am "probably disinvited from her passing." Strangely, this latest intense level of verbal abuse was instigated when I took umbrage at being cursed out in front of company. I did not back down. I expected an apology and some indication that these cursing binges leveled at me would be controlled. I know they can be controlled because ONLY Dan and I get this level of abuse. I received no feeling of remorse, no indication that there would be an attempt to change the behavior. When I removed myself from the open shooting range, I was told that Britt's friends had diagnosed me on the verge of a psychotic breakdown. So, I leave tomorrow. Gary will stay until a friend or Dan arrives.

Donna responded:

What you and Britt are going through is literally mind-bending, an awful reality to comprehend, absorb and deal with. Regroup. Give yourself some room to breathe. To relish the months of joys you have shared. To mourn.

Sarah responded:

I have been thinking about you and feeling so badly for the maelstrom you are living in. I am so sorry for her as well, as even though she can contain herself while her friends are around for short periods, she is obviously unable to regulate her emotions at all and must be living in a very angry place. Let Gary take care of you!

I left early the next day. I was crying as I tiptoed past Britt's closed bedroom door. I cried all the way to the airport as Gary drove.

"Deb. Brittany told me last night that she has the entire next month booked with one friend after another. Maudie is just the first of a parade of guests," he said.

"She never told me about this." I looked out at the traffic inching along.

"Part of you getting kicked out is that she needs our rooms for the Brittany Bed-and-Breakfast. It'll be good for you to get away from your role as proprietor, head cook, and personal laundry service for the parade of guests."

"It *is* hard work," I whispered.

"Well, Amber is coming for almost a week, followed by four other friends."

"This is already arranged?" I asked in surprise. At least Britt would be in better spirits with guests her own age.

"Yes. Sweetie, you need to go home and let Britt have a month of visiting friends. You've been holding down the fort long enough."

24
FREE BIRD

2011, Age Twenty-Seven

Birds have wings; they're free; they can fly
where they want when they want. They
have the kind of mobility many people
envy.
— Roger Tory Peterson, *Field Guide to
Birds of Eastern and Central North America*

Everyone was in good spirits after our
activity-packed "Brash" Christmas in Colorado. Brittany got a bread maker for Christmas, so she baked in domestic bliss. In late
January, Britt and Cash celebrated a year of
togetherness.

Brittany was recommended for a ten-
month Fulbright grant and review by Nepal's Foreign Scholarship Board, but she
decided to make her own plans. She contacted several orphanages, and decided she
would go to Kathmandu solo for four

months.

Gary and I insisted that she get an apartment in a gated, guarded building. We discussed our fears and concerns, knowing that Britt would go with or without our approval. She was a free bird and would fly where she wanted to. All we could do was encourage her to stay in safe housing.

Brittany was gathering clothing, shoes, and donations for orphans. She solicited Cash's help in getting these hundreds of pounds of items to Kathmandu. However, Cash was extremely busy with work and didn't have a lot of downtime to help with the difficult shipping challenge.

I got a sobbing phone call from Brittany. "Momma, Cash really shouted at me."

Every nerve in my body jangled. "Are you all right?"

"He said, 'Brittany, why the hell can't you just be happy?' "

A twinge of pain twisted my heart. Gary and I had discussed this very thought so many times at dinner. How no matter what we bought her, where we took her, how much we adored her — it never satisfied her. Britt seemed unable to relax and accept that she was attractive, smart, and loved. There seemed to be a gaping maw of neediness, restlessness, and an endless process of striving for more of everything. My husband and I knew that happiness came from within; not from a mate or partner, and not from things. In her mid-twenties, Britt still seemed convinced that happiness was something others could give or take away from her. She didn't own her own happiness yet.

"Brittany, you and Cash aren't getting into physical fights, are you?" The level of her sorrow made me worry that she'd been struck.

"Cash would never hit me." Her voice cracked and she sobbed again. "But he said our relationship isn't working. It's over," she wailed. I don't think that any of Britt's beaus had ever ended a relationship with her. She was always the one who'd called it quits. Hadn't she felt an undercurrent of discord in the midst of all the Christmas fun? Gary and I thought we'd sensed an eddy in the audacious stream of fused energy and love that defined them as "Brash."

My protectiveness sprang into high gear. I found some free boxes on Craigslist, told her to call her friend Nina, and that I'd be there soon. The three of us got all her things packed up in short order. We loaded the boxes and furniture in a rental van, drove it south, and stored it in our garage, meaning that Gary would have to park his car outside. Britt and I teased him, saying that parking outside from February through June in Southern California was a real bitch.

Brittany mourned the loss of her relationship. "I still love him," she sobbed on my shoulder. "I've never had so much fun with another human being in my life."

I patted her back. "Our hearts don't turn on and off like a water spigot. Naturally it's going to hurt for a while." I wondered if there would ever be a man who could keep things fun enough for Brittany. I worried that my child had some kind of personality disorder that kept her from ever being deeply contented. Gary and I had discussed that it would take a patient man to live with Britt. Naturally, we never once thought that Britt's inability to be happy — her "no filter" style of communication; her tactless style of blurting out hurtful comments; her increasing inability to empathize with those she loved, while at the same time feeling deep compassion for the charitable causes of perfect strangers or injured animals — might be the result of a brain tumor.

While she mourned, she also packed her days with activity. There were only a few weeks to survive heartache before she was on a plane bound for Kathmandu. Britt shopped for expedition-weight cargos and boots. She booked a two-week trek on the Annapurna Circuit and leased a secure apartment.

On March 1, 2011, Britt flew out of LAX, and Gary and I began a three-month period of nonstop worry and prayer for her safety. We kept Bella for a while, until Dan picked her up.

We knew that Britt was still in contact with Cash, so it was a little surprising to see Dan reappear. As he drove away with the dog, Gary said, "I've got a feeling Dan just got a toe back in the door."

Britt started a blog to keep us advised about her travels in Kathmandu: http://brittanygoestonepal.blogspot.com/.

She was struck by the love and life in such poverty, the pitiful beggars eking out an existence from garbage, darting in and out of traffic. She explored the city, paraglided in Kathmandu Valley, and got food poisoning twice, the second time when she was trekking on the Annapurna. The hike involved difficult trails, jungles, rice paddies, and snowcapped mountains. She explored small villages and survived a freak snowstorm as well as an avalanche.

Something she wrote on her blog makes

me incredibly sad to read today:

> A couple of times along the trail I spotted couples in their 60's and 70's taking their time to explore a new area. How amazing to be trekking and traveling at that age . . . I certainly hope that my future husband and I will be the type of couple that treks through Asia at any age on holiday.

After her trek, Britt volunteered in the Bal Mandir Orphanage, which housed over two hundred children and lacked adequate staff and supplies. The babies' room consisted of rows of cribs tended by only a few women. Toddlers walked around unclothed and unsupervised. Britt spent hours holding and feeding the babies. She also jumped off the world's tallest bridge swing in a one-hundred-meter free fall. On April 18, she wrote:

> Living here in Nepal . . . and getting to know so many amazingly resilient children has been the best experience in my life. Despite their various tragedies, they have such capacity for joy.

April 29, Britt summed up her trip:

Hey mom . . . love you, miss you. Thank you for loving me so much as a child, protecting me from harm, and teaching me about the value of compassion for others. You were always a model of tolerance; standing up for what is right, compassion, and love.

My complicated, sometimes maddening daughter had been looking for love throughout her twenties. Brittany was a marrying kind of girl. She wanted children, which was so crystal clear to me and Gary that we bought a home with grandchildren in mind, with a pool and room for them to visit comfortably.

As I communicated with my passionate girl, I realized that she was still searching for a man to love. She was looking for someone to love her just as she was, to make her happy. In looking for love, she had become a citizen of the world. Brittany had opened her heart to the underdog. She championed those who were judged, spurned, or held in contempt because they were different. I was proud of any part I'd had in creating an environment for her heart to grow and expand.

On May 5, Brittany left Kathmandu for Thailand with another young volunteer from the orphanage. Britt visited several cities and went on two open water dives, but the most vivid stories were about volunteering at a Thailand elephant sanctuary.

The elephant refuge was run by a British charity. My daughter became an assistant to a mahout (elephant keeper) for six days a week. She bathed and washed her charges in the river each day and cleaned their enclosures. Britt paid a modest fee to cover her housing and food, and shared a bungalow with her new friend. Each day they woke at 6:30 a.m. to harvest pineapples, corn, bananas, or sugarcane, chopping and dragging the fodder for some distance. The elephants captured Brittany's heart. She loved the soulful way they looked at people, and she never tired of watching them use their trunks to grasp things.

Brittany arrived home exhausted and feeling torn about what she wanted to do next. We left almost immediately for a family getaway in Montecito, California. There she started combing the Internet for a teaching job anywhere in California, but the nonexistent job market created by school budget cuts continued. In fact, teachers with no tenure were being laid off in droves. Britt decided to study for the LSAT and get an apartment in Oceanside, not too far from our home. She found a roommate to share expenses, and they landed an apartment with a view of the Pacific Ocean. Bella would remain with Dan because dogs weren't allowed.

That summer, Britt managed to study hard, schedule some diving excursions, date another handful of guys, and take up paddleboarding. On September 4, she did an impromptu skydive.

Britt took her first LSAT test and scored in the ninetieth percentile. She was disappointed in the score, even though full scholarship offers started rolling in from a handful of the fourteen law schools she'd applied to. One has to wonder what her score would have been without a brain tumor.

Brittany also filled out paperwork to take my maiden name, Ziegler. She was ready to let go of her former name forever. Together we planned a trip to Greece, a mother-daughter adventure. I organized every single minute of this trip with such hope of reconnecting with my daughter, and deep longing for Britt to discover that happiness was a choice that only she could make. I hoped that this trip would help my daughter face the question that was clearly tormenting her. She had a bachelor's and master's degree, and yet no fulfilling job, or even an idea of what to do besides teach — which would require a move out of state. What was she going to do with her life? How was she going to support herself? Was a career in law a good fit?

We flew to Greece on the very day a new government was formed. My mum called me at the airport as we waited for our flight. "Cancel the trip. There's too much unrest. You're buying into Brittany's unsafe travel patterns."

"We're going to Greece, not Somalia. We'll be perfectly safe. Love you. Gotta go."

We checked into our room in Athens at twilight. The man at the desk told us to call Gary immediately, and we rolled our eyes at each other. Worrywart Gary had probably heard about the strikes and unrest.

When we opened the French doors on our balcony, our exhaustion faded along with the memory of the reminder to call Gary. There, lit up against an inky Greek sky, on Acropolis Hill, was the Parthenon, the most dramatic, sacred, eerie sight I'd ever seen. Britt and I exhaled sounds of appreciation.

"I booked dinner on the roof." I looked at her, and we smiled.

The phone rang. I ran for it as Brittany

said, "We forgot to call Gary."

"Gary. Oh my god, the Parthenon. It's so close, we can almost touch it. It's all lit up!" I wouldn't let my husband get a word in edgewise. "We're just about to go eat dinner on the roof."

Britt lingered on the terrace and I stared at the temple even as I heard Gary say, "Deb, your mother was killed in a car accident. You and Brittany need to come home. I tried to catch you in Paris, but —"

The phone fell from my hand. I sank to the floor and curled in a fetal position on the carpet. I remember thinking, *What in the hell was that horrible noise?* "No . . . no . . . no!"

Brittany had the phone. "Gary, we can't turn around and catch the first flight out. Momma needs a good night's rest. Wait, someone's at the door."

From the floor I saw Brittany answer the door, and a man was asking, "Is everything all right?"

"We just got some very bad news. Give us a minute."

I was sure that he'd heard the same ghastly noise that I had . . . that howling, screaming woman.

Britt came over, phone in hand, and bent down. "Momma! Breathe. Stop that noise.

We're going to get kicked out of our room."

It slowly dawned on me that I was the source of the awful noise. I put my hand over my mouth. "Never speak badly of your mother," I said. "I wish I'd never said anything negative about her."

"Can you talk to Gary?" She handed me the phone.

"We'll take a flight out tomorrow afternoon. Mum is dead. Getting on the next flight out will not change that. We need to rest." I hung up. A series of phone calls came. My brother. My sisters.

"Britt," I said, "Can you get us to Dallas? I'm not thinking clearly."

"No worries, Momma. I got this. But no regrets. You were good to your mother, and she was a royal bitch sometimes."

"No regrets," I said softly.

We flew to Dallas for the funeral, and afterward I brought my father back to California to live with me.

Britt celebrated Thanksgiving with her grandpa at my house, and then took off just days later for Tokyo, Singapore, Laos, and Vietnam. She was meeting the same girl that had traveled with her to the elephant refuge. I simply couldn't worry. I had my ninety-year-old father to care for, and it was becoming apparent to Gary that I was sinking under this weight. We were looking at assisted living care centers.

Both my father and I were deeply depressed. He was hard to rouse from bed. Although my mother had been difficult, it hadn't diminished my love for her. My mind kept revisiting her body being thrown from the car. Had she been conscious? She had not been dead on arrival. Did that mean she had suffered?

I could only take it one day at a time, and meanwhile pray for Brittany's safety.

Brittany ran a marathon through ninety-degree Angkor Wat. The locals stood and watched the crazy Americans run in the sweltering heat. On December 1, Britt posted a selfie with a snake around her neck. She called to tell us that she rode bikes with her friend through rural Laos, and then hiked into a huge cave where there were no other people. Gary lost his temper and said, "There is adventuresome, and there is downright stupid. This falls in the latter category." It was a short phone call. Britt's last words were something along the lines of she didn't care what we said; it was one of the most exquisitely beautiful days of her life.

From Laos, Brittany traveled alone to

Vietnam. Her itinerary: Vientiane to Pakse to Ho Chi Minh to Nha Trang to Ha Long Bay to Hanoi.

My father was waking in the middle of the night and dragging furniture from his room into the hall. Gary and I were at our wits' end, and had terrible backaches from trying to assist him in and out of the bath.

Brittany was causing a level of worry that we couldn't even fathom. She had booked a week on a junk in Ha Long Bay, in which she'd be the only passenger with an all-male crew. Brittany sipped Vietnamese coffee as the captain skillfully threaded the junk between towering limestone islands covered in jungle vegetation. She swam off the side of the boat and feasted on a fresh seafood meal prepared just for her. Later she described the pure joy she felt as she explored grottos in a small bamboo boat.

When she came home, I felt like kissing the ground.

The next thing I knew, Brittany made plans to meet with Dan and Bella. They decided to spend New Year's weekend in Sonoma Valley wine country.

Gary couldn't suppress his grin. "Told you Bella was a way to keep in touch."

25
PRE-GRIEF IS A NASTY BITCH

September 2014

I don't care how hard being together is,
nothing is worse than being apart.
— Josephine Angelini, *Starcrossed*

Separated from Brittany, I cried many times
each day. I didn't care what I wore or what
I looked like. I didn't attempt to hide my
grief. My face was etched with pain; my
feelings were raw, naked, and exposed.
Complete strangers asked if I was all right,
provoking an outburst of tears. "No, I'm
not, but there's nothing anyone can do to
help me."

Every muscle in my body ached. I told
myself to grieve, get it out of my system, so
that I could go back to Oregon and be the
mother my daughter needed me to be. The
sorrow, the well of tears, and the agony of
knowing what was coming . . . endless. Wave

after wave of excruciating pain knocked me down as soon as I wobbled to my feet. I wanted to throw myself into it, drown in it. I wanted grief to kill me, and some days I thought it might.

I couldn't concentrate, couldn't remember names of people that I knew well, couldn't sleep. The dream about Britt inserting the knife into my torso was on a repeat cycle, haunting me several times a week.

My therapist told me that I must not expect an apology. He asked me to remember the last time that Brittany apologized, and I couldn't. It had been years.

"The 'apologize' part of her brain isn't there anymore. It hasn't been there for a while, hon," Gary said, reaching for my hand.

I thought about Brittany's brain, and how some of it was missing and some of it was tangled and choked with the tentacles of her tumor.

I vacillated between feeling like the worst mother on earth and feeling like an abused mother. Finally I found it therapeutic to make a book of photos of Brittany and me. I decided to design the book around a baseball theme, since Brittany had told me that I hadn't knocked motherhood "out of the park." It was my way of trying to heal myself and reach out to her at the same time.

The title of my creation was *Hitting It Out of the Ballpark — Being Brittany's Mother.* On the cover was a photo of me giving Brittany a kiss as she ducked to avoid me. Inside were impish photos of her as a child, photos of us over the years, and quotes that I thought related to both baseball and motherhood.

I wrote, in part:

I do see some similarities between mothering and baseball. Of course it would be great to knock the ball out of the park, but that's not what professional players are usually trying to do. They simply train themselves to strike the ball well, and they can do it almost without thinking. . . . Occasionally they do manage to strike it just perfectly and it flies like a rocket. Oh, to have felt that moment. I don't think I've hit mothering out of the park. I did eat, sleep, and breathe mothering. I showed up, played pretty smart, and swung with everything I had.

The last page of the book was a photo of me whispering in Brittany's tiny shell of an ear when she was little. I wrote, "How many times have I whispered 'I love you' in Brittany's ear?"

I had a copy mailed to Brittany in Oregon, hoping it would soften her heart.

In early September, I sent an email to Brittany. I felt strange being in Southern California, tending to my ailing father's needs and letting others tend to her care. But I was sure that at this moment, her young, intelligent, and resilient friends were doing a better job with Brittany than I had been doing. This wasn't fun to acknowledge; in fact, it hurt like hell. I continued to email my daughter, trying to let her know that her kicking me out of the house had not changed my love.

One thing of which you may be sure. I love you. I have loved you since I first felt you move beneath my ribs. I understand that at this time in your life you find more confidence and comfort in the presence of others. I am grateful to anyone who commands this respect from you — who can be that rock for you. For some reason, old worn out patterns of the mother daughter dance are especially grating on your nerves right now. If you really love someone — you step aside so that that person can be calmed and comforted by those who do a better job than you do. It doesn't mean that there weren't thousands of times that I was exactly the right person to give you care. It just means that right now — in this instant — I am not. It was clear in the days before I left that I was irritating you and providing little if any added value. I think of you each day, each hour. I pray unceasingly.

Brittany emailed me back on September 8.

I just got this and wanted to say I LOVE YOU SO MUCH MOM. It's not fair . . . it's not fair . . . it's not fair. Your emails bring me to tears but they are a tear that must be shed. They have to come out. I am so sorry I am dying. I am trying so hard to be brave and do what is right.

I love you, that love will ALWAYS be with you, nothing can ever take it away. Ever.

Your daughter,
Britt

I booked a flight back on September 31, following the directions that Brittany had screamed at me. She had said she didn't want to see me until October. It came as a surprise to me when she later said, "Everyone loves the book you did for me, but no one gets why you used baseball quotes." I bit back an answer, realizing that Brittany might not remember saying that I hadn't knocked motherhood out of the park, that she didn't want to see me again for a month, if ever. It happened over and over again: my thinking she meant what she said, and her not remembering it at all.

My on-and-off attendance in my father's life had created problems, although since his eyesight and hearing had also degenerated over the last year, it was hard to know what the source of his rage and depression was. Dementia had steadily built plaque between the synapses of his brain, causing it to harden and shrink.

Prior to Brittany's illness, my steady presence seemed to stabilize his moods. I think I made him feel safe and needed. I knew all of Daddy's stories, could finish his sentences. Sometimes I knew how to make him feel that he was still a contributing member of society — something very important to him. I convinced him that his job at his caregiving center was to thank all the musicians who came to perform. I encouraged him to clap and call out "yee-haw!" at songs that were particularly good. Dad referred to the caregivers as "people he worked with" and where he lived as "a pretty good outfit to be employed by." He wore a different cowboy hat each day of the week. All seven hats hung on hooks in his room, and at night he would count them before going to sleep.

Although our friend Pamela graciously moved into our home and visited Daddy daily, his mood and weight had dropped significantly in the last nine months. We were blessed to have such a caring, loving person step in to care for my father in our absence, and Daddy's life had been as stable as possible, given the circumstances.

Try as I might, I didn't think I could fool my father, now ninety-two and losing his memory. I think that like everyone else, he could sense my grief and pain. But it wasn't appropriate to tell Daddy anything other than "Brittany is sick, and sometimes I have to go away and take care of her."

I tried to coax Daddy into eating. I made him chocolate milkshakes with Ensure and ice cream. Sometimes he spat or sprayed the shake on me, and I ended up wearing it home. In the caregiving world, it seemed that everyone I touched was dying.

I watched Brittany's visits with friends on Facebook, having become a voyeur of my daughter's life.

Finally I emailed another letter to Brittany. I wanted to let her feel that doing what she needed to do, including not having me around, was all right.

Darling daughter — (these are words from my heart — I don't want these words to make you cry with weakness — if you weep, let it be tears of strength . . . you are fiercely strong.)

You are flesh of my flesh, bone of my bone, a matching soul in the universe. We know each other so well, and yet in some ways we are mystified by each other. You are the first thing I think about when I wake up. Even pregnant, I'd touch my tummy and think of you. I have prayed for your safety and happiness more than I've prayed for my own.

You are the only human being that if by offering my life I could give you more time to live in joy, I would sign up in a flat second.

I want to soothe your soul, smooth your brow, massage your legs, feet, shoulders. I don't want to make you angry or anxious. If you need me — I will come. If it is easier to do fun things with friends — be with those who are of your own age who are good at sharing youthful fun and laughs — I will come later.

This is excruciating. Yes, we need to get all dolled up and go out on the town. Laugh about some old memories. For me, I think pain is etched upon my face, but I will try to shake it off and live "in the moment" with you.

You are beautiful. You are smart. You are a giver. You are the bravest woman I know. I thought I had a pretty big pair of cojones, but you are much bolder — much braver than I am. You will die as you have lived, with no looking back — you will just look forward and overcome every obstacle — creating the person/ soul you will be for eternity . . . I'm convinced that the next journey you take will be full of beauty and understanding. You will look back at all the exploring and traveling you did here on earth and smile. Each bit of this world that you explored prepared you for the best journey of all. This is my heart's under-standing. This is my heart's joy.

I know that this is not fair. You are too

young. The first thing that goes through my mind sometimes is that there was a quickening, a knowing, inside of you so early in life. You lived more life in less than 30 years than most of us live in a lifetime. Somewhere inside your old soul — you knew. You went for everything with such gusto . . . no trepidation.

Now you ready yourself for another journey. You will travel light. Your body no more than a favorite soft, warm garment that you enjoyed wearing and were so reluctant to part with. As beautiful and feminine and strong as that body was — it cannot hold a candle to your fearless spirit. Your warrior princess iron will. The will to . . . Improve . . . Move forward . . . Know more . . . Love more . . . Accept more . . . Challenge yourself more . . .

Nothing can put out the flame inside you . . . though this illness is trying. You will not be diminished. You will not be brought down. You will be lifted up. I lift you up.

If I can be a calming steady presence by your side — I will come to you. If my presence brings up old angry feelings, I don't want to be a vehicle for those feelings. As you plan these special coming days, weeks, months — put me where your heart and gut tell you I will be of greatest solace to you. Leave me out when you think that my grief will be an additional burden to carry. You need steady — steadfast — perhaps less emotional people with you at times.

I have been everything I knew how to be to you for almost 30 years. Now I must trust that you know what will be best for you in this stressful time. I want you to have the dignity that this whole medical option is built around. You are wise far beyond your years. I have nothing I need to prove. My agenda is not important. With all my heart I want to free you of a feeling of obligation. Do what you need to do. Know that I am with you in spirit, whether we can touch each other, or speak to each other. You are the last thing I think of at the end of each day. I pray for a peaceful night for you, for you to know that you are loved; I pray that I will be in the presence of your spirit always and forever. Just as I could hear you call "momma" over a din of other children's voices, I will hear you in a breeze, or the call of a bird, or the sound of the ocean. I long to shed my body and join your traveling spirit. It

406

will be just a minute amount of time that we are separated. I will know your spirit above all others in the universe. It is spirit of my spirit. Always my beautiful daughter.

Giant hugs and kisses,
Momma

One September 22, Daddy was taken to the emergency room with a gash on his head from falling. I rushed to meet the ambulance there. I found myself thinking that my father and my daughter were going to die almost simultaneously. I was flying to Portland at the end of September, come hell or high water. Hopefully, Daddy would be healed and stabilized by then. I had about a week. I called my sister for help, and Donna agreed to come out and give Pamela a break. This allowed Gary and me to fly up a few days sooner, in time for Brittany's two-year wedding anniversary on September 29, 2014.

There was pressure from the caregiving staff to put Daddy in hospice care due to his forty-pound weight loss, three falls, and emergency room trips. Dad's little legs couldn't hold him up long enough to transfer from the wheelchair to the toilet. A contraption called a "Hoyer" was brought in, and Dad was understandably terrified of being lifted in the air. I managed to convince him that the Hoyer was an Army Corps of Engineers invention, and pretty soon, he told the caregivers it was an "army contraption."

I signed the hospice papers for Dad before I flew. It didn't feel right to me, but what the hell did I know? There was no solid ground anymore.

26
Mountain Climbing
and a Wedding

2012–2013, Age Twenty-Eight

Today is your day! Your mountain is waiting, So . . . get on your way!
— Dr. Seuss, *Oh, The Places You'll Go!*

Early in 2012, I booked a trip for Britt and
me to go to Rome, the Amalfi Coast of Italy,
and Austria. I was trying to re-create the
trip that Britt and I had missed in Greece,
but we weren't ready to face Greece again.
The memories of my mother's death were
still too raw. Brittany suggested that Gary
join us. She also asked if Dan could join us
for a few days, and I said of course.

I had been so busy with Daddy that I
hadn't noticed that Britt had stayed closely
in touch with Dan since Christmas. With
her applying to law schools all over the
country, I didn't see how this relationship
would make it. But if she wanted Dan to

409

come with us on vacation, that was okay with me and Gary. Since we'd be gone for three weeks, I arranged for my sister, Sarah, and my friend Pamela to come and take care of Daddy.

Before we left, Brittany received admittance letters to UC Berkeley Law School and to University of Washington School of Law. She received offers of scholarships from University of California Irvine's Law School, and the law schools at University of Colorado and University of Chicago. Brittany was glad to get the acceptances, but also stressed about the choices.

Gary, Britt, and I left for Italy in early April, and Dan joined us in Rome. After a few days we left to tour Pompeii. It was as if Mount Vesuvius embalmed a slice of Roman life. Britt and I spoke of our sadness as we realized that volcanic ash had beautifully preserved the city for so long, but now exposed, it was endangered by pollution and tourism.

We continued south to the Amalfi Coast. One evening Gary and Dan went out together, and Brittany and I went to a different restaurant. At dinner, Dan asked Gary's permission for Brittany's hand in marriage. Caught off-guard but charmed by the gesture, Gary was his gracious and honest self.

"Are you sure that's what you want to do?" Gary asked.

From the look on Dan's face, apparently this was not an expected response.

"Brittany is a very difficult woman to please. We've found her very difficult to live with since her late teens." Gary gazed at Dan. "Did you know that about the woman you want to marry?"

Dan smiled and said that he did. "Well, then, congratulations!" Gary raised his glass of wine for a toast.

That night Gary told me of this dinner conversation, and said that perhaps Dan's extra years of maturity would help him ride through Britt's storms. We both truly wished them happiness.

We took a boat out to the Isle of Capri. Dan and Brittany enjoyed a leisurely day of shopping while Gary and I rode the tram to the highest point on the island. The ocean had never looked bluer. After Capri, Dan headed home as we headed for Austria.

In Vienna, Britt's mood seemed to change. One day she threw an absolute conniption fit because I wanted to visit the Lipizzaner stallions at the Spanish Riding School. I'd read about the horses as a girl and had always wanted to see them, but after yelling at me that it was animal abuse, Brittany stormed off to the hotel.

Knowing that she was planning to get married, I worried and felt a profound protectiveness that I could do nothing about. Law school would be out, at least for the foreseeable future. Dan didn't want to wait another three years to start a family. Britt felt that law school would be hard enough without having a baby in the middle of the process. So Brittany would be walking away from some important dreams and some significant scholarship money. I hoped she was sure about giving it up.

When we returned to California, Brittany and Dan began an exhaustive house search. They settled on a quaint home with an enormous backyard and pool. Yet I sensed my daughter struggling with the idea of settling down in suburbia.

The next thing I knew, Britt had booked a trip with her friend Mina to New York, Boston, and Massachusetts. The bigger news was that she had also booked a trip to Kilimanjaro, and was beginning to train for the climb.

When she returned from the East Coast, Dan and Britt signed the closing docs on their new home and Dan officially popped the question. I asked Brittany if Gary and I could host a dinner with Dan's parents to toast their engagement.

Gary told Brittany that our big backyard would be a beautiful place for an intimate outdoor wedding. He pointed out that we could arrange parking at the nearby school and shuttle guests from there to our home.

Britt wrinkled her nose. "We're planning on having the wedding in Sonoma Valley, at Beltane Ranch," she said.

"Really?" Gary's eyebrows rose.

Afterward, he and I had several conversations about how we wanted to handle Brittany's upcoming wedding. Traditionally the parents of the bride footed the bill for the festivities. It was clear that Dan and Brittany had already discussed and settled on plans that we weren't conferred with about, or on board with. Renting an entire ranch in Sonoma for a wedding in September at the height of the wine season? Obviously I wouldn't be playing a big part in planning the wedding, because Britt had chosen to have it in the San Francisco Bay Area, and I was the primary advocate and caregiver for my elderly father 450 miles south of there.

We weren't interested in taking on a wedding of imprudent proportions, nor did we think Brittany would function well under the pressure of an ever-ballooning event. Gary and I felt strongly that the last few receptions we'd been too were overly elaborate and stressful. We had heard the comments about the grinding machine of the wedding industry and had no intention of getting crushed in the gears of florists, photographers, and caterers.

After much discussion, we decided to offer a fixed amount of money toward a wedding, or whatever they wanted to spend it on. Having recently come into a chunk of cash from a distant relative, Brittany could match our offer and have a very nice wedding.

We agreed to rent two large homes to house family members and friends. One of the homes could sleep ten, and the other could sleep six. I also hosted a spa day for the bridesmaids.

After making our monetary contribution, we didn't get a thank-you note from Brittany until we called her on it. Although it was unspoken, we felt strong vibes that our contribution was seriously deficient. She tried several times to get me pulled into the wedding machine. I resisted each time, telling her that she could use the money we'd given her in any way she wished. "Oh, that's long gone," she said.

By this time, Gary and I were inured to this kind of treatment. We continued to hope that Britt would mature out of this type of behavior. Hindsight is painful, knowing what we know now about what was happening in her brain. Hindsight brings self-recrimination. Had we missed gradual personality changes because they occurred so slowly? Or had teen behavior blended into behavior changes caused by the tumor? Britt's tumor was estimated to be nine years old by the time she got married. A lot can happen in nine years.

I watched the wedding grow bigger and bigger. Certainly Gary and I knew that we had no power to change the course Brittany chose. In late May, Brittany wrote me an email that showed signs of stress. She talked about having a panic attack, sobbing, and the fact that she was losing her law school option as of June 1.

One of my favorite evenings during the months of preparation was the engagement dinner at the end of June. Gary and I hosted Dan, Brittany, Carmen, and Barry. The dinner was warm and pleasurable, and Dan's parents calmed any concerns I might have by their very presence, their inherent goodness. A boy brought up by this compassionate man and witty woman would surely do right by my charming but challenging daughter.

When it came to wedding dresses, I was clearly not on the same page as Brittany. I had been emailing her suggestions in the $800 range. Brittany was looking at gowns six times that expensive. She chose a dress that was truly breathtaking. It was majestic, even regal, with a bodice that hugged her curves and a voluminous tiered skirt. Each tier was heavy with a three-dimensional, swirling-fabric floral design. Brittany looked stunning in it. Underneath she wore a pair of cowboy boots.

I didn't ask how much this dreamy confection cost because I was sure that the price for a couture wedding dress out of New York would have shocked me. Brittany told me that she was going to save the dress so that each flower that flowed from her hips to the ground could be sewn later onto her future baby girls' Easter dresses. "I'll photograph the girls each Easter in dresses created from my wedding dress," she said.

On July 5, Brittany left for her Kilimanjaro trek. At least she would be traveling with a girlfriend and the friend's boyfriend.

Given that the whole escapade was intrinsically risky, having friends along could only be an improvement over traveling alone. I prayed fervently for Brittany's safety and asked everyone I knew to pray. I couldn't help feeling that something was very wrong. Why would my daughter go to Africa and engage in a dangerous mountain-climbing expedition in the middle of planning her wedding? When she was already experiencing a great deal of stress? What was driving her to travel to such far-flung places?

It seemed like every time life started to calm down, Brittany stirred it up again. She hated stress, and reacted physically to it: neck ache, backache, headache, tears, muscle fatigue. Yet in many ways, she created her own anxiety.

I blamed myself. How had I set her up for this? Had I been too strict, or not strict enough? Had I been too protective, or not protective enough? What the hell had I done wrong? I read that some people were born with a personality trait called "sensation seeking," and that it was about 60 percent genetic. But I knew of no one on either side of Britt's genetics that fit this description.

In mid-July, we finally got an email from Brittany. It was addressed to Gary, Dan, and me. Brittany's email captured a bit of the danger and risk-taking involved in summiting Kilamanjaro. She said that the climb was beautiful but very challenging, and that it made trekking through the Himalayas with giardia look like "a cake walk." She got an intestinal infection and a "skull-splitting headache," as well, and one of the guides got pulmonary edema and had to be hospitalized. The whole thing sounded torturous to Gary and me, but Brittany later told us with great pride that her guide said she could accomplish anything she set out to do because she was able to achieve a mind-over-matter mentality.

Brittany took fantastic photos of the safari she went on after her climb. I was happy she was safe, and that she had taken a break. When she returned in early August, she'd have to hit the ground running before her big wedding day.

Despite the hectic preparations, the wedding itself was gorgeous. Brittany had created a dream wedding, and she and Dan looked like a dream-come-true couple. Bride and groom smiled at the camera with great hopes, and every reason to think the future would be bright.

As guests and family sat smiling on folding chairs surrounded by the natural beauty of Sonoma, we had no way of knowing that under the bride's carefully coiffed hair, beneath the veil I'd helped her choose, a large tumor bloomed like an oversized orchid.

27
TWENTY-NINE YEARS
October 2014

Life will undertake to separate us, and we
must each set off in search of our own
path, our own destiny or our own way of
facing death.

— Paulo Coelho,
Manuscript Found in Accra

On the flight up to Portland, I thought
about Brittany being only twenty-nine years
old. I realized she was the age that I was
when she was just a babe in my arms. My
daughter was dying at a time in life when I
had been bringing life into the world. I was
almost twenty-nine years older than Brittany. My father, for whom I'd just signed
hospice paperwork, was ninety-two, the
inverse of Brittany's age. Today was the 29th
of September, the day that Brittany was
married only two short years ago. If I were

a numerologist maybe these numbers would have had some import, but instead they were another mystery piling on top of all the other unknowns in my life. *I don't understand.* That thought went through my mind over and over again.

I don't understand.

When I entered the house in Portland, I ran upstairs to find Brittany. Her face had changed so much from the medication while I was away, she was almost unrecognizable. I reached my hand out to cup her dear cheek and looked into her eyes for a moment with all the love I could transfer in a gaze. I hoped that my face, my eyes, said "You are always beautiful and I love you."

That night, Gary and I were to babysit Charley and Bella, who had been brought up to Portland to spend the last days of Brittany's life with her. Brittany's head ached so much that we ordered takeout and ate next to her on the couch, on her and Dan's second wedding anniversary.

I brought a book about massage and tried to use the techniques as I massaged her neck and shoulders, which were giving her great pain, along with the headaches. We were also gifted massages by several friends. Medicine had failed us in every way possible. The doctor running the dendritic vaccine study had not even told Brittany why she was rejected as a candidate for that experimental treatment. The doctor who'd had some success using a polio vaccine had not responded to my emails. We were down to the last thirty days, with no hope on the horizon. Britt now polished the plans, not for a funeral, but for a "life celebration": music, type of chairs, and what poetry was to be read. She asked to be cremated and have her ashes spread in the redwoods of California. All of this was too concrete for me. Even now, fat, hot tears blur my vision if I think about my twenty-nine-year-old daughter planning every detail of her death and its aftermath.

Brittany had begun falling. Her foot couldn't send signals to her brain fast enough about an uneven walking surface. She didn't crumble and fall; she did face-plants. Her legs, ankles, and feet were bruised and swollen, making it even more dangerous to walk. However, when we took walks she wouldn't let me, or anyone else, hold her arm. She fell again. And again.

Brittany was very self-conscious about her facial swelling, and she asked me to help her write something for the filmmaker to put in the YouTube video. I emailed Britt the following suggested statement. However, no explanation was given in the video for her "moon face," and this distressed Britt a great deal.

Brittany Diaz's brain tumor is being treated with several strong drugs designed to reduce swelling of the brain and to try to minimize debilitating seizures. Unfortunately, these drugs come with their own frustrating set of side effects including weight gain and swelling of the face, referred to as "moon face." In spite of some shyness regarding her new drug-induced appearance, Brittany agreed to be interviewed regarding Death with Dignity because her belief in this basic human right was more important than her vanity.

I emailed my sister Sarah about my fears of Brittany's passing. An excerpt is below:

What will I do, Sarah? Try to keep anyone from removing Brittany from my arms? Walk out the door and down to the woods to scream and cry? Will I faint? Will I strip my clothes off, scratch my own skin until it bleeds? Will I crawl in bed and take lots of sedatives? If so, where will I get them?

Will I be out of it? Having to be led from room to room?

On October 5, Brittany met with her palliative doctor regarding her latest MRI. Nothing was said that made her want to change her plan. She still planned for a November 1 passing. Britt, Dan, Gary, and I left for a trip to the Columbia River Gorge, where Gary had rented a vacation home. It couldn't have been a better time to get away.

On October 6, People.com posted an article on their webpage. It went viral, with more than 16 million people reading Britt's story. The reporter assigned to the story, who stayed with it for the duration, was refreshingly transparent, up front, and compassionate. The photo they used was of Brittany with Charley, the Great Dane.

The six-and-a-half-minute video that the New York director made with Brittany, me, and Dan regarding Brittany's choice to use the Death with Dignity law was released almost simultaneously on YouTube, and that also went viral.

On October 7, from the rental house in the gorge, Brittany requested that her Facebook friends avoid media and decline to be interviewed. News crews had already hit our home, Dan's parents' home, and the home of Dan's parents' friends in Portland. We had no idea what was happening at the yellow house, but we suspected it was a good time to be away.

By October 8, Brittany's YouTube video had more than 3 million hits. There was also someone on Facebook who'd created a website impersonating Brittany, and they had seven thousand followers. We were freaked out about that.

We busied ourselves taking a picturesque thirty-six-mile drive through what is known as the "fruit loop" of Oregon, the nation's largest pear-growing region. It was lovely, and there were fruit stands and vineyards to explore. Unfortunately, Brittany experienced a mild seizure on a train ride that made her tired and anxious to get home. Even so, it was clear to all that she did better when plenty of outdoor activities were planned.

October 13 was a long day for Brittany. She filmed with CBS all morning, explaining her dismay that not all Americans had the right that she was exercising with Oregon's Death with Dignity Act. The spunky New York gal, who made the first YouTube video, filmed a follow-up video with Britt, Dan, and me. By the end of the day, Brittany was as tired and in pain as I'd ever seen her. She told Dan, Gary, and me that she wanted all the film crews to leave. She also told them to cancel the Meredith Vieira interview that they had scheduled. "I'm done. The only thing I'll do tomorrow is the video testimony for legislators."

I went downstairs to heat up Brittany's neck buddy, and found a film crew outside our kitchen window. I slid the sash window up and asked, "What are you doing?"

The two young men looked up at me in surprise. "Hi, ah . . . we're filming B-roll."

"You need to leave. Brittany is ill. She's resting now. She wants to pad around in her pajamas and slippers."

"Can we get some footage of your kitchen?"

"No!" I shut the window.

When I went upstairs to give Britt her warm neck buddy and a drink, she began crying. "I'm so tired. No more. I can't do any more, Momma."

That evening Brittany posted a note on Facebook that broke my heart.

Thank you friends for all the genuine support as I am dying . . . My medication/steroids has made be [sic] gain weight uncontrollably and blown me up into someone I can barely recognize in the mirror in recent months. As a woman who has worked really hard to fight petty vanities, this is still so hard. My wedding ring is difficult to slide on my swollen finger, it hurts. Add that to an increasing level of intense physical and emotional pain beyond words, terrifying seizures, temporary post-ictal losses of speech, headaches that make my world split open, nausea, ironically loss of appetite . . . To then sit down in front of a major network's news video camera, be vulnerable about my brain cancer, healthcare choices, logic, fears, my life . . . deep breaths . . . I do it only because I feel this is a HUGE ethical issue and problem in our country. People NEED to talk about it, need to advocate for change, need to vote for equal rights for all terminally ill Americans. No one this sick deserves to be robbed of choices available to some and not others, options. I am exhausted, so tired, and feeling so sick. So sick of looking in the mirror and seeing this hideous cancer staring back at me. I am fighting to stay strong while I can. Then it will be time to say goodbye with as much grace as possible to all those I love with a ferocity beyond words.

If I could've granted Brittany anything before she died it would've been love of self, because as hard as she was on us, I knew she was harder on herself. With blurry vision, I commented:

My beautiful daughter. Always. Cancer ca [sic] not diminish you. It will try but your sprit [sic] burns bright. Forever.

The next morning I heard a car door slam outside and got up to look out my bedroom window. A giant television van with a satellite dish on top sat directly in front of our house. We had told everyone who interviewed Brittany to be as discreet as they could possibly be, because we didn't want the location of our house revealed. There were too many crazies trying to be heard.

This was not discreet.

Already we had dealt with all manner of irrational people, both trying to help and trying to hurt. Phone calls from complete strangers with cures like drinking and eating nothing but carrots. Packages left on our doorstep with homemade vegan juices and colon cleanses. Emails begging Brittany not to take her medication, from religious fanatics threatening her with eternal brimstone.

A couple of other cancer patients, with cancers that by definition were unlike Brittany's, because everyone's illness is different, wrote open letters addressed specifically to Brittany (that the media published and spread), telling her how to handle terminal illness and begging her not to take medication to lessen her suffering by hastening death. These letters were the worst.

I peeked in to see if she was up, and heard her sleepy "Momma."

I thought I'd better break it to her rather than let her find out the way I had. I sat on the edge of the bed and stroked her hair. "Sweetheart, there's a news van with a satellite dish outside. Did you and Dan discuss this again?"

She sat up and threw back the covers. "No fucking way!" She stared out her bedroom window.

I was still in my pajamas when Gary joined me in my room, looking out the window from between the slats of the blinds. Dan appeared outside and began talking to the crew. Brittany, too, peeked through the blinds. "I'm dying, and don't feel well enough for another interview."

While we stood watching Dan talking with the crew, Brittany's interview with CBS correspondent Jan Crawford aired on national television. Facebook lit up with people who had seen it.

Later, after the satellite van left and we'd had breakfast, the team from New York arrived to film Brittany giving her testimony for legislators. This is what Brittany said:

My name is Brittany Maynard. I am twenty-nine years old, and I am terminally ill.

On New Year's Day 2014, to my great shock, I learned I had brain cancer. Despite the efforts of advanced medicine, my cancer is aggressive and currently without any cure. On New Year's Day, I was told I may have a few years to live with a Grade 2 astrocytoma. This was a great shock to my family and me.

Then, post-op from a January craniotomy, my April MRI showed significant enhancement, indicative of a higher grade change. I was told I most likely had six months or so to live, my imaging was very indicative of a Grade 4 glioblastoma based on MRI interpretation. A GBM4 is the most dangerous form of brain cancer. My world fell apart.

I moved to Oregon shortly after with my family from California because it is one of only five states that do authorize the patient right to a choice of death with dignity. I'm heartbroken that I had to leave behind my home, my community, and my friends in California. But I am dying, and I refuse to lose my dignity. I refuse to subject myself and family to purposeless prolonged pain and suffering at the hands of an incurable disease.

Death-with-dignity laws authorize the medical practice of aid in dying. They give mentally competent, terminally ill adults the option to request life-ending medication that they can choose to ingest if their dying process becomes unbearable. The freedom in this patient right is choice.

Besides Oregon, only four other states authorize the medical practice of aid in dying: Washington, Montana, Vermont, and New Mexico. Making aid in dying a crime creates undue hardships and suffering for many people who are terminally ill and suffering tremendously. It limits our options and deprives us of the ability to control how much pain and agony we endure before we pass.

People have asked me whether I explored the medical practice of palliative or terminal sedation. Some claim it is an equally gentle alternative for patients whose symptoms cannot be controlled.

The procedure involves drugging the patient into a coma. Nutrition and fluids are withheld until the person dies from the disease or dehydration. No one can tell when that would happen. But each patient is different, and deserves the autonomy and freedom to make this most personal choice for themselves.

I can't imagine what that experience would be like. I may be minimally conscious, still suffering and unable to move or speak. That terrifies me. Death with dignity is a much swifter and peaceful way to pass. Logic motivates me to choose this for myself instead.

I refuse that procedure because I want to live fully until I die. The rest of my body is young, fit, and retaining fluid, so I would likely hang on for days or even weeks before I died. I don't want that.

Also, palliative sedation usually requires hospitalization. I want to be sure my husband and mother are with me when I die. I want to leave this earth in my home, in the arms of my husband and parents.

I can't change the fact that I am dying, but I am living my final days to the fullest, spending time enjoying family, friends, and the great outdoors. And I am preparing to experience the best possible death.

Achieving some control over my passing is very important to me. Knowing that I can leave this life with dignity allows me to focus on living. It has provided me enormous peace of mind.

The inevitability of death is universal; the widespread support and overwhelmingly positive response to my story represents [that] our community is ready to have a new conversation about death.

The decision about how I end my dying process should be up to me and my family, under a doctor's care. How dare the government make decisions or limit options for terminally ill people like me? Unfortunately, California law prevented me from getting the end-of-life option I deserved.

No one should have to leave their home and community for peace of mind, to escape suffering and to plan for a gentle death.

For the vast majority of people, that is not even a remote possibility because of the cost of moving, the inconvenience to the family, and the time it takes to change your residency status, find new doctors, confirm your eligibility, and obtain the medication. This must change.

Every one of us will die. We should not

have to suffer excruciating pain, shame, or a prolonged dying process.

The laws in California and forty-five other states must change to prevent prolonged, involuntary suffering for all terminally ill Americans. As elected officials, you have the power to make this happen. Please take action.

Every terminally ill American deserves the choice to die with dignity. Let a movement begin here, now. Access to this choice lies in your hands; freedom from prolonged pain and suffering is the most basic human right.

Please make death with dignity an American healthcare choice.

Thank you.

It was a cloudy, gray day, and Brittany was feeling so fatigued from the long previous day. Filming takes many hours, just to get a few minutes of usable footage. It was a short interview to watch, but it required grueling hours of having the house rearranged, lights set up, and so much film that wasn't used. The one bright spot of the long day was when Brittany and I went back to visit Gary, where he was holed up in the small office with the dogs. He had the windows closed, curtains drawn, and music playing softly, trying to keep Bella and Charley quiet while filming was being done. Charley had had gas. All day.

"Oh . . . My . . . God." Brittany waved the air with her hand. "It smells terrible in here!" She bent to hug Gary. "You are the most patient, kind man in the world." And then she started laughing, as only Brittany could. I started laughing, too. The film director came in to shush us, and she also started laughing. We needed that moment.

The gloom turned into rain. After they packed their equipment up and left, I made banana pancakes for dinner. Brittany and I sat on the sofa, watching the rain slash at the windows.

"Momma." She reached for my hand. "With my diagnosis — this is as good as it gets. What we're doing here in this little yellow house, is as good as it gets."

And for a little while, it was.

The next day *People* magazine hit the stands, and Brittany was on the cover, with the title, "My Decision to Die." There for the entire world to see was my heartache, my all, my only child — beautiful, clear-eyed Brittany staring straight at death.

Brittany had mentioned in an interview that she would like to see the Grand Canyon before she passed, and a man who owned a helicopter tour company reached out to try to make it happen. Dan spent a great deal of time arranging this. Kind people were reaching out, trying to support my child. On October 19, we left for Vegas, where Brittany and Dan had been comped a gorgeous suite. Gary ordered room service the first evening, and we dined in the privacy of the suite.

The next day, I received a kind email from Katie Couric, wishing me strength and comfort. I was extremely touched because Katie had lost both her husband and sister to cancer. She knew the pain of losing loved ones before their time. Katie, a mother of two daughters, shared that she could not fathom losing a child. It was a note from one mother to another.

Our Vegas hosts treated us to dinner and Cirque du Soleil. The next day, we were picked up in a limousine, and Brittany was treated with the utmost care and respect by the helicopter touring company. Her privacy was guarded, and our pilot had been hand-picked for not only his expertise, but his temperament.

As we hovered over the Grand Canyon, Brittany and I smiled at each other. Even Gary, with his fear of heights, appeared to be in a state of bliss. The ginger-, cinnamon-, and curry-colored striped bands of rocks perhaps 70 million years old lay below us, in contrast to a turquoise sky laden with cumulus clouds. Brittany took a photo of her shadow stretched across the antiquity of time, and I appreciated the symbolism. We, too, were trying to stretch time on this day, to slow it down.

As shadows lengthened, the blue of the sky deepened, and time seemed to be the lesson we were there to learn. We live our lives thinking we have time. I looked back and realized that some of the time that I thought I'd wasted was actually the best time spent in my life. Giving someone you love your time, if you are really present with them, is the greatest gift. My girl and I had little time left, and the clock seemed to be ticking louder and faster.

It was a day for pushing aside fear. At the Grand Canyon Skywalk, a horseshoe-shaped bridge with a glass floor, we walked above a vertical 800-foot drop to the ledge below. The muddy Colorado was 4,770 feet down. Gary even walked on the terrifying loop of glass. Death was near now, making its presence known no matter what we did.

We all seemed to have a little bit of Brittany's bravado. So what if death came a few days early, a few weeks early? Death had already enfolded Brittany in a clinging embrace — she was already gone. "Momma, I'm only living for others. I no longer live for myself. I just want to get to Dan's birthday and then move on."

I thought of death all the time; Brittany's and mine. The level of fear, tension, and sorrow I lived with was a servant to cancer. I imagined stress mutating and damaging cells even as I looked past my feet through the glass floor at the canyon. I felt that it would not be long before I followed Brittany. This thought neither frightened nor saddened me.

What mother wouldn't feel the same abject terror that I felt? The same helplessness and despair? The same desire to go with her child? All my friends assured me that they would be in worse shape. "At least you aren't curled up in a fetal position," one friend said. "That's where I'd be if I were losing my daughter."

My sister and Gary arranged for me to see a Portland therapist who could assist me with stress using a technique called eye movement desensitization and reprocessing (EMDR). The technique, used with post-traumatic stress disorder, involved moving my eyes from side to side while thinking of disturbing situations. EMDR seems to create positive consequences with regard to how the traumatized brain processes information, especially moments that the brain has "frozen in time" due to shock or anguish. Eye movement can reduce the intensity of disturbing repetitive thought. Even though I only saw the therapist a couple of times, it was helpful to learn of this technique because I continued EMDR therapy with another therapist in San Diego after Brittany's death.

Not long after we returned to the hotel, Brittany had a seizure in her room with Dan. I was called down to keep her company, while Gary and Dan set about procuring food for dinner. Brittany shared a description of this seizure on Facebook, which thankfully didn't occur in the helicopter above the Grand Canyon:

> I just had the worst seizure of my illness in this last hour. Felt it coming on like something different and thankfully sat down, tried to call for my husband Dan but couldn't remember or say his name aloud. Then apparently lost consciousness, bit my tongue, bled all over the bed and shook and twisted. When I woke, I didn't know where I was, had to ask why we

were here in Vegas . . . That was scary, so much pain and confusion, tears. Life has really been unfair at times (for many I realize) but I have tried to be brave, embrace what is real and prepare, advocate for other terminally ill rights. How dare those who haven't stood in the shoes of the terminally ill try to argue we deserve to suffer more physical and emotional pain, fear, and loss in the face of inevitable death? I can't even dress alone right now and things will only get worse.

Unfortunately, no one could keep Brittany from reading the hateful things that were posted online. I tried not to look at the comments, but I was like a crazed bird attacking a reflection in a mirror or window. I read horrifying, cruel statements. I couldn't stop deliberately raking my talons at the image of my own religious past. I read hundreds of statements that made me ashamed to have ever been affiliated with such judgmental thinking, such small-mindedness. In the beginning it was a window collision, me accidentally banging into the reflection of childhood beliefs, but eventually I intentionally flew right into the ugly image, bloodying my heart in the process.

I sent Brittany articles written by loving,

logical Christians. I couldn't help myself. I didn't want her to end up hating *all* Christians. For the first time in my life, I was ashamed to call myself a Christian, because there was nothing Christ-like in much of what I read.

Brittany was raised in the church. She went to religious schools; we prayed together, and she had begged for God's intervention and grace at many different times in her life. But as she faced death, many members of the church treated her unkindly. It was impossible for me to defend that behavior.

Any mention of prayer, the church, or belief in God now enraged her. And why wouldn't it? In a haze of pain and painkillers, she read the most odious hatemongering imaginable — from people who called themselves "Christians." Who wouldn't be angry? I certainly was.

We returned to Portland on the 23rd, and surprise . . . it was raining. Gifts cheered Brittany in this gloomy weather, and flowers and a handmade CD of music from a middle school friend helped chase away the blues. The next day, she had a doctor's appointment. If things went as planned, it would be the last appointment with the palliative care doctor. The mood was somber because it was a goodbye.

October 24 was not just gray; it was dark. With nothing on the schedule, time seemed to tick forward as if someone had wound the clock too tight. Time whirred by, and yet it seemed frozen. As we faced the last week before Brittany's death, it was like being on the edge of a black hole, frozen forever in a countdown of misery.

Brittany cuddled in her bed. I joined her with the book we'd been reading and a warmed neck buddy. "It's really raining," I said.

"Again? I'd hoped that we could go for a walk," Brittany murmured. She sighed as the heat from the neck buddy soothed her. "Can you turn on the aromatherapy machine? It seems to help my headache."

I filled the basin of the diffuser with warm water and sprinkled in fragrant oil. Slipping back into the bed, I opened the Kindle and read to her until I was almost hoarse. The rain spattered against the windows louder, and trees swayed in the wind. I shivered as a lightning bolt lit up the dim bedroom. A low rumble was followed by a crash that seemed to shake the house. Another lightning bolt flashed. The lights flickered off.

"Damn," we said in unison. I got up again and lit some candles. We'd dealt with outages before, but not in cold weather. I decided to read to Brittany a little longer. There was nothing else we could do. Eventually I closed the book and Britt rolled over on her side, facing the window. Rain sluiced down the old paned glass. The house had grown dark and cold. I wondered if the electricity would be off all night. Gary and Dan were, I assumed, still downstairs.

"It will be just endless blackness and towering stacks of dead babies, their stinking carcasses filling the air," Brittany said.

"No, Britt. Don't say that!" The image struck close to the bone, re-creating an image I had been trying to erase from my childhood. I had been trying so hard to overcome beliefs that were implanted in my mind by my parents and teachers; attempting to unravel what I was told as a child. I'd sifted through and rebelled against the beliefs that I didn't choose.

I'd tried to undo almost sixty years of teaching to arrive at a place of acceptance. A place where I could resist the urge to cling to my daughter and beg her not to take the medicine. A place where a higher, wiser, kinder part of me could comprehend that what Brittany was feeling and planning actually made a great deal of sense. A place where I would sit and watch her die by her own hand.

She and I had been on eggshells about this subject ever since the day of the diagnosis. I'd repeated over and over that I supported her, that I was not afraid for her. Just as I could spot her voice in a crowd of noisy toddlers, I told her that I would find her bright light and energy anywhere in the universe. I tried to stay away from specifically talking about God, although I couldn't help but tell her I believed I would be with her again.

But this was what I said. "I know that you have different beliefs than I do, but I do not believe in hell. I don't believe in damnation." I struggled to push the covers aside and sit up, but Brittany was already standing, facing me in the flickering candlelight.

Her face contorted, twisted with fury. She screamed, "You fucking selfish cunt!"

It felt like she had slapped me, hard. I was confused. Shocked. What had I said or done to deserve this?

I jumped up. "What did you just call me?" I said, fists balled at my sides.

"You heard me. You are a fucking selfish cunt." Brittany swiped at me with her arm, pushed past me, and left the bedroom.

I followed her, trembling in anger and hurt. "Why are you talking to me like this?

444

You haven't wanted to talk about religion. I've tried to respect that."

"Oh, really." She turned at the top of the stairs. "You've fucking tried?" She started down the stairs for the kitchen, and I followed.

Someone had lit candles in the hallway and the kitchen. Brittany filled a glass at the sink faucet and drank a swig. "You fucking selfish cunt! Always thinking of your fucking self." My daughter's bellicose face was half in the dark, half lit by the flickering candle. Thunder clapped as if to punctuate her sentence. She slammed the glass down on the counter. She paced in the dark of the kitchen.

Suddenly, I knew that Brittany wanted to hit me. I knew that she needed to hit me. *What have I done to deserve this level of rage?* I thought. I looked steadily at my child and said, "You want to hit me, don't you, Brittany?"

She lunged toward me and cuffed my head. "Fucking bitch!"

The words hurt so much more than the cuffing. "You're not finished, are you? Do you still need to hit me?" I asked.

"Bitch!" she screamed. I saw her come at me with both fists balled above her head. I took the pummeling, not moving my arms.

"Do you want my head to hurt as bad as yours does?" I asked as I bent my head, almost as if in supplication, and this time I covered it with my arms. I was still asking my daughter questions, thinking she was capable of lucidly answering them.

The blows came like the rain. I started crying. "Help me. It hurts."

Gary and Dan arrived simultaneously, and Dan pulled Brittany off me.

"Brittany, you can't resort to violence. You cannot hit your mother," Gary said, taking me into his arms.

Brittany lunged at us, this time swiping at Gary. Dan was having a hard time holding her back. "You always stick up for her, no matter what."

I watched Britt struggle in Dan's arms. "Look," I said as though I were noting scientific evidence. "She still wants to hit me." Britt continued to try to lunge. "Go ahead. Hit me." I looked straight at her when I said this.

Brittany broke free and started hitting me again.

"Hit me again," I said through my tears.

Britt flailed so wildly, it took Dan a couple of tries to grab both of her arms and pull her off. I remember thinking how strong she was.

"I never struck her or called her a name," I told Dan through my tears as I turned to climb the stairs. "She really hurt me." As I started up the stairs, I realized I had to get out of that house. It was dark and cold, and I was trembling from head to foot. My head throbbed, and my heart was ripped to bloody shreds.

"She asked for it," I heard Brittany tell Dan.

Gary and I packed quietly in the dark. I called my sister, one hand cradling my head, and described what had happened.

"I was worried, Deb. Remember she called me a 'fucking selfish cunt' when I was last there? It's the tumor, honey, and the meds." Sarah cried softly on the phone.

I couldn't stop sobbing and shaking. My sister's logical words didn't erase any of what had just happened. Gary took the phone from my hand. "Sarah, we're in a blackout. Can you call around and get us a reservation at a hotel that's *not* in the blacked-out area of Portland?"

Sarah called back with a reservation, and once again I tiptoed past my daughter's door and down the stairs with my suitcase. I wept like I would never see my child again. I truly didn't know if I would. This might be her way of severing the cord. Maybe between the meds and the brain tumor, this seemed easier than a tender goodbye. Whatever the case, she had hacked the invisible cord that bound us into a bloody stump.

We loaded the car in the cold rain and drove to the hotel. The next day, we flew home to recover our sanity and decide how much, if any, of the last week of Brittany's life we would be a part of.

28
MARRIED LADY

September 2012–December 2013,
Ages Twenty-Eight and Twenty-Nine

There is no spectacle on earth more appealing than that of a beautiful woman in the act of cooking dinner for someone she loves.
— Thomas Wolfe, *The Web and the Rock*

Brittany threw herself into being married with her usual energy and resolve. She was a great cook, and Dan enthusiastically ate her meals. Carmen was a good cook, too, and Dan wanted Brittany to learn some of his mom's recipes.

Christmas was upon us before we knew it. Gary and I flew up for a few days to celebrate with the newlyweds. My father had hernia surgery scheduled on December 27, so the visit was short. Daddy did very well for a ninety-one-year-old.

In January, Brittany and Dan left for a belated honeymoon in Patagonia, where they hiked and kayaked. Gary and I started planning a trip for May with another couple, to the Piedmont region of Italy and the Catalonia region of Spain. We found that caregiving was both rewarding and draining. We needed a vacation dangling in the future, something to look forward to.

Brittany made plans for a mountain climbing trip because Dan was working full-time and was also remodeling their new home after work and on weekends. Bored and restless, she took flying trapeze lessons and went on hikes. In late February, she took off for mountaineering school in Ecuador, with plans to summit Cotopaxi, at 19,348 feet the world's tallest active volcano. She got some bad food in Quito and went down for the count for an all-night vomiting session. When dawn broke, Brittany noticed that her vision was blurry; in fact, she couldn't read the clock. She had been taking Diamox for altitude sickness, so she thought perhaps the blurry vision and nausea were from the drug, not bad food. She stopped the Diamox, but couldn't go on the first hike. Within another twenty-four hours, her vision was back to normal and she rejoined the class.

Brittany was determined to learn the self-arrest technique, rappelling, rope management, navigation, roped glacier travel, and ice-climbing techniques. Her class did an acclimatization hike to 14,100 feet, and the next day, with eight male climbers and a couple of male instructors, Britt climbed to the glacier at Cayambe. At midnight on February 28, they left to summit Cotopaxi. The twelve-hour climb became an ice climb as the weather took a turn for the worse. Meanwhile, I went for a bike ride at the beach, braked too hard, and flew over the handlebars, breaking my arm. Brittany and I saw the irony in this.

Mina met Britt in Guayllabamba, Ecuador, where they hiked another active volcano before heading to Galápagos National Park. My daughter was euphoric about this leg of the trip, which was such a switch from the terror of the ice climbing. She summed it up on Facebook.

Our Galapagos trip was AMAZING! Swam and played with dozens of friendly sea lions, snorkeled with giant sea turtles, saw giant 100 year old tortoises, marine iguanas, blue footed boobies, and woke up to blue skies and water everyday [sic]. It's a beautiful world.

Back in the States, Brittany visited us and then went out for St. Patty's Day with Mina and Colette. She talked a lot about wanting to get a Great Dane. *Of course,* I thought, it would need to be an extremely large dog.

When she returned, Britt had to adjust to being home alone most of the day. She volunteered to teach an English-as-a-second-language class at the local library, and she also volunteered at the humane society. I knew that Britt was not easy to live with, and that Dan was very busy with the remodel. What none of us knew was that by this time Brittany had a deeply rooted brain tumor that was about nine years old.

On April 9 Brittany purchased a Great Dane puppy. Charley was an adorable, wrinkled, blue-gray Dane with every allergy known to mankind. He was also a picky eater, so Brittany tried various foods and coaxed him to eat from her hand. Deciding to take a break from the construction zone, she rented a cabin at a nearby lake for two weeks. Dan's parents drove out to visit her, and a friend visited the cabin to keep her company.

In mid-July, Britt flew to visit Mina. In August she flew to Southern California to visit Maudie, and I drove to Santa Monica one evening so we could go to dinner. In

September, Brittany was back on the flying trapeze with a friend, and planning to do a white shark cage dive off the coast of California. Gary and I were very worried. Our daughter had just spent a good portion of the first year of her marriage traveling and away from home. It didn't seem to bode well for the newlyweds.

Brittany took a part-time tutoring job with a company near her home. She was making a difference with children again, and that gave her a sense of fulfillment.

In October, I flew up to spend some time with her. While hiking in Redwood Regional Park, we came upon many thousands of ladybugs. Brittany and I watched in amazement as they converged for their winter hibernation. When Britt was a little girl, I'd always told her that if a ladybug landed on her, it would bring her good luck. On this day my beautiful girl was surrounded by ladybugs, and I hoped that they were blessing her with a happy marriage and children. That moment will live in my mind forever.

Brittany had been to see a neurologist about her on-again, off-again headaches. At first we'd thought that they were from allergies, or maybe the remodel had stirred up some toxin that she was reacting to. But now the house was all put back together, and still she had these terrible headaches. The doctor had told her that sometimes women stopped having headaches after they had children.

On November 1, I was so concerned after a sad phone call from Brittany that I wrote her a very heartfelt email. My daughter seemed depressed and unhappy, and I advised her to seek professional help.

Brittany was not open to my suggestion; indeed, my comments had offended her, and she retorted that she didn't need professional help. She was right about one thing. She didn't need to be treated for depression; she needed treatment for a giant malignant brain tumor. No one — least of all Brittany — knew that her moods, quick temper, unhappiness, and headaches were side effects of a tumor.

Britt started ordering locally grown organic produce. She was eating as healthily as possible, hoping to alleviate the headaches. She planned to celebrate her twenty-ninth birthday in San Francisco. She booked a hotel and massages for Dan and herself, and planned to meet some friends for dinner and see a documentary.

On November 18, the eve of her birthday,

I posted a baby picture and wrote this on Facebook:

At about 10:00 in the evening on November the 18th in 1984 I went to the hospital in Anaheim, California. My baby wasn't due until Dec 17th. Turns out — the doctor told me — it's happening now. I watched the operating room clock. At about 10 minutes after midnight, they held up my daughter. Brittany Lauren.

Before she was conceived . . . I wanted her. Before she was born . . . I loved her. Within seconds of seeing her face . . . I would've died if it meant saving her life. That feeling remains the same today.

This miracle happened to me. I am forever grateful.

The birthday weekend seemed to go well, because Brittany posted a happy message on Facebook.

Thank you friends and family for all of the warm birthday messages! I am very grateful to be entering this final year of my 20's beside my hard working, smart, funny, and loving husband, Dan. We are blessed to be supported by our wonderful family and amazing friends both near and far. We

455

couldn't ask for better parents in Deborah, Gary, Carmen, and Evaristo. Feeling truly grateful for all of the blessings and opportunities the past 28 years of life has brought forth . . . and looking forward to 29.

I flew up again to see Brittany after her birthday, then she returned to Southern California with me. On November 21, after a surprising rain shower, there was a gorgeous rainbow. I pulled over to photograph what I thought was a sign of God's promise to me that my child, my one and only girl, was at last going to be well and happy. I thanked God for that promise, and later I posted the photos and these words:

Have your [sic] ever prayed about something and then God answered. We don't get these often here in Carlsbad, CA. And God, I got the message — loud and clear.

Britt helped me move my father from assisted living care, where he was semi-independent, to memory care, where doors were locked and the caregiving to resident ratio was much lower, and helped me turn a fairly institutional-looking room into an inviting home. She also spent time with Mina, her "sister that life gave her."

When Brittany returned home, she was still having headaches. I sent her an early Christmas package of warm pajamas and other goodies to try to cheer her up. In the meantime, I was extra-involved with my father as he adjusted to his more confined life on the memory care wing.

In mid-December, Brittany said that she was having insomnia and difficulty sleeping. She was planning on hosting us for the holidays at her house and wanted to have a white-elephant gift exchange. I decided that I would win this gift exchange challenge by finding the most loathsome gift of all.

On December 11 Brittany was over the moon with excitement because she had ordered a Jeep. She would make monthly payments from her tutoring salary because her personal money was depleted from travel and the wedding.

When Gary and I arrived at Britt and Dan's, she had made her home a Christmas wonderland. She made a beautiful and delicious Christmas Eve dinner, and afterward we played games. The next morning she had a full breakfast ready when everyone got up. We felt pampered and loved. The smell of cinnamon buns in the air was a strange and wonderful role reversal for me.

I don't remember Brittany complaining of

a headache at all over the holiday. She was a gracious vision of Christmas delight. I watched Dan walking around with Bella the beagle in his arms, showing her this and that. I dreamed of grandchildren, and Brittany and I joked about what they would call me. We settled on "Mimi," although Brittany thought the name was absurd. "What's wrong with Grandma?" she asked.

I smiled, knowing that I'd answer to whatever a little one called me.

Dan and Britt were going away for a couple of days for the New Year to Healdsburg, California. I thought perhaps they would get pregnant.

It was a lovely, relaxed Christmas. The promise of a new year, potential grandchildren, and a happy, more settled marriage for Britt danced like sugarplums in my head.

29
I WANT HER BACK

*October 25–November 1, 2014,
the Last Days Before Britt's Death*

"Yes, Mother," she says simply, embracing
me. "I can see you are flawed. You have
not hidden it. That is your greatest gift to
me."

— Alice Walker,
Possessing the Secret of Joy

When I got back to my own bed in California on October 25, I crawled under the covers in a fetal position and slept.

When I woke up, it was midmorning. I
had slept for over fourteen hours.

Gary fielded angry text messages from
Brittany.

"Where's Mom?" she demanded.

My husband told me it was best that I not
read the messages.

"What could hurt me more than what

459

already happened?" I asked.

"Well, for starters, she wrote that next time you ask someone to hit you, to expect it to be harder. She only used a fraction of her strength this time."

I held my stomach, thinking I might be sick. "And?"

Gary sighed. "And, you are not invited to the funeral. It is invitation only."

"And?" I insisted.

"Deb. Stop." My husband held me in his arms.

In a few days, my daughter was going to take a prescription and die. I thought about the fact that in spite of all she and I had been through together in the last twenty-nine years, Brittany had said I was a "fucking selfish cunt." I cried ceaselessly. I cried while drinking, eating, showering. The well of tears was bottomless, and the act of crying was something I didn't even think about. I cried when Gary took me to the doctor's office, I cried at the pharmacy while they filled a prescription, and I cried while I put a tiny white pill between my lips and swallowed it. Then I slept again.

When I woke up, Gary tried to talk to me. "Deb, this is going to be just like when Brittany said you hadn't knocked mothering out of the ballpark, and you made her a memory photo book based around that very theme. She didn't get it. She didn't remember saying anything about baseball."

"I think she needed to cut the cord," I said. "I think she chopped at everything that bound us together. She's already left me. I don't think she wants me there."

"Maybe you shouldn't be there," Gary said. "Maybe it would be easier for Brittany if you weren't there. Have you thought about that?"

Those words, heavy with pain — Gary's pain, my pain, and Brittany's pain — made me realize that I had to be with my daughter, no matter what. But I didn't know how I could experience her leaving, her passage, and not scream and cry. "I don't want to hear people crying," Brittany had said repeatedly, looking specifically at me.

How would I stop myself from slapping the cup out of her hand, as I'd once slapped a syringe out of her hand as a child when she'd picked the filthy thing up at the beach? How I could refrain from knocking the poison all over the room — I didn't know. How could I keep myself from getting down on my knees and begging her not to drink it? How could I keep from grabbing it and downing it myself? I wanted to

461

know why I couldn't go instead of my girl who still had so much life to live.

I wanted to let go of this burden of loss and pain and grief. I wanted to escape. Run until I couldn't breathe. Run until my heart burst for lack of oxygen. Run into the ocean with stones sewn into my pockets and let the water pull me down.

If I could have struck a deal with Satan himself to keep my daughter with me, I was selfish enough to do it. I would take care of her, read to her, help her to the toilet, give her endless massages, if she could just stay here on earth with me.

I texted Brittany. I asked her to forgive me for the times that I might have caused her pain or let her down. I told her that I was grateful for the gift of being her mother, and that I was thankful that as a parent I had learned so much from her. Finally, I told her that I forgave her for hitting me and calling me horrible names.

I told her that I would be returning to Portland on October 30, and that I would promise not to cry if she wanted me to be with her at the time of her death. I wish I'd said that one does not cry tears of sadness, only tears of joy, when a caterpillar morphs into a butterfly. I wish I'd been that wise.

While I was curled up in a fetal ball in my

bed or crying endlessly, Brittany took a walk with Dan and her friends, and had another seizure in the woods. She fell to the ground among the trees she loved so much, and jerked and shook. She also had more uncontrolled rage. This time the target was the New York film director and the nonprofit who'd released the YouTube video. Brittany was furious because she felt they'd cut and spliced the film taken on October 13 and 14 so that it seemed like she was changing her mind about the day she would die. To make this worse, one of the top networks took the video and spun it out with a headline something along the lines of "Terminally Ill Brittany Maynard Changes Her Mind."

Brittany completely lost all control, raging at Dan, her friends, and various people on the phone.

In Southern California, I naïvely thought that they might be trying to protect Brittany by misleading the media to keep them away from the yellow house on the day she planned to die.

When I came back to Portland on October 30, two days before her planned death on November 1, Brittany was still upset about this misleading release of information.

We went for a walk on October 31. We

were a party of eight people and two dogs. I studied the dogs' soulful eyes. Did they know they were about to lose their momma? I think they did. Brittany wrapped her arm around my waist and told me that she was glad I was there. She said, "I just could not apologize, Momma."

"Nothing to worry about, love." I put my arm around her, and we walked a short distance together in this way.

Britt wanted a night out on the town, so Dan, Gary, and I hosted Brittany, three of her friends, and my dear friend Sherri for dinner in downtown Portland. It was surreal. A last meal out on the town was too much like a prisoner's last meal before execution. How does one step out of the shock, denial, dread, and fear, and "be there" at the dinner of a child who will be dying the next day? It was an out-of-body experience. I simply wasn't there.

November 1 was a mild day for Portland. Gary and I joined the six young people staying at the house. Some people were gathered around the table having brunch. After breakfast, we went for a walk. Yes, my child walked through the woods on the day that she chose to slip the bonds of this earth.

Did Brittany take no medication, less medication, more medication, or a different combination of medications in those last hours of her life? Or was she perhaps simply blessed with equanimity before death? My sweet girl marveled at nature's beauty as a group of friends and family wandered with her through trees that were over a hundred years old. We switched places by her side, rotating in and out, everyone longing to be close to her. Tranquil and serene, on the razor's edge of death, Brittany took in the loveliness of her last day. To decide to notice beauty, to decide to be the most that she could be — and then to leave before everything that defined her was diminished — made Brittany the bravest and most intelligent woman I have ever known. As I walked next to her, I told her that if she wasn't ready, it didn't need to be today. It could be tomorrow. Or another day.

"No, it will be today. People need to get back home on Sunday. I'll be ready later today."

The lump in my throat was so big that it was almost impossible to swallow. "Okay, darling." I allowed Gary to take my spot next to Brittany, and I hung back and walked with Amber for a while.

Brittany had been very specific about how she wanted her death to be, who she wanted in the room with her, where she wanted them to be, and what she wanted to hear. Britt was especially worried that she might lose consciousness and yet be able to hear us for some time afterward. She specifically instructed us not to weep, make sad noises, or discuss her dying until everyone was sure that she had expired.

She selected poems written by Mary Oliver, her favorite poet, to be read to her in the minutes after she ingested the medicine.

When we returned to the house, a hundred capsules were being broken open at the dining room table, and the powder was collected in a small glass. What little bit of hell it must have been to handle the medication. I hurried past, not wanting to see. I was grateful that I didn't have to do it.

Brittany was propped up high on pillows in her four-poster bed, writing cards. She handed me a card. I left the room to read it. This is the last thing my daughter wrote to me with her beautiful tapered fingers. The last thoughts that she shared with me.

On the front of the card, there was nothing but the following quote:

It's not the years in your life that count, it's the life in your years.
> — Abraham Lincoln

Inside the card, she had penned these words:

The quote on the cover of this card makes me think of the wooden sign in our Portland kitchen. They are words I truly believe to be true. Mom, I don't have enough words to tell you how much I love you, how much of a huge loss we are suffering. Thank you for being such a wonderful mother. I love you with every cell in my body. I would do anything to make this pain go away and rewind life . . . but that is not possible. So here we are coping like the strong, smart, caring women and family we are. MORE THAN ANYTHING I want you to be able to feel this pain but then let it go, travel, love Gary, seize each day of beauty on this gorgeous earth. I will find some way to be watching down on you.

I will smile as your plane touches down in Peru.

Love with every fiber inside me, your
daughter
Britt

I wrote something for Brittany. I returned to her room and handed the note to her. People were carrying chairs into the room and talking in the background. In the note, I told her that I would find her . . . her light . . . that I'd know her spirit anywhere. I signed it "Godspeed." Brittany read my note and carefully placed it in a giant Ziploc bag of cards and notes from friends and family. She looked at me quizzically and patted the area behind her on the bed. "Here, Momma."

I realized that this meant that I would have to sit with her pillow and head on my lap or chest as she died. She had talked before about Dan and me being on either side of her on the bed when she died. But Brittany wasn't in the middle of the bed. I think my daughter was asking me to get behind her in a straddle birthing position, because the nightstand would have prevented me from having my legs to the side. I think she wanted her head on my chest. Maybe she thought it would be better not to see my face? I had never thought this through.

I was not supposed to cry, but if I sat that close to her, she would feel me crying. Even now, I was praying that I could somehow cry silently, not wail loudly.

If I sat that close, I wouldn't be able to shudder, gasp, or tremble, or react in any way as my child left this world. I'd be sitting so close that she would be able to feel me disobeying her repeated order not to cry. I moved my head the tiniest bit, and my eyes must have answered. Brittany busied herself propping more pillows up and just said, "Help me write my goodbye on Facebook."

I nodded yes and pulled my chair a little closer to the bed.

The blinds were open, and the late-afternoon sun shone through them. Five chairs were suddenly filled. Brittany looked around and said, "Where's Gary?"

"You told him he couldn't come," I choked out. "You never said he could be here."

"Go get my dad. We need another chair." Brittany had invited several dear friends to be with her in her last moments. It comforted Britt to know that Maudie, a urologist, would know how to find her pulse and tell the rest of us when it was no longer there.

Brittany wrote a goodbye post on Facebook, reading what she was typing out loud. We all listened.

Goodbye to all my dear friends and family that I love. Today is the day I have chosen to pass away with dignity in the face of my terminal illness, this terrible brain cancer that has taken so much from me . . . but would have taken so much more. Thank you to all those who have without hesitation helped me, been there, a shoulder to cry on (although rarely), it is more often a fellow smile to break into laughter with. The world is a beautiful place, travel has been . . .

Brittany paused.

"My greatest teacher," I said.

Britt nodded, typed, and repeated:

. . . my greatest teacher, my close friends and folks are the greatest givers. I even have a ring of support around my bed as I type. I love you Dan Diaz (my sweet, smart husband), my mother Deborah Ziegler (my selfless, giving example), Gary Holmes (best stepdad ever), . . . Goodbye world. Spread good energy. Pay it forward!

"You are loved, Brittany," I said as she settled her head on her pillow. There was an immediate response of "yes, yes" from others in the room.

Someone brought a small glass with the prescription mixed in water. Brittany took the glass, looked at it briefly, and drank the medication in one prolonged swallow. She grimaced and said it tasted bitter.

She ate a small bite of ice cream and then said, "Wow. This is going to happen fast."

Britt rested her head again on her pillows. "Tell me a good story, babe," she said softly to Dan, who lay on his side next to her. Before Dan could get even two sentences into a story, my daughter settled lower on her pillow and snored once, very deeply. Someone handed me a laptop, and I read several of Mary Oliver's exquisite poems in a shaky voice. I kept reading through tears as if my voice could keep Britt here, keep her with me.

At some point, Maudie, who held Brittany's pulse point, tapped me on the shoulder and whispered, "She's gone. Her heart has stopped."

I set the laptop down and ran to the landing of the stairs outside Brittany's room. I turned in a circle. "No . . . no . . . no . . . ," I said. One of the girls tried to reach out to me. I said, "No. . . . No. . . . No." I ran downstairs and outside into the nearby woods. It had begun to rain gently. My husband followed me. We stood under the shelter of the trees, and he held me as I wept and screamed.

The sky wept. Brittany, my beautiful brave

girl, passed away purposefully and peacefully, just as she planned. Death was kind, graceful even, and spared Brittany a great deal of physical pain and mental anguish. But in this moment, none of that mattered. Because selfishly I wanted her back.

"I . . . WANT . . . HER . . . BACK!" I screamed at the trees, the rain, and the sky. "I want my baby back!"

Gary helped me walk down the short stretch of road to the house. I looked up at the sky once more and climbed into the car. I never went into the little yellow house again.

30
DUST TO DUST

November 2014–October 2015,
the First Year After Britt's Death

No person is your friend who demands your
silence, or denies your right to grow.
— Alice Walker

I don't remember one thing about the day
after Brittany died. Nothing. I know I was
in a hotel. I know Gary and my friend
Sherri were there. I know that, but I don't
remember it. I have no recollection of that
day at all.

On November 3, we flew home. I remember feeling angry that I had to fly so soon
after my child's death. People in the airport
looked as though they were on the other
side of a watery glass pane.

On Nov 4, I posted this on Facebook:

I went to the ocean today and stood on

the end of a jetty. I screamed two words until I was hoarse. "Why?" and "No." The waves crashed back and forth with such regularity that I eventually heard the answers in my heart. "Why not?" and "Yes, it is true . . . she is gone."

The next day I wrote:

All day today I kept thinking, like a child, "I want . . ." I want to spin the earth backward . . . I want my baby back . . . I want to talk to her again . . . I want this to be a bad dream . . . The wanting is endless.

I arranged to continue the therapy I'd started in Oregon for patients who have undergone high stress. It seemed to have a calming and positive effect on my thinking. The eye movement desensitization and reprocessing therapy definitely interrupted the cycle of images that kept replaying in my mind, and allowed me to see where I was stuck in an unhelpful circular thinking pattern.

One of Brittany's friends offered to set up a celebration of her life.

When we went to spread Brittany's ashes in the redwoods, I dropped to my knees in the dirt and scooped a tiny bit of her ash up and held it. My friend Sherri knelt in the dirt with me as Dan sprinkled some of the ashes beneath a stately redwood tree. I read the Mary Oliver quote I'd been asked to read. It was about loving a corporeal being, and letting that earthly life go when the time came.

When I got up to leave, out of the corner of my eye, I saw a red fox darting through the woods, its thick white-tipped tail twitching as it leapt over underbrush, its black-tipped ears swiveling as though it could hear my sobs. I wanted to show Gary and Sherri, but when we looked back, it was gone. Whether I imagined the fox or it was really there, I took comfort from the image.

Our brave niece, Erica, was still fighting for life. She was in the middle of what she called her "everything but the kitchen sink" chemotherapy treatments in Illinois and had already undergone multiple surgeries. Erica was in her thirties, and had two beautiful daughters. "Aunt Deb," she wrote, "I'm going for quantity of life — not quality. I've got girls to raise." (Erica fought valiantly at great personal cost, and thankfully she is living and loving her girls at the writing of this book.) On January 9, Gary's brother had an emergency heart transplant in Dallas (and he is also doing well).

I will never again ask the universe, "What

more can happen? How much more can this family take?" I keep those words locked in my throat, or at worst jammed behind clenched teeth. When life falls apart, sometimes we cannot solve or surmount the problem. Sometimes the falling apart is not our problem to solve. Sometimes when we feel that we "deserve" an answer, that we "deserve" a miracle, we make everything worse for ourselves and others who are hurting.

When the ground shakes beneath us, when answers evade us, when we hold out hope when there is none, we rob ourselves of the moments that we do have left. If I could do anything again, it would be to try to have more of those seconds, minutes, and hours with Brittany where we both quietly accepted the script that life had given us and just softly lived with that knowledge. When we just looked about ourselves and soaked in the beauty around us in those precious instants of time that we were given, instead of wasting precious life with worry, terror, and false hope.

I'm amazed and proud that we were able to grasp any of the love and joy in her season of death. It is only because of my daughter's brilliance, stubbornness, and wisdom that we did. She planned the last months of her life. She tried valiantly to experience times of harmony and beauty in the midst of fear and terror. She requested that we visit places in nature that would allow us to get used to the idea of her death and would provide a distraction so we could focus on texture, color, light, and movement. We could feel flashes of unadulterated joy. All of this was possible because of the Death with Dignity law in Oregon. We were able to appreciate some respite from the never-ending thoughts of death because Brittany had a plan. She had options that made her feel safe enough to enjoy some parts of her remaining days. Without this law, we wouldn't even have had those fleeting moments of peace.

In this time of mourning, the wonder of Brittany's determination did not escape me. Even with a giant tumor, in the face of death, she was able to do such careful planning. I marveled at her resolve, her fortitude, her capacity for understanding — even as her brain was being altered by both disease and medication.

Only two days after Brittany's death, the Vatican's top ethicist, Monsignor Ignacio Carrasco de Paula, condemned my daughter's death. "Assisted suicide is a reprehensible absurdity," said the man from a religion my family didn't adhere to, who knew nothing of my daughter's diagnosis or struggle. "Brittany Maynard's gesture is in itself to be condemned . . ." Ignacio said to Ansa, the Italian news agency. Then on Saturday, November 15, Pope Francis threw out his two cents' worth, saying that the right to die movement was a "false sense of compassion" and a sin against God and creation.

This was a tipping point for me. It wasn't just the Catholics; other religious institutions had made inappropriate, cruel, and harsh statements about Brittany's choice. I wrote a general response:

I am Brittany Maynard's mother. I am writing in response to a variety of comments made in the press and online by individuals and institutions that have tried to impose their personal belief system on what Brittany and our family feel is a human rights issue.

The imposition of "belief" on a human rights issue is wrong. To censure a personal choice as reprehensible because it does not comply with someone else's belief is immoral. My twenty-nine-year-old daughter's choice to die gently rather than suffer physical and mental degradation and intense pain does not deserve to be labeled as reprehensible by strangers a continent away who do not know her or the particulars of her situation.

"Reprehensible" is a harsh word. It means: "very bad; deserving very strong criticism." Reprehensible is a word I've used as a teacher to describe the actions of Hitler, other political tyrants, and the exploitation of children by pedophiles. As Brittany Maynard's mother, I find it difficult to believe that anyone who knew her would ever select this word to describe her actions. Brittany was a giver. She was a volunteer. She was a teacher. She was an advocate. She worked at making the world a better place to live.

This word was used publically at a time when my family was tender and freshly wounded. Grieving. Such strong public criticism from people we do not know, have never met — is more than a slap in the face. It is like kicking us as we struggle to draw a breath.

People and institutions that feel they have the right to judge Brittany's choices may wound me and cause me unspeakable pain, but they do not deter me from supporting my daughter's choice. There is currently a great deal of confusion and arrogance standing in the way of Americans going gently into the good night. I urge Americans to think for themselves. Make your wishes clear while you are competent. Make sure that you have all the options spelled out for you if you are diagnosed with an incurable, debilitating, painful disease. Do your own research. Ask your family to research and face the harsh reality with you. Ask your doctor to be brutally honest with you. Then make your personal choice about how you will proceed. It is YOUR choice.

The "culture of cure" has led to a fairy-tale belief that doctors can always fix our problems. We have lost sight of reality. All life ends. Death is not necessarily the enemy in all cases. Sometimes a gentle passing is a gift. Misguided doctors caught up in an aspirational belief that they must extend life, whatever the cost, cause individuals and families unnecessary suffering. Brittany stood up to bullies. She never thought anyone else had the right to tell her how long she should suffer. The right to die for the terminally ill is a human rights issue. Plain and simple.

Debbie Ziegler
Brittany's Momma

The letter was read in its entirety on *The Last Word with Lawrence O'Donnell* on MSNBC. Then other media sources picked up the story. The message must have struck a chord with some people. Headlines with words like "Mother Lashes Out at Vatican" or "Mother Delivers Sharp Response to Vatican" spun the story further.

On November 18, the day before what would have been my daughter's thirtieth birthday, my sister Sarah and I decided to get tattoos in honor of Brittany. They would be on the instep of our right feet and say, "Be soft." Mine would have Brittany's birth date, and Sarah's would have the day of her passing. It was our way of honoring Brittany.

I had to remind myself every day not to let Brittany's death harden me and turn me into a bitter woman. I knew that she wouldn't want me to let losing her destroy my love for the beauty of the world.

Sarah came again with her husband and daughter for Christmas. Christmas without Brittany. It seemed all the joy had been sucked out of the holiday. Brittany, who only last year had decorated her house to the nines, was so very, very missing. My child had chosen three Christmas gifts for me before she died. I opened them, and then ran into the hall to lie on the floor and cry.

The first gift was a pair of shoes with "live your dream" printed on them. Brittany wrote a note with the shoes, telling me that she hoped that I'd wear them to Machu Picchu one day. The other gift was a long, soft pink shawl. Woven into the fabric was white lettering that said, "Dear Mom, I love you more than words can express. Your love and devotion has made me who I am today. Thank you for not only being my mother but also my friend. I feel so proud and blessed to call you MOM. I love you today, tomorrow and forever! XOXO, Me."

The third gift that Brittany selected took a while for me to understand and accept with joy. She ordered one year of "fruit of the month" to be delivered to Gary and me. The first time I found a box of fruit on the porch, when I saw that it was from her, I dropped to my knees. Inside the box, nestled in separate compartments, were pears from Oregon. Our trip along the Columbia River Gorge came rushing back to me. Each pear was huge, and one of the nine pears was wrapped in gold. They looked like giant pink-tinged tears. The fruit inside was so juicy, you could eat it with a spoon. I couldn't swallow the fruit. It was still too alive with her touch. My girl didn't want to be forgotten — as if that were possible. Her gifts stretched forward into the future, bringing her love in such a tangible way to my door every month.

From mid-January onward, Gary and I did what we could to testify on behalf of California's proposed End of Life Option Act, drafted and championed by two amazing Californians, Senator Lois Wolk and Senator Bill Monning. We donated money and time to the cause.

In March, I did several newspaper interviews, one with a doctor who'd lost his daughter the long and hard way to cancer. I also testified in Sacramento before the Senate Health Committee. It was on this trip that I met a new friend. Her name was Christy O'Donnell, and she was at the capitol with her beautiful daughter, Bailey. We liked each other immediately. Christy was an attorney, former police officer, and a single mom. She and I both had given birth to one and only one beloved child. We both had one daughter. Our situations were reversed, but in a sense the same.

Over dinner, Christy expressed the thought that we were both being separated from our daughters by cancer: in my case, cancer had taken my child; in her case, her own cancer would steal her life.

Over the next year, Christy and I would grow very close as I moved through grief and grew stronger, and while she grew weaker and died. We testified together, picketed for "death with dignity" together, took Bailey to high tea, went for massages and facials. As Christy grew more and more ill, I took my father's old wheelchair up for her to use, and then arranged for a special hot air balloon ride for her over the vineyards of Temecula.

I cleaned her house, brought her food, and at the very end, I sat on her bed and fed her. Our friendship had been encouraged by a kindhearted reporter, and to this day, I can never thank Nicki at *People* magazine enough for suggesting that Christy and I had the makings of a forever friendship.

I think Christy held out a flicker of hope that she would benefit from the legislation she campaigned so hard for, but in her heart she knew that in all likelihood she would die before the law was enacted. (She died on February 6, 2016, at age forty-seven, about four months before the End of Life Option Act went into effect on June 9.) Christy was a dignified woman, and she and I had discussed that all death, no matter the path we must take, is in some way dignified because death is in and of itself a sacred passage. Even a soldier who cries for his mother as he dies on the battlefield is dignified. In the end this thought was of little comfort because Christy shared with me repeatedly that if she were legally able, she would choose to use medical aid in dying, rather than suffer the terrible seizures and loss of autonomy that she experienced in the end.

Christy told me that the greatest compliment I ever gave her was when I said she gave me a glimpse of what Brittany might have been like at Christy's age. The two of them were so wickedly smart, funny, and strong.

In May, the California Medical Association changed their position about the End of Life Option Act. Christy and I were overjoyed to hear that they admitted that sometimes medical discoveries and excellent medical care weren't enough for the terminally ill. They left the decision to be made between the doctor and the patient, removing their objection to patients seeking end-of-life options. This was an important day, and I felt Brittany's powerful energy all around me.

On June 4, Gary and I were in Sacramento

again with a photo of Brittany when the California Senate passed the legislation. We met with reporters after the vote. It was an emotional day for everyone, and I knew Brittany would have been proud.

For the last two weeks of June, I'd planned a surprise for my niece Erica. We were taking her and her family to the redwoods, staying in San Francisco for a few days, and then driving down the coast of California, ending up in Carlsbad. I knew that Brittany would have loved every detail of the trip. I felt her energy and blessings for her cousin as I planned it. While in the redwoods, we got a call to drop everything and come to the capitol for testimony for the House of Representatives.

Before Gary and I rented a car and drove the seven hours to Sacramento, we had a blissful day with our niece among some of the oldest redwoods in California. We found a momma redwood scarred from fires. She was bumpy and hollowed out a bit, but still standing — reaching skyward, green and beautiful. Erica was hollowed out from her fight with cancer, and my heart had a huge Brittany-shaped hole in it. As we looked up at this tree's branches, we both drew strength as we studied burls and scars of a tree that had survived hundreds of years.

I would need to remember this tree because on this trip to Sacramento, one of California's representatives told me that there was "beauty in suffering." I was so taken aback, I could hardly speak.

When I could stammer out an answer, I said, "I can assure you that Brittany's suffering was *not* beautiful. There was nothing beautiful about it." What I really wanted to do was plant my high heel in the middle of the representative's forehead about an inch deep and then say, "Here, I want you to have a beautiful day. Isn't suffering great?" The bill stalled out in the Assembly Health Committee, and Gary and I flew back to meet our family for the rest of the vacation.

In July, Gary and I went to British Columbia for my birthday. Grief hit me hard, making it difficult to breathe. I kept thinking that I shouldn't be having more birthdays, if my daughter couldn't. Grief is not kind or rational. Grief is not careful about timing. Grief can ebb and flow. You can become complacent thinking that the worst is over, and wham! Grief will knock the air out of you. You drop to your knees. You feel grief tugging at your insides, twisting them, ripping them out of your body.

We stayed on a farm. Sarah, her husband, and her daughter joined us there. There

were figs everywhere. We picked fresh raspberries, blackberries, and blueberries. My
sister baked the figs with cheese and drizzled
local honey over them and sprinkled them
with roasted bits of walnut. She made a
berry cobbler. Brittany had left me three
gifts for my birthday. I simply couldn't open
them. I needed to keep the brightly wrapped
packages until another time. I would know
when it was right.

When we returned, I was vacuuming our
sofa, and I pulled off the cushions. A silver
bracelet that I'd bought Brittany glimmered
in the sunlight. The bracelet said, "Live in
the moment." You can call it what you want:
Chance. Luck. Coincidence. I called it
"grace."

More and more, as I grieved, I gravitated
to something C. S. Lewis wrote. He said essentially that we are souls. We don't possess
a soul; instead, we are souls that briefly possess a body. I began to feel that human beings are energy, light, and love. This thought
was bigger than anything I'd learned at a
church. Yes, there was an eternal quality to
this new truth I was feeling, but it wasn't at
all about heaven or hell. It wasn't about
angels with wings or streets paved in gold.
It was much bigger than all of those childhood teachings.

In August, Brittany sent me peaches. I opened the ninth box of fruit from my daughter. All these painful months later, I could now put the fruit to my mouth and eat. Each succulent bite was like a sacrament, an act of love. Eating a peach from Brittany was like taking her love inside me, swallowing joy and light and love. She was sending me what I needed to write our story, my precious peach of a girl. I would draw energy and love through the velvety surface, the fuzzy skin with the golden flesh that melted in my mouth. The peaches reminded me of warm days and sunbleached branches.

One day as I was writing this book, it began thundering, lightning, and raining. Not a great coincidence to some, except that I live in Southern California, where we were in the middle of a long drought. No area was feeling this severe drought more than San Diego. We could go for months, even years, without lightning.

It was rare enough that I stopped writing and went outside. I stood faceup toward the sky. I smelled the rain and the thirsty earth, and I got soaking wet. I whispered to the rain, "Brittany." I didn't want the storm to end, but it lasted only a few minutes.

I hadn't danced in the rain, but afterward I wished I had. I recalled the time when Brittany was little and I took her hand and we danced in the rain in our backyard. But on the day I wrote this, she was gone, and there was no dance left in me. I just let the sweet rain pour down and mix with my tears. I promised my daughter that I'd dance the next time.

The week of September 7 was a tense one as Christy, Gary, and I urged representatives in Sacramento to pass the End of Life Option Act. On September 9 the bill passed in the House after a moving message from one of its authors, Susan Talamantes Eggman. The Senate passed it on September 11. We were exhausted but hopeful. The bill now needed to go before California's governor.

Christy and I marched on the governor's office in Los Angeles. Katie Couric had a crew filming some of our work together. Christy was failing, and knew that the bill would never pass in time for her to utilize it. My friend reminded me so much of Brittany near the end. It was like their life flames quickened for days and weeks as they exuded energy and purpose in their dying moments. I had seen this in Brittany, and marveled that many people are driven by a goal tougher than their cancer or illness, and that cause gives them resolve and perseverance until the very end.

On October 5, 2015, Governor Jerry Brown signed the End of Life Option Bill, which to me was "Brittany's Bill." Gary and I wrote letters to Governor Brown and had them delivered by overnight express.

In an extraordinary signing message, the governor touched my heart. Governor Brown had clearly searched his conscience, and consulted with experts and religious leaders. He had even spoken with Archbishop Desmond Tutu. In the end, the governor understood why terminally ill people would be comforted by having options. I admired him for his courageous decision. I would like to give him a hug, straight from Brittany. She'd had an opportunity to speak to him before she passed away, about how much harder it made everything about dying to have to leave your home and friends and move to a different state.

Although glad about the bill's passing, I was emotionally wrung out, and dreading the one-year anniversary of Brittany's death. I told Gary that there was only one place on the planet that I thought I might be able to draw in oxygen on that day: Machu Picchu, where Brittany had asked me to meet her.

I experienced several terrible crying jags. After a particularly bad one, my husband took me in his arms. I could feel how badly he wanted me to come back to him. I could feel his unwavering love in the way he cradled my head and the quaver in his voice when he said he would make Machu Picchu happen.

And he did.

EPILOGUE:
MACHU PICCHU

*November 1, 2015, Exactly One Year
to the Day After Brittany's Death*

It's one thing to feel that you are on the right path, but it's another to think that yours is the only path.

— Paulo Coelho

Somewhere a noise nudged me awake, softly at first, along the edges of my awareness, then more insistently. *What was it?* I struggled to surface. My throat felt a bit tickly and my eyes itched. *Where was I?* Ah, the smell of an indoor fire gave it away. Thanks to the compassion and generosity of a Peruvian hotelier, I was in a casita at Inkaterra Hotel. The noise I heard was rain, and it was stirring up smoke fumes in my fireplace.

Our hosts had met us in Lima, taken us

out to eat among ancient ruins, given us a detailed guide on how to catch the plane, train, taxi, and bus that we would need to take to the tiny town of Aguas Calientes. These two beautiful women understood that this was much more than a vacation. Kindness shone from their eyes as they recounted how they had seen Britt's YouTube video, where they first heard about my daughter's request for me to meet her in Machu Picchu after she passed. They had looked at each other and said in unison, "We can make this happen." And so it was that a Peruvian hotelier gave us not just shelter, but the kind of welcome and attention that allowed healing. We came to them in broken jagged pieces. They handled us with kid gloves.

The steady thrumming on the roof tiles grew louder, then softer as the rain came in waves. I fell back against the pillows and reached for my watch. It was 4:05 a.m., the hour we'd originally planned on getting up to leave for Machu Picchu. I pulled my thick comforter up around my neck and snuggled deeper into the pillows. I was glad we'd decided to tackle the mountain midday, as our guide had suggested, but if the rain continued, I had brought the proper boots, hat, and slicker. Nothing was keeping me away from Brittany. I fell back to sleep smiling.

By the time we met Carmela, our guide, the rain was nothing but a sprinkle. Carmela smiled. "It rained hard from four until seven a.m. The early risers had a rough trip up the mountain. I called it right this time."

We'd spent about ten minutes the evening before explaining what we hoped to accomplish among the ruins of the Lost City of the Incas. It would be up to Carmela to intuit when to talk and offer information, and when to hang back and let us commune with our daughter. Clearly she understood that this was not an ordinary tour.

As we walked down the terraced hills on a winding stone pathway, we saw six different types of hummingbirds. These tiny, joyful birds, wings whirring, seemed always to appear when I was missing Brittany the most. Sweeping down for bites of bananas tied to the limbs of a tree, blue-and-black tanagers caused sudden showers of rain from the waxy green leaves. Growing low and lush were milky white orchids. We walked past a waterfall and heard the rushing Vilcanota River somewhere below. We trudged on in the light rain through the narrow streets of Aguas Calientes.

Soon we clambered aboard a packed bus

for the ride up the mountain. The road was narrow, with almost vertical drops plunging down into the Vilcanota Valley. The bus had to pull to the side when meeting another bus coming the opposite way. During the ride I caught glimpses of pink and orange orchids in the Rain Cloud Forest, called Wiñay Wayna, which means "forever young." At one point in her illness, Brittany had said that the only good thing about dying was that she'd never get wrinkles; she would be forever young.

When the bus pulled to a stop, we headed for the entrance and the self-stamp station for our passports. The stamp is brag-worthy, and I know Brittany was proud of hers. It is a drawing of the lost city and the mountains in the background. The sound of the stamp — "Parque Arqueologico Nacional De MACHU PICCHU Nov 1, 2015" — exactly one year from Brittany's death, marked my commitment to meet her here.

We pushed through turnstiles and began our odyssey. The vegetation was exotic and shrouded the citadel, a true lost city when Hiram Bingham stumbled upon the ruins in the early 1900s with the aid of a peasant. Carmela pointed to the crowds in this area of the city. "I know a very sacred spot on the way up that is not heavily visited. You may find a connection there in privacy."

"I read that the Intihuatana stone, or solar clock, is full of energy. That if you put your forehead on the stone, you can feel it. Would that be a good place?" I huffed and puffed as I tried to speak while climbing the steep steps.

"We will go to the Intihuatana, but you may be disappointed. You will not be allowed to touch the stone. There is a guard and it is roped off. Also, that is a busy place here. There is no privacy. But I am taking you to a special place. It is on the trail to the sun gate, but it's a much more private spot. It is the place where they found the bones of a young Incan girl and her dog who were buried here during the 1400s."

I shivered.

"Brittany loved her dogs so much," I commented as we followed Carmela's compact khaki-clad form up the worn stone steps. I shuddered again, thinking it was likely that at some point I would step exactly where Brittany had trod on these narrow winding trails. There was an eerie sense of how many people had stepped on these stones, wearing them into a cup shape.

"I think you will like this spot," Carmela said. "I thought carefully last night about where you might be able to feel enough quiet and peace to enter into the mysterious communication we're capable of on this sacred mountain."

The stones of the trail and the buildings seemed almost alive, as if they could speak. The Incas were expert stone builders, using a type of construction called "ashlar" in which stones fit together so perfectly that not even a knife blade can fit between them, and no mortar was used.

We took lots of rest breaks, during which I looked out at the terraced slopes. Sixty percent of the engineering of the terracing and the city was underground, an elaborate drainage system that insured that the city would live forever, even on steep slopes with seventy-seven inches a year of rain.

As I climbed, it never crossed my mind that Brittany might not be here. I simply knew with certainty that she would meet me. My daughter and I had always gone out of our way to keep our promises to each other, both big and small.

After climbing for forty-five minutes, we stopped at a large overhanging rock. In front of the huge boulder was a low terraced wall, with four steps in the middle.

"This is where they found the young girl's bones," Carmela said. "She was holding her dog."

I climbed the steps and searched the face of the wall. I found an oval tipped at a slight angle, like the shape of a face in the stone. I turned, and Gary took me in his arms. We were both vibrating. I heard a sob, something I'd never heard before from my husband.

"Do you feel it?" I asked him.

"I do," he said.

"She's here." Turning from him, I tried to hug the wall of rock.

You can love me lightly. Momma, you don't have to hold so tightly. My daughter's voice was kind, loving, and slightly bemused. I pulled one arm away and then the other, until only the tip of my pointer finger touched the stone. She was right. I felt her all around me just as strongly as when I'd tried to embrace the rock.

We are one. Her voice bubbled in my head, sounding happy and content. *We are love. I am in you, and you are in me.*

This was not a thought I'd ever contemplated. I'd thought about mankind, how we all cry, laugh, bleed, but I'd never thought of us being one. I'd definitely navigated my way through life as a separate, individual, even lonely being, and if ever there was a girl who was independent, separate, and autonomous, it was my daughter. Now

Brittany was telling me that we were one? Intuitively I knew she was talking about a collective "we," not just mother and daughter.

All is as it should be.

I wanted to scream *"No . . . no . . . no!"* But no words escaped me. I just stood quivering like a drawn bowstring. I felt the energy inside me of the arrow waiting to fly. I wanted resolution. I wanted the answer, but I was unwilling to hear this one.

Gary rustled around in his backpack and pulled out a mysterious cardboard tube. As I stood full of unleashed energy, full of longing, my husband unrolled a banner he'd had made as a surprise for me. "Brittany is here!" was printed boldly in letters two inches tall under a photo of Brittany with me, and another photo of her taken when she was in Peru. As Gary showed me what his love had created, I stood dumbstruck, not moving.

Although tears blinded me, I managed to grab one end of the banner, and we stretched it across the face of the rock. We placed our free hands on the wall, fingers splayed. Carmela discreetly took several photos and simply waited for us to receive what Machu Picchu had to give.

I love you. We are one. You took good care

of me, Momma.

Finally, I turned from the wall. Gary released his end of the sign and gave me a big hug. My husband was soaked with sweat from the climb. He trembled as he held my trembling, and I worried that this experience was just too much for him. "Are you all right?" I asked, my face buried in his shoulder. I felt him nod yes.

As we started away from the wall, Carmela approached and said she'd like to show us something else.

"In Peru, we make little cairns like this called *apuchettas,* meaning 'little mountains.' " She pointed to a pile of balanced stones with leaves strewn on top. "I thought you might like to make an *apuchetta* in honor of your journey to meet your daughter."

As I collected stones and balanced them on top of one another, I felt a deep connection with the earth. I could barely see what I was doing through my tears, but I kept placing the rocks on one another with rapt attention until they balanced. I didn't know it yet, but I was also balancing things inside my soul. There was still a buzz of energy in the air as I balanced stones, engrossed in my task, honoring my daughter. While I built the *apuchetta,* I came to realize that I was also honoring my journey toward accepting and understanding Brittany's death. Placing the stones on top of each other, I felt my burden of grief lighten.

Carmela disappeared for a couple of minutes and returned with a pink begonia in her hand. I placed the blossom on top of my rickety hill of rocks.

I wonder if the stones have fallen by now, and if their falling represented a huge breakthrough in terms of my grief. If so, they must have fallen while I was traveling down the mountain on the bus.

Gary, Carmela, and I spent the rest of the afternoon looking at the amazing Lost City Citadel. Here there were more people, tourists, and classes of students doing tours. Even in the midst of tourists, it was impossible to lose the feeling of mystical spirituality. Carmela explained that Machu Picchu means "old mountain" in Quechua, or the "people's language." It is a mystery how the Incas were able to drag enormous blocks of stone up the mountainside without using wheels and they lacked strong draft animals. Their engineering brilliance dazzled Gary and me as we walked the beautifully paved and well-drained roads of the citadel, and traced the interlocking patterns of the stones with our fingers, feeling how tightly they fit. These walls had withstood disastrous earthquakes in the region. It was clear that the Incas had built this flawless city to last forever.

There was a feeling of perpetuity, of timelessness, that permeated my thinking as I walked the ancient city. We climbed narrow steps while below the white Urubamba River coiled like a snake at the foot of the mountain. Above us, white clouds against a cerulean blue sky came and went, enshrouding the mountaintops. Sometimes we found ourselves in the midst of a cloud, waiting patiently for white water vapor to reconfigure itself so that we could see enough to proceed.

The Intihuatana stone, or "hitching post of the sun," was the highest spot in the citadel, up even another seventy steps. It was also the most desired tourist spot. The stone was roped off, and a guard stood watching to make sure no one touched or climbed on the stone.

We were among the last visitors leaving the park, and the bus to take us down the hill was packed. Gary, Carmela, and I had to share seats with other bus passengers.

I sat down in the first available seat, next to a young girl who collected her things quickly as the bus began to move. The bus was careening around corners. This ride was much more nerve-wracking than the ride up.

As we descended the hill, it felt like Brittany was being ripped away from me again. The pain was equivalent to my memories of birthing contractions. I placed one hand over my stomach and bent forward, tears splashing on my knapsack as I dug for Kleenex. It was impossible for those close to me not to know I was crying. I hid behind sunglasses and cradled my knapsack to my chest. I couldn't stop the tears or the shaking. My mouth soundlessly quivered, chin wobbling and nose running.

This painful process went on for at least half the journey down the hill. The persistent and childish thought I'd had so many times before returned to me. *I want her back. I want my daughter back.* For some reason, this repetitive line of thinking always undid me completely. It was an emotion that harkened back to memories of mothering Brittany through some spectacular toddler meltdowns. That was how childishly strong my wanting was.

I sat blubbering and sniveling, wishing I could stomp my feet, kick wildly, and throw myself on the floor of the bus. I wanted to scream, as toddler Brittany used to scream,

"It isn't fair."

Momma, all is as it should be.

I'd heard Brittany's voice say this twice already in Peru. Once in Lima, looking down from a high-rise at rhythmic gray waves; and earlier today, at the burial site on the mountain. Now I heard it again as I struggled to breathe in the middle of a full-blown anxiety attack. I concentrated on inhaling and exhaling through my mouth, puffing like a pregnant woman in a childbirth class.

We are one. Nothing can separate us. Not spouses. Not friend or foe. You are my forever mother.

I stopped crying because I so badly wanted to understand. "We are one." I mouthed the words.

Yes. Again, she sounded so happy and gently amused. *We are one. We are love.*

I thought how very much I loved her . . . how very much I wanted to be with her . . . how much I didn't want to leave Machu Picchu.

This is a sacred place, and you don't want to leave. But our love is sacred, too. My love will always be with you.

This statement took me by surprise. It almost sounded religious. It didn't sound like something Brittany would have said

505

when she was alive. But careening down the muddy road, I suddenly remembered that Brittany had written a similar message to me not long before she died. She had made a site on Shutterfly where she'd placed thousands of photographs as a gift to me. She had also written this message to me on the site:

Live your lives well. Accept the sorrow with the joy, the ineffable grief with the love, humility with accomplishment. Don't take a single moment for granted. This is it. This moment is all that you have. Don't squander it. . . . Remember me in the sunset and the sunrise and the birds and salty ocean breeze, and the crisp pines. Remember me in my laughter and in my shadows that dance between the clouds. Remember me in the gentle furrows of your face, archiving the ebb and flow — the beauty and pain — of life through the years. I am you and you are me. We are one. And I will love you beyond this world and into eternity. Quiet your mind and listen for my voice. You will hear me whisper, "I love you and I miss you, precious family" and you will know that it is true. Believe in your heart that I am with you always, and I will never leave you. I will be waiting for you to come one day, far off in the future. I will be waiting with grandma, and my dearest grandpa when it is his time. And one day we will all be together again. . . .

She also wrote on the site:

To my dearest Mother —
Remember to love yourself. Embrace happiness. Pursue your dreams. You are in control of your own future and the people you choose to share your rich and wonderful life with. You are secure in yourself and that is a blessing. Don't let my death change who you are deep down Inside.

There is no road map to heal from the loss of a child but you should trust your instincts. No matter how powerful and painful the heartbreak, that breaking is opening up a door to a new life. One that is not better, but different and not necessarily worse, just changed because of this pain. I know your strength because I have seen it, I have felt it, it has changed my life. It will carry you forward on to more greatness in life . . . that is who you are.

All my love always,
Your Daughter Brittany

In my all-consuming grief, I had forgotten about her words. Her beautiful gift of the photographs. I had all of that to read and look at and enjoy because of my daughter's thoughtfulness. I smiled and swiped my face with the sleeve of my rain slicker.

Love yourself, Momma. When you love yourself, you love me. We are one.

Again, Brittany's voice was saying things a little foreign to the Brittany I knew, and foreign to my own thinking. We hadn't been big on daily affirmations, positive thinking, or creative visualization. Brittany and I were doers; we observed problems, and then solved them. Life was a long string of challenges to be met head-on and conquered. Brittany had always felt a sense of urgency, and was more impressed with forthright action than with purposeless discourse about what to do. Using her wit and intelligence, Brittany got things done.

Love yourself, Momma, as I love you.

Brittany had struggled so hard with this very issue: loving herself. She and I were always better at loving others than we were at loving ourselves. How many times had I scrutinized her beautiful face, longing for her to love herself, to be kind to herself?

Loving yourself is the way to get well. Get well, Momma. You have more life to live.

I was infused with a feeling of exhaustion but well-being. I felt things slipping out of the realm of my care, and certainly out of my control.

After months of grieving, it dawned on me that Brittany didn't remain behind in her ashes. Instead, she was in butterfly-wing kisses as they flitted overhead. Brittany was in the breeze caressing my face. Brittany was in the embrace of a sunny, beautiful day. This knowledge came in a flash, and I felt muscles in my shoulders and neck loosen.

It was so simple. My child — her message, her essence, light, and love — was very much alive and all around me. I felt toxicity, anger, and grief rushing out of me. They no longer had a home in my heart.

You are love.

A smile widened on my tear-soaked face. I had been the best mother I knew how to be. I had given birth to, nurtured, and raised a tempestuous, beautiful soul who tried to make this broken planet a better place to live.

Brittany had gained enough self-worth in

life to believe that she didn't owe anyone pointless suffering. What a brave, bright flame. My child had grabbed all the life she could grasp, and lived — really *lived*. Then, when faced with sure and torturous death, she had loved herself enough to know that she deserved to die with more peace and dignity than the brain tumor would leave her if she didn't intervene.

She didn't just say it; she did it.

As the bus pulled into Aguas Calientes, I pledged to start loving myself more. I promised to live more joyfully, and with less fear. I owed it to my daughter to not waste a second of it. And I vowed to write the book I'd set out to write about mothering Brittany.

As we walked up the hill to the hotel, I felt a cool drop of rain. When I lifted my face to the gray sky, a drop hit me squarely on the forehead. I felt changed, washed clean. Life was hard, but exquisitely beautiful. No one was going to wag a finger in my face, or tell me I was a bad person for supporting my child's choice about the way she would die. I would not listen to those who told me to be quiet, or that I must keep my daughter in glass slippers as I told the story of her wild and precious life.

Brittany was always more of a hiking boot kind of girl anyway.

ACKNOWLEDGMENTS

I'd like to thank my youngest sister, Sarah, for standing by me in a million ways big and small through Brittany's illness and while I wrote this. I'm grateful to my sister Donna, for her steady encouragement about writing over the years. Thank you to the Holmes clan, who surrounded me with steadfast support and love.

Very special thanks to my agent, Jennifer Gates, for her compassion, vision, and purity of purpose; to my editor, Leslie Wells, who was the best birthing coach a mother could hope for through intense and painful labor as I delivered this book; and to Emily Bestler, the editor in chief of Emily Bestler Books at Atria, who believed in the power of a mother's story about her wild and precious daughter from the very beginning. For the spare, and elegant, wildness of the cover art, thank you, Albert Tang.

Many thanks to thousands of hardworking

advocates who support death-with-dignity laws throughout the world; to the kind and generous men and women who reached out to make a dying young woman's requests come true at the Grand Canyon, Machu Picchu, and various other places; to clinicians and scientists who continue to look for cures for the terminally ill; and to brave readers who carry on exploring options for a better life and death, even when there isn't a fairy-tale ending.

I am profoundly grateful to my husband, Gary, who so freely gave my daughter unwavering support and steadfast love and in doing so loved me beyond measure.

ABOUT THE AUTHOR

Deborah Ziegler was born in Albuquerque, New Mexico. Her mother was a British immigrant and her father was a child of the Oklahoma dust bowl. One of four children, she received her BA in secondary education. Deborah went on to enjoy teaching for fifteen years. She received her MA in science education in California, where she currently lives with her husband, Gary, and two cavipoos named Bogie and Bacall. Ziegler started a successful woman-owned engineering company after retiring from her teaching career. Being Brittany's mother is without a doubt Ziegler's proudest accomplishment in life. Currently, Deborah speaks on behalf of end-of-life options in the hopes that one day all terminally-ill Americans will have the right to aid in dying if they so choose.

The employees of Thorndike Press hope you have enjoyed this Large Print book. All our Thorndike, Wheeler, and Kennebec Large Print titles are designed for easy reading, and all our books are made to last. Other Thorndike Press Large Print books are available at your library, through selected bookstores, or directly from us.

For information about titles, please call:
  (800) 223-1244

or visit our Web site at:
  http://gale.cengage.com/thorndike

To share your comments, please write:
  Publisher
  Thorndike Press
  10 Water St., Suite 310
  Waterville, ME 04901